D0906554

418.007
L26

ESL.

Language Learning in Intercultural Perspective

Approaches through drama and ethnography

edited by

Michael Byram and Michael Fleming

Nyack College Library

PUBLISHED BY THE PRESS SYNDICATE OF THE UNIVERSITY OF CAMBRIDGE
The Pitt Building, Trumpington Street, Cambridge, United Kingdom

CAMBRIDGE UNIVERSITY PRESS
The Edinburgh Building, Cambridge CB2 2RU, UK
40 West 20th Street, New York, NY 10011–4211, USA
477 Williamstown Road, Port Melbourne, VIC 3207, Australia
Ruiz de Alarcón 13, 28014 Madrid, Spain
Dock House, The Waterfront, Cape Town 8001, South Africa

http://www.cambridge.org

© Cambridge University Press 1998

This book is in copyright. Subject to statutory exception
and to the provisions of relevant collective licensing agreements,
no reproduction of any part may take place without
the written permission of Cambridge University Press.

First published 1998
Reprinted 2002

Printed in the United Kingdom at the University Press, Cambridge

Typeset in Sabon [CE]

A catologue record for this book is available from the British Library

Library of Congress Cataloguing in Publication Data
Language learining in intercultural perspective: approaches through
drama and ethnography / edited by Michael Byram and Michael Fleming.
p. cm. – (Cambridge language teaching library)
Papers presented at two seminars held 1995, University of Durham School of
Education; the first was entitled Intercultural Dimensions of Foreign
Language Teaching and Learning; the second Drama, Cultural Awareness
and Foreign Language Teaching.
Includes bibliographical references and index.
ISBN 0-521-62376-6. – ISBN 0-521-62559-9 (pbk.)
1. Language and languages – Study and teaching – Congresses.
2. Multicultural education – Congresses. 3. Drama – Study and teaching –
Congresses. 4. Ethnology – Study and teaching – Congresses.
I. Byram, Michael. II. Fleming, Michael (Michael P.) III. Series.
P53.45.L357 1998
418′.007–dc21 97-47530 CIP

ISBN 0 521 62376 6 hardback
ISBN 0 521 62559 9 paperback

#38067616

Contents

Preface

The origins of this volume lie in two seminars held at the University of Durham School of Education early in 1995. The first, 'Intercultural Dimensions of Foreign Language Teaching and Learning', was initiated by the British Association for Applied Linguistics which invited one of the editors (Byram) to organise a seminar under its auspices. It was supported financially by a grant from Cambridge University Press which enabled us to invite Claire Kramsch to give a keynote paper. It was also organised to follow immediately on a meeting of a research network led by Geneviève Zarate (ENS Fontenay/St Cloud, Paris) and financed by the LINGUA programme of the European Commission. This ensured that the seminar had a strong international representation which was valued by all the participants.

The second, 'Drama, Cultural Awareness and Foreign Language Teaching', was initiated and organised by the editors of this volume, with the generous financial support of the Goethe Institute, the French Embassy and the University of Durham School of Education. We are particularly grateful to Klaus Krischock and Didier Paris who not only supported our request for financial assistance to invite participants from Germany and France, but who were also active participants in the seminar itself. One day of this seminar was spent as a workshop, led by Dorothy Heathcote, with teachers and pupils of Shotton Hall Comprehensive School, Peterlee, County Durham, and we are grateful to the headteacher, his colleagues and pupils for their willingness to co-operate in this venture.

Finally, but not least, we are grateful to Alison Sharpe, of Cambridge University Press, who participated in the drama seminar and encouraged us to take the next step of developing papers from both seminars for publication.

Michael Byram and Michael Fleming
Durham, May 1997

Acknowledgements

Cambridge University Press, the editors and author are grateful to the authors, publishers and others who have given permission for the use of copyright material in the text. Every effort has been made to identify, or trace, sources of all the materials used, but in some cases this has not proved possible. In such cases Cambridge University Press would welcome information from the copyright owners.

Rich, A. Part IV of poem 'North American Time' from *Your Native Life Your Life*. Copyright © 1986 by Adrienne Rich. Reprinted by permission of author and WW Norton & Company Inc. on p. 31; Sallmann, S. 1983. *Ein Ausländerproblem* from *Nichts Besonderes*, Verlag Dirk Nishen on pp. 182–3; Duncker, L. 1995. *Spiel und Phantasie. Eine kreative Form der Weltneignung: Spielzeit-Spielräume in der Schulwirklichkeit. Friedrich Jahresheft XIII*, Erhard Friedrich Verlag: Seelze on p. 180 and 187; J. Degraeve cartoon from *Knack* nr 29, 20th July 1994 Published by Roularta, Belgium on p. 275; Behal-Thomsen, H., Lundquist-Mog, A., Mog, P. 1993. *Typisch Deutsch, Arbeitsbuch zu Aspekten Deutscher Mentalität*, Langenscheidt-Verlag, Berlin und München on p. 276; Hog, M., Müller, B., and Wessling, G. 1984. *Sichtwechsel. Elf Kapital zur Sprachsensibilisierung. Ein Deutschkurs für Fortgeschrittene*. Copyright: Ernst Klett International GmbH. Stuttgart on pp. 277, 284–5, 288; Anders, G. 1982. *Der Löwe* from *Blick von Turm* Munich: Beck on p. 278; Gardenghi, M. (ed.) 1994. *Ausländer in Bayreuth*. In *Der Eszettelkasten Volume* 2 (series editor U. Jung). Bayreuth: University of Bayreuth Language Centre on pp. 280–82.

Introduction

Michael Byram and Michael Fleming

Culture and language learning

The purpose of this collection of chapters is to enrich our understanding of the nature of language learning and the potential of language teaching. The chapters focus on the fact that in learning another language students are exposed to, and inevitably learn something about, one or more other societies and their cultural practices. The nature of the learning, the desirability of such learning and the ways in which it can be shaped by particular teaching strategies are some of the concerns shared by all the contributors, whatever their starting point and perspective. Their perspectives include different national and international viewpoints, different disciplines and different degrees of emphasis on teaching and learning. Moreover, as our sub-title suggests, there are two themes which cut across these varied perspectives: 'drama' and 'ethnography'.

The former arises from a deliberate attempt on the part of the editors to take a new look at drama in language learning and consider the potential for cultural as well as linguistic learning. This was done through an international seminar at which the papers were not simply presented, but part of a very practical and exciting workshop. We hope some of the flavour of the workshop will be conserved by putting the papers in a separate section.

The presence of 'ethnography' was not planned deliberately, but the fact that it is to be found in a number of chapters is an indication of how the focus on cultural learning has led a number of language teachers and researchers independently to an appropriate new source of ideas and inspiration. Ethnography is the methodology originally developed by anthropologists and later adopted by other disciplines as a means of understanding the cultural practices, meanings and beliefs of unfamiliar social groups. When language teaching begins to take seriously the concept of learning a language as the means of communication and interaction with people of another society and culture, it is not surprising that it turns to ethnography to provide a 'thick description' (Geertz 1975) of a context in which the language is used. Some of our contributors also show that ethnography can be a method which learners themselves can acquire in order to develop their understanding of other contexts and other languages in context.

The concern with the cultural dimension in language learning is not a new one. It is evident in the history of *Landeskunde* in Germany and *civilisation* in France. It was part of the post-1945 development of audio-lingual and audio-visual methods in the USA and Western Europe, particularly in France (Steele and Suozzo 1994; Puren 1988). This remained, however, unsatisfactory because there was a tendency to separate the learning of a language as a grammatical system from the provision of information about one or more countries where it is spoken. Learning the grammar of a language remained the important focus and the rest was 'background', to use the term common among British language teachers (Byram 1991). It is only as a result of a greater emphasis on language learning for communication and, even more importantly, social interaction, that it has become evident in recent decades that a fresh perspective was necessary.

If communication is to be successful, the people involved need to share the same referential meaning of the words they are using. When this is the case, they can send messages to each other through the medium of a given language, and particularly when they are at a distance and using the written language, they can assume that an efficient exchange of information has taken place. However, when the exchange of information takes place in face to face interaction, it becomes more evident that communication is not merely an exchange of information. There, the people involved have a number of social identities (Le Page and Tabouret-Keller 1985). These identities bind them to particular social groups and their cultural practices. The language is not merely a means of reference to what is in an objective world, but also carries the shared connotations and associations which help to maintain a speaker's sense of belonging to particular social groups.

When people interact in a language which is foreign to at least one of them, the shared meanings and values it carries for those involved cannot be taken for granted in the way they are when those involved are from the same language group. Learning a language as it is spoken by a particular group is learning the shared meanings, values and practices of that group as they are embodied in the language. However, precisely because they are shared and only made explicit when there is a breakdown of communication and interaction, learners find it difficult to discern them and understand their significance. Only after a process of discovering those meanings and practices can learners negotiate and create a new reality with their interlocutors, one which is new to both learners and interlocutors, a shared world of interaction and experience.

The contributions to this volume are all concerned with the ways in which language learners need to go beyond the acquisition of a linguistic system, and language teachers need to find new ways to help them do so. This makes language learning and teaching more demanding than ever. The more we understand about the nature of language and its function in society, the more the task becomes complex and difficult. Yet, as these chapters will demonstrate, there are new approaches and methods being developed, where language teachers are prepared to go beyond the traditional reference disciplines of applied linguistics and psychology.

We do not propose to go any further in tracing the developments in language teaching and learning within which this volume lies. The purpose of this introduction is to focus on some of the conceptual issues which form a framework for it. We shall do so by starting from the perspective of the English education system. For although there is common ground and mutual influence from one language teaching situation to another, conceptual developments and curriculum changes are never context-free, and it is better to relate an analysis to a specific case in which more general changes are realised and their significance revealed.

'Cultural awareness': an example from the English National Curriculum[1]

The statement of the educational aims of 'modern foreign language teaching' within compulsory education is similar to what can be found in policy documents in many countries. Most of the aims are familiar to the language teaching profession, and they can be divided roughly into four categories:

- those which focus on the development of *practical communication skills*;
- those which focus on an understanding and *awareness of language*, and how languages are learnt;
- those which encourage *positive attitudes towards* and *understanding of* speakers of foreign languages and their way of life;
- those of a *general nature* which develop learning skills and capacities which are also found in other subjects in the school curriculum.

[1] We refer here only to England since the situation is different in other parts of the United Kingdom, where each country has its own education system.

What is particularly interesting and new, however, is the introduction of an educational aim which turns learners' attention back onto themselves and the way of life which they take for granted and seldom question:

> to develop pupils' understanding of themselves and their own way of life (DES 1990:3)

This is a major innovation, in England at least, because language teaching is for the first time explicitly stated to have what might be called a 'reflexive impact', a focus on learners' own culture and not just a view outwards to other cultures.

This was the consequence of proposals by a working group who use the phrase 'cultural awareness'. They do not give a definition of cultural awareness, but they emphasise that it is a significant aspect of language learning, and indeed that without cultural awareness, a language cannot be properly understood:

> A growing awareness of the people who speak the language of study is intrinsic to the learning of it [...] Without the cultural dimension, successful communication is often difficult: comprehension of even basic words and phrases (such as those referring to meals) may be partial or approximate, and speakers and writers may fail to convey their meaning adequately or may even cause offence. (DES 1990:37)

When they discuss teaching methods for cultural awareness, they link the understanding of other and native cultures through the notion of comparison:

> The context of the language community, whether in this country or abroad, derived from a variety of authentic sources, plays a substantial role in classroom activities. In this, comparison between the learner's own way of life and that of the other language community is an essential means to better understanding of both. (DES 1990:37)

It is the comparison of own and other cultures which begins to help learners to perceive and cope with difference. It provides them with the basis for successful interaction with members of another cultural group, not just the means of exchanging information. There is of course one school of thought, we should note in passing, which argues that teaching should emphasise similarities, our common humanity, whatever the cultural differences. The problem with this view is that it does not help learners to overcome the problems of interactions, and yet interaction is crucial to their experience of a sense of common humanity.

The working group also identify other methods for developing cultural awareness: from 'contact' with otherness, to comparison and 'appreciation' of similarities and differences, to 'identifying' with otherness, and finally to take an 'objective view' of their own culture. Referring to students in the first three years of language learning, they say learners should have frequent opportunities to:

> – work with authentic materials deriving from the communities/countries of the target language and especially from links with schools abroad ...
> – come into contact with native speakers in this country and where possible abroad
> – from these materials and contacts, appreciate the similarities and differences between their own and cultures of the communities/countries where the target language is spoken
> – identify with the experience and perspective of people in the countries and communities where the target language is spoken
> – use this knowledge to develop a more objective view of their own customs and ways of thinking. (DES 1990:36)

This list suggests an underlying concept of progression which presupposes a theory of cultural learning not made explicit. In particular, it is the notion of 'identifying with' which introduces potential links with ethnography and drama. It implies, we would argue, teaching techniques which are not widespread, and psychological processes which are new to language teaching.

Finally, in their recommendations for older students – in the fourth and fifth years of learning – the working group add three other points:

> Learners should have the opportunity to:
>
> – investigate and report on a particular aspect of the communities/countries of the target language
> – plan a visit abroad, if possible with a view to carrying it out, but at least as an exercise
> – make general and specific comparisons between their own country and the communities/countries of the target language. (DES 1990:37)

Here, the notions of investigating and reporting, of visiting and exploring another country and community, suggest a link with the ethnographic methods which have served anthropologists well in precisely this task of understanding another society and its culture, and seeing its relationship to one's own.

There are thus many implications of this kind of reassessment of language teaching but the implications are not thoroughly discussed. Teachers are left to make of it what they can, and the need to explore these issues more thoroughly was one of the reasons for the seminars on which this volume is based, and since we believe that the situation is not untypical, for the re-working and publication of the papers.

The 'intercultural speaker': a new purpose for language-and-culture teaching

Although a particular case, the perspective represented by the English National Curriculum documents is part of the changes in language teaching as a whole which we outlined above. It suggests that language learning should lead to insight and increased understanding of the society and culture of speakers of other languages, but also of learners' own society and culture and the relationship between the two, a cognitive learning process. It also suggests that language learning should lead to positive attitudes towards speakers of other languages, an affective change. Although attitudes towards learners' own society and culture are not mentioned, it is probable that they are assumed to be positive already. It is, however, possible that a perspective on one's own society and culture from the vantage point of another leads to a critical reassessment of what has hitherto been invisible because all-too-familiar.

The methods suggested in the documents are also representative of those in use elsewhere. They include comparison, a particularly significant means of acquiring a new perspective on one's own language and culture. It questions the 'naturalness' and taken-for-granted nature of the culture into which learners are socialised, in the home and in the school. Just when pupils are in the midst of the process of primary and secondary socialisation, they are introduced to a new way of doing things, a new conception of reality, a new set of values, which are just as 'natural', at least for those who have been socialised into them. This meeting with otherness which challenges and 'denaturalises' the learners' own culture, might be called 'tertiary socialisation' (Byram 1989a; Doyé 1992). It involves an implicit, and sometimes explicit, questioning of learners' assumptions and values; and explicit questioning can lead to a critical stance, to 'critical cultural awareness' (Byram 1997a). The process and the teaching methods associated with it need, of course, to be supported by and related to learning theory in general and to theories of psychological change in the face of experience of otherness in particular. There is no space to develop that here, but we have begun to do so in other publications (e.g. Byram, Morgan *et al.* 1994). The methodological question which then arises, is how this process of tertiary socialisation and decentring from one's own taken-for-granted world, can be structured systematically in the classroom. As later chapters will show, this is another starting point for a dialogue with drama, ethnography and other modes of experiential learning.

The framework for language learning and teaching we have developed to this point has three aspects:

- an integration of linguistic and cultural learning to facilitate communication and interaction;
- a comparison of others and self to stimulate reflection on and (critical) questioning of the mainstream culture into which learners are socialised;
- a shift in perspective involving psychological processes of socialisation;
- the potential of language teaching to prepare learners to meet and communicate in other cultures and societies than the specific one usually associated with the language they are learning.

The next stage of our argument is to introduce the concept of 'intercultural communication'. The starting point for this is again linked to the notions of identity and interaction. Whenever we are engaged in interaction with others, we perceive and are perceived ourselves in terms of our social identities, one of which is our ethnic identity (Tajfel 1981). In British society and those similar to it, for example in Western Europe, the ethnic identity of the dominant majority coincides with their national identity. This in turn sometimes coincides with state citizenship, although the second coincidence is less frequent.

Each person has a number of social identities, social groups to which they belong, and cultures, cultural practices, beliefs and values to which they subscribe. Which identity is dominant in a given interaction depends on a number of factors in the situation: the language in use, the relationships with the other, how the participants identify each other. When the other with whom we are interacting is from a different state with a different national identity, symbolised in a different language, it is our national identity which comes to the fore, at least in the initial stages. It is therefore important to understand the national group and culture to which that person belongs. Any international interaction will refer to national identities and cultures which are therefore embodied in the mutual perceptions of the actors involved. It is for this reason that language teaching puts an emphasis on national cultures and the mutual perceptions of national groups, attempting to ensure a proper analysis of national stereotypes. When an interaction takes the people involved beyond this stage and into relationships where other social identities – for example, gender, social class, age group – become significant, then it is necessary for the participants to know, or be able to find out, about the other social groups to which their partner in the interaction belongs. Language teaching thus also needs to anticipate what learners need to know or what skills they need to acquire in order to discover other identities and groups – and their cultures – for themselves. In the first instance, however, learners usually perceive others and are themselves perceived by others as belonging to a national group and culture.

It is not possible, nor desirable, for learners to identify with the other nor to deny their own identity and culture. Yet in terms of linguistic learning this has been the implicit aim for many years. We have judged the best language learner to be the one who comes nearest to a native speaker mastery of the grammar and vocabulary of the language, and who can therefore 'pass for', or be identified as, a native, communicating on an equal footing with natives.

When considerations of social identity are introduced into the debate a different kind of judgement of the good learner is implied. It is the learner who is aware of their own identities and cultures, and of how they are perceived by others, and who also has an understanding of the identities and cultures of those with whom they are interacting. This 'intercultural speaker' (Byram and Zarate 1994) is able to establish a relationship between their own and the other cultures, to mediate and explain difference – and ultimately to accept that difference and see the common humanity beneath it. The concept of 'intercultural speaker' is thus one of the fundamental themes of this volume. It is developed by Kramsch in the first chapter, and though not used as a term by others, many of the chapters are concerned with how the competence for intercultural communication can be defined and promoted inside and beyond the classroom.

The 'intercultural speaker' and English Language Teaching

Risager identifies in a later chapter of this volume four approaches to language teaching, each of increasing complexity as the issues of cultures and cultural identities are recognised by the teaching profession. She suggests that a 'transcultural approach' is emerging as cultures interpenetrate each other as a consequence of extensive migration, tourism and international communications. One aspect of this is the development of the *lingua franca*, in particular English. The debate about which, if any, standard form of English should be the reference for learners throughout the world is made more complex when it includes the question of which culture(s) learners might be exposed to.

How the question is to be answered is an issue for teachers and learners themselves, and will vary according to their situation. They may decide to focus on one country and the social identities and cultures present there, with which they may come into contact. They may argue that there is a sufficiently international '*cultura franca*' for them to treat this as the basis of their teaching, although this would be to ignore the various social identities of speakers of English as a *lingua franca* which operate in any interaction.

The emphasis of this volume on approaches through ethnography and drama does not pre-suppose one answer to the debate, but rather offers a means by which learners can be prepared to interact with speakers of English irrespective of whether they are native speakers from the United States, Australia, Britain or elsewhere. The 'intercultural speaker' is someone who has a knowledge of one or, preferably, more cultures and social identities and has a capacity to discover and relate to new people from other contexts for which they have not been prepared directly.

The 'intercultural speaker' is thus someone who is learning to become independent of the teacher and the limits of what can be achieved in the classroom (Holec 1981). It is a process which can take place whatever the learners' age, and the chapters of this volume describe research and development with school pupils and adults, in formal education and in the workplace. It is not a process which is ever totally complete, and teachers and researchers themselves continue to learn and develop their capacities as intercultural speakers. This is an advantage. Teachers who take seriously the cultural dimension of language learning as we have described it briefly here, will not expect to know and teach everything about a specific society and its culture(s). They will place more emphasis on developing their learners' and their own awareness of the nature of intercultural interaction, and the skills and competences which allow them to relate to cultural difference. In the final analysis, even teachers who have never personally experienced a particular society and the people of many different social identities within it, can help their learners to engage with texts and documents where those identities are expressed. Their task, and expertise, as teachers is to enable learners to enquire into the beliefs, values and cultural practices they embody, and it is this approach which is represented in the chapters of this book.

Overview of the following chapters

We have divided the chapters into three parts and provided separate introductions for each. We suggested above that improved understanding of the nature of intercultural communication and interaction leads to increased demands on the learner. In the first part, the focus is upon learners and on further definition of what is required of them, what they bring to the learning, and descriptions of teaching and learning approaches which aim to fulfil those requirements. The second part explores the contribution to intercultural learning which can be made through particular approaches to drama and theatre. It will be of interest to language teachers but also to drama teachers who believe in using drama as a means of exploring other subjects in the curriculum. The third part focuses on the teacher, for we must not forget that our improved understanding of intercultural communication also places new requirements on them, as well as on their students. This section describes how teachers and researchers experience intercultural interaction, and how they might be helped to develop their own competences, both intercultural and pedagogic, to meet the challenges of language teaching into the next century.

Part 1 Approaches through ethnography: learner perspectives

Introduction

In the last hundred years or so, since the Reform Movement and the beginning of modern languages teaching, the task of the learner has become both more difficult and more easy. As our understanding of the nature of language has improved, it has become more apparent that language is extremely complex, not only in terms of grammar, but even more in terms of the human interaction involved in language use. Indeed, the argument that knowledge about grammar can inhibit fluency, as learners try to manipulate consciously and in real time the rules they had been taught in the studied quiet of the classroom, applies even more to knowledge of the complexity of interaction revealed by conversation analysis and pragmatics.

Of course, people manage to learn languages despite this complexity. Sometimes, it seems that they learn better if they are not taught, but simply exposed to a language in natural ways, in a natural environment. Yet there are many examples of people who have lived most of their life in a particular language environment without apparently mastering more than the rudiments of the grammar or the pragmatics.

All this is familiar ground, and need not be argued in detail here. What we have witnessed in the last decade, however, is a further recognition of complexity, as research on cross-cultural communication has developed. It has become apparent that human interaction across cultural frontiers introduces new difficulties. As well as the linguistic, learners must be aware of the cultural dimension of their interaction with others. There is little they can assume they know about those with whom they are communicating, for despite the growth of international tourism, business and trade, social groups manage to maintain their separate identities by putting their own interpretations and meanings on cultural objects or practices they have in common with or have borrowed from others. Learners can take very little for granted; everything has to be borne in mind, consciously or otherwise. The problem of consciously taking into account what others may take for granted or what may in fact be quite different preconceptions, is no less difficult than trying to remember all the rules of grammar one has learnt over many years in a classroom.

One way in which all this has nonetheless become easier for those learners who have to rely on what they can gain in the classroom, is that new methods of 'communicative' teaching have suggested that learners should value real time communicative fluency as much as classroom time grammatical accuracy (Brumfit 1984). It is possible to extend this argument to knowledge of the difficulties of cross-cultural communication, all the more so since our knowledge of the underlying regularities of cross-cultural communication is very limited. What can be learnt in the classroom should inform but not inhibit interaction with others outside the classroom.

A further development making things easier for learners, or at least different, is a change in our perception of what they should be aiming to achieve. Instead of the assumption that learners should model themselves on 'the native speaker', it is becoming apparent to teachers and their learners that successful cross-cultural communication depends on the acquisition of abilities to understand different modes of thinking and living, as they are embodied in the language to be learnt, and to reconcile or mediate between different modes present in any specific interaction. This is not the 'communicative competence' on which people using the same language in the same, or closely related, cultures rely; it is an 'intercultural communicative competence' which has some common ground with communicative competence, but which also has many unique characteristics. Precisely what these are is one of the current preoccupations of theorists and teachers, and we have not yet seen the same kind of detailed analysis of this competence as that which was devoted to the analysis of communicative competence.

However, learners cannot await the results of scientific analysis and teachers must provide them with the best they can currently understand. The chapters in this first part represent current developments in both our analytical understanding and our approaches to teaching.

In the first chapter, Kramsch develops in detail the analysis begun here and in our general introduction. She argues that the native speaker's traditional privilege of being the model for learners, ascribed by teachers and readily accepted by learners themselves, has to be re-evaluated and in fact withdrawn. She does this through a close analysis of language in use, where the nature of privilege of a different kind – based on social class or economic status – is shown to be understood differently in different cultures. She discusses what other model is appropriate and begins the description of the competence of the 'intercultural speaker' which is essential to future developments of theory and teaching practices. That description needs to draw upon academic disciplines other than applied linguistics and psychology, already familiar to language teaching, but she concludes her chapter by emphasising that teaching practices should not lose sight of the centrality of language, of the need to ensure that intercultural competence is related to *communication* across frontiers.

In the second chapter, Byram and Cain describe an experiment in teaching and learning practices which attempts to integrate some of the insights into the nature of cross-cultural communication into classroom teaching. As suggested above, the assumptions about shared and taken-for-granted preconceptions become less justified as the distance and difference between speakers of different languages grows. Even between English and French languages and cultures, where a common European heritage might imply similarity, learners can assume less than they might at first believe. Indeed, the apparent similarity is arguably as difficult to deal with as obvious difference and distance, when individuals seeking to communicate across cultural frontiers are immediately aware of the problems they face. The experiment described in this chapter took place in secondary education and had to focus mainly on what can be done in the classroom. It also had to take into consideration the fact that language learning within general secondary education has many functions in addition to developing intercultural communicative competence. It has, for example, to follow society's requirement that learning be evaluated, assessed and certificated. The chapter therefore also raises the difficult issue of assessment of intercultural competence in a context of communication, offering some examples but certainly not claiming to have solved the problems.

The third and fourth chapters also deal with language learning in an institutional context, but at higher education level, where some of the language learners will become the teachers and researchers we shall consider in more detail in the third part of this volume. One of the distinguishing features of learning at higher education level is that the constraints of the classroom are more easily broken; language learners may – and in Britain *must* – learn not only in real time but also in the natural environment of the language in question. Coleman's research investigates the effects and efficacy of this dimension of learning. He has analysed elsewhere the gains and losses in terms of mastery of the linguistic system, but in this chapter he focuses on the effect of residence abroad on learners' perceptions of the people and country where they spend a substantial period of time: an academic year. His findings are not all encouraging. Learners may return with stereotypes reinforced, or even with more negative impressions than when they first set out.

There are clearly implications in Coleman's findings for the 'pedagogy of visits and exchanges' (Alix and Bertrand 1994; Byram 1997) and

Barro, Jordan and Roberts' chapter proposes an approach which may lead to different responses to the experience than those which Coleman found. Like Byram and Cain, they describe an experiment in the classroom, but one which links classroom time and place with real time and place, and one which also draws upon the other disciplines which Kramsch argued are necessary for the advance of language teaching and learning. They argue that ethnography can provide a link between the disciplines of anthropology and sociology on the one hand and the needs of language teaching on the other. They describe a course in ethnography for language learners which ensures the centrality of language which Kramsch demands. It nonetheless helps learners to understand the natural environment in which the language in question is used, and how that environment relates to the environment in which they are accustomed to interact through their own language. Learners do not only acquire improved understanding, but also the tools and concepts through which to become independent researchers in another culture – and their own – thus acquiring one of the skills required to be competent in intercultural communication. We suggested in our general introduction that language learners should reflect upon their own language and culture and its relationship to others. This 'reflexivity', to use these authors' terminology, is a fundamental part of their course, as is evident from the concrete and detailed examples of classroom work they describe.

The classroom and the need for reflexivity are also the focus of the fifth chapter. Jin and Cortazzi consider the relationship between native speaker and foreign language learners from a complementary perspective to that taken by Kramsch. They argue that classroom work should not only include acquisition of understanding of the preconceptions of speakers from other cultures, and the development of real time skills, but should also lead learners to analyse their own language environment. They share this position with other authors in this part of this volume, but their research has the advantage of examining the interactions in classrooms where learners and teacher are from obviously different and distant languages and cultures, from the West and China. Even the modes of learning, the assumptions about what will happen in a classroom, are different, and this needs to be taken into account by both teachers and learners. Moreover, it can be the basis for reflection on self, for the 'reflexivity', which is fundamental to success in intercultural communication, and in this sense, Jin and Cortazzi demonstrate how teachers can incorporate insights into cross-cultural communication even though a systematic understanding of it is far from complete.

The final chapter in this part is also concerned with gaps and difference between distant cultures, and also focuses on the issues arising from Chinese speakers learning English. However, Cooper takes us out of the classroom and into the workplace, an example of the real time and place demands which contrast with the classroom. She describes research which was at first perceived as an audit of language needs. It quickly became apparent that this was too narrow a definition, and that employers need to be aware of the significance of cultural competence just as much as linguistic competence. Cooper, too, draws upon anthropology and ethnography but this time as a researcher trying to describe and analyse what is needed for successful intercultural communication, putting into operation the kinds of skill and concepts acquired by students in the course described by Barro, Jordan and Roberts. Cooper thus demonstrates how the link between education and the workplace is more than the preparation for the latter by the former, that there are links of substance between the two, that not only researchers but also learners and workers may benefit from the disciplines new to language teaching to which Kramsch drew our attention in the first chapter.

1 The privilege of the intercultural speaker

Claire Kramsch

Introduction

The learning and teaching of foreign languages has traditionally been predicated on the distinction between native speakers and non-native speakers. Non-native speakers are supposed to learn the rules of the native speaker's standard grammar, vocabulary and idioms. In turn, the native speaker is supposed to provide the norm against which the non-native speaker's performance is measured. This norm corresponds to the linguistic intuitions that are claimed to make speakers of a language into native speakers. Native speakership brings to its speakers a certain authority associated with authenticity and legitimacy of language use. As a rule, native speakers are viewed around the world as the genuine article, the authentic embodiment of the standard language. This authority carries distinct privileges. Because they represent a whole community of speakers, native speakers are endowed by non-native speakers with credibility, trustworthiness, respectability.

In recent years, however, the notion of native speaker, that seemed so uncontroversial some thirty years ago, has become much more complex. Who is a native speaker? the child as well as the adult? the university professor as well as the worker on the assembly line? and what native speaker norm should we teach? Not only have scholars started questioning the *identity* of the native speaker (see for example Paikeday 1985; Davies 1991; Widdowson 1994), but recent years have also seen a slow but sure erosion of his unquestioned *authority* (see for example Phillipson 1992; Byram and Zarate 1994). An increasing number of scholars are even questioning the *appropriateness* of the one native speaker norm in a time of large-scale migrations, cross-national and cross-cultural encounters, and increasing linguistic and pragmatic differences among speakers of the same language (e.g. Peirce 1995; Blyth 1995; Holliday 1994; Kramsch and Sullivan 1996). Byram and Zarate (1994) have proposed that learners of a foreign language, rather than trying to approximate the native speaker, should be taught instead how to become 'intercultural speakers'. It is this shift from the native speaker norm to an intercultural speaker model that I want to explore in this chapter. But first I want to illustrate the dimensions of this shift with an example.

Of privileges, rights and prerogatives

At a teacher training seminar conducted some years ago in Leipzig for English, French and German teachers from the United States, France and Germany, one French teacher suggested to her American and German colleagues that they use a 1992 advertisement from the reputable Paris department store, the *Bon Marché Rive Gauche*, to teach French in the United States and in Germany. The ad shows one elegant looking woman with a diadem in her hair, holding up a credit card and looking straight at the viewer. Above her, the statement: 'Rive Gauche, il existe encore des privilèges que nul ne souhaite abolir' (On the Left Bank, there still exist some privileges that no one wishes to abolish). This ad is complex in its message and the various interpretations given of it by teachers from different cultures illustrate well the potentially intercultural place of the non-native speaker attempting to learn another person's language and culture.

For any native speaker of French, the ad's allusion to the night of the 4th of August 1789, the famous 'nuit du quatre août', is clear, in which, as we know, the nobility abolished its birthrights on the altar of the Revolution. The ad knowingly uses the very words that one can find in any history textbook: 'la nuit du quatre août' collocates in the French native speaker's imagination with 'l'abolition des privilèges'. In addition, the mere mention of the Left Bank of the Seine evokes for a French native speaker the Quartier Latin with its May '68 demonstrations for social justice and its fights for civil rights. In this ad, however, both privileges of birth and civil rights have, courtesy of the *Bon Marché*, been replaced by the prerogative (Lat. rogare, 'to demand') of the credit card. The teacher who had suggested using that ad to teach French in the United States and in Germany, suggested that it be juxtaposed with a one-franc coin bearing the inscription: 'Liberté, égalité, fraternité', thus illustrating how historical myth and historical reality can coexist side by side in present-day France. Privileges of birth, she said, might have been abolished in 1789, but today, France still has a class system, where membership of the upper class can only be acquired by being born into the right circles. Equality in the motto, inequality in the facts.

The non-native teachers who taught French in the United States and in Germany had quite a different interpretation of what 'privilèges' might consist of. For the American teachers, a privilege here referred simply to what you can buy with a credit card if you have the money. It had nothing to do with birth. It was the prerogative that comes with the card-bearing membership in a community of consumers. The West German colleagues had yet another notion of privilege than either 'birth right' or 'membership prerogative'. They had rephrased the ad for themselves into an equal opportunity issue: A privilege, they said, is what you acquired through meritorious work; it is your just reward for services rendered in a *Leistungsgesellschaft* or performance-oriented society. If you can afford to buy things at the *Bon Marché*, it is because you have served hard and therefore you 'deserve' it. Neither birth nor money, only merit is the right entitlement, they said.

Note that the interpretations of those American and West German viewers were not wrong. Indeed, all three meanings are potentially enclosed in the French ad. The *Bon Marché* offers its customers the birth rights of the elite by alluding to the night of the 4th of August; by evoking the icon 'Rive Gauche', it offers them the social rights gained through revolutions; and by holding up the *Bon Marché* credit card, it grants them the prerogatives of modern-day consumer society members. The polysemy of the ad allows it to be read and understood by multiple audiences, who each have the right to see in it what they please. What is interesting is not so much whether the non-native speakers of French were 'right' or 'wrong' in reading this ad differently from educated native speakers, but, rather, how different sociocultural contexts elicited different readings.

For Parisian viewers, this ad is an echo of their high school history textbooks and of politicised student life. It was multiplied on the walls of the Parisian metro with varying captions that all offered the viewer the same ambiguous reference to pre-1789 reactionary times, 1968 civil rights demonstrations and 1992 commercial practices, thus constructing in the French cultural imagination a historical continuity between privileges of birth and consumer prerogatives. No doubt, different French speakers resonate differently to the ad's multiple meanings, according to their occupation, their level of education, their gender, their ethnic origin, their age. A French woman, who had participated in the events of May '68 in the Latin Quarter, remarked cynically at the sight of the poster: 'Le mythe de la Rive Gauche a la vie dure!' (the myth of the Left Bank is tenacious). A North African or a Portuguese immigrant living in France would possibly have another reading than a native French person.

If this ad is exported, as it was suggested that it might be, to teach French around the world, the diversity of potential readings will increase. Native speakers and non-native speakers will find in this ad a different confirmation of their own world views and a different interpretation of what distinguishes a privilege from a right, and a right from a prerogative. American viewers might draw on their own prior texts to interpret this ad. They might project on the woman someone they know, for example Jackie Kennedy or any of Andy Warhol's 'Reigning Queens'. Because a publicity poster is a genre they know well, American viewers may feel that they understand this advertisement perfectly, as being just another sales pitch for a piece of plastic. Teachers raised and educated in the former GDR might either draw on the pre-1989, party-line cultural schemata of the GDR, where such mottos as 'Ich leiste was, ich leiste mir was' (I produce, therefore I can afford to buy) were inculcated from an early age in generations of East German citizens, or they might draw on early socialist revolutionary notions of equality as humanitarian ideal. The former reaction would lead the East Germans to feel more affinity with their West German counterparts, the latter would bring them closer to the French reading.

This example illustrates the differences between the perceptions of native and of non-native speakers regarding cultural events and texts. What is the position of foreign cultural readers of such texts and where should we teach them to position themselves? Should they try to read the poster as a French native speaker, if we can define who that may be? I shall first review the current controversy about who is entitled to count as a 'native speaker' and what kinds of privileges are associated with the title. I shall then reflect on the notion of the 'intercultural speaker' and the pedagogical goals associated with this notion.

Who is a native speaker?

It is only in the last ten years that linguists have started to examine critically the construct of the native speaker (e.g. Paikeday 1985; Quirk and Widdowson 1985; Kachru 1985; Davies 1991; Widdowson 1994, Kramsch and Sullivan 1996). Thomas Paikeday in his little book *The Native Speaker is Dead!*, self-published in 1985 and circulated under the table by linguists and educators, was the first to give the topic 'a good airing', as he says. Through his interviews with over forty linguists, including Chomsky himself, Paikeday passed under systematic scrutiny the usual definitions of the native speaker. Here, I shall use the example of the multiple readings of the *Bon Marché* ad discussed in the preceding section as a metaphor for three types of privilege that have traditionally been associated with the native speaker: entitlement by birth, right acquired through education, prerogative of membership in a social community.

Native speaker by birth?

Originally, native speakership was viewed as an uncontroversial privilege of birth. He who was born into a language was considered to be a 'native' speaker of that language. Native speakers in that sense have grammatical intuitions that non-native speakers do not. For Chomsky, the mere fact of being human was enough to endow one with the ability to know grammatical right from wrong. However, Chomsky's native speaker/hearer was such an idealised abstraction, that his entitlement was inoperative. Chomsky's native speaker had no social reality.

The notion of birth rights remained, however. Even though native speakers became creatures of flesh and blood, they were still viewed as the infallible arbiters of grammaticality and social acceptability. Recently, with the increased legitimation given to non-national, non-standard languages, the ability of any person born into a language to make correct grammaticality judgements about her language has been severely put in question. In his interview with Paikeday, Crystal urges researchers to distinguish between the intuition of the native speaker, who is linguistically naive, and the intuition of the linguist, i.e. the analyst. The two 'intuitions' work in different ways: the native speaker, he says, may have a good 'feel for the language' but it is not always as accurate and especially not as precise as the linguist's analyses (Paikeday 1985:43).

If then it is not enough to be born into a language to count as a native speaker, is it enough to have been born into a national speech community that claims this language as its national language? If, however, we take 'native' to mean 'national', as many people do, then all those born into a Welsh or Scottish family would automatically know standard English, and all children born in the United States of, say, Chinese-speaking immigrants would automatically qualify as native speakers of English, which, as we know, is not the case. Is it enough to be born of English native speaking parents? If the parents don't choose to speak English to their children, or don't speak it at home, children may never become native speakers of English. If these children were displaced in adolescence and never acquired full native proficiency in their second language, they may even become people without a native tongue, having faulty 'intuitions' in both. Paikeday sums it up: 'One could have a mother tongue and as many first languages as circumstances permit and never be able to use any of them as a "native speaker" because of lack of aptitude for language learning, lack of educational opportunity, displacement from one's native land, etc.' (*ibid.* p. 5).

If one is not entitled by birth, is one entitled by education to be a native speaker? It may be indeed that native speakers are made, rather than born.

Native speaker by education?

Some scholars acknowledge that the social environment plays a role, but they view that role as an unconscious one. McDavid, for example, suggests to Paikeday that one is a native speaker by virtue of having acquired the language 'from early and continuing exposure rather than from conscious study' (*ibid.* p. 47). However, others disagree. At the end of his study of the native speaker in applied linguistics, Davies (1991) comes to the conclusion that although non-native speakers, have *not*, by definition, had early childhood exposure to the language, they *are* capable of acquiring all other capacities of native speakers, i.e. intuitions about grammar, discourse and pragmatic control, creative performance, interpreting and translating capabilities.

What sounds plausible from a psycholinguistic point of view might not be true from an educational perspective, however. How much education and what kind of education is necessary to speak, read and write *socially acceptable* language? The notion of 'mature educated native speaker' tries to remedy this vagueness, but we are still left uncertain as to what kind of maturity and education is needed to qualify as a mature educated native speaker.

Defining native speakership as the result of education transforms it from a *privilege* of birth into an educational *right*. It is the fact of having been socialised into a given society, schooled in a given educational system that gives you native speaker rights. Thus education bestows upon one the right not only to native speaker status, but to a middle class, mainstream native speaker status. Indeed, one acquires native speaker rights through a competence acquired in school. Some scholars therefore suggest using the term 'proficient or competent-user' rather than 'native speaker'. But the next question is: *Who* evaluates the competence of the competent-user? who judges the social acceptability of the educated language user's ways with words?

Native speaker by virtue of being a member of a native speaker community?

If native speakership is more than a birth privilege, if it is an educational right, who decides which native speaker norm obtains? Davies (1994) has recently given quite a radical response to that question.

> It is probable that what is most enduring about the concept [of the NS] has nothing to do with truth and reality, whether or not individuals are native speakers; what matters most is the enduring native speaker myth combining both knowledge and identity: in that myth the two views have an equal role.

And he goes on to quote Bartsch (1988:182) who says:

> We have, at least presently, no method to decide whether two speakers of a language have the same linguistic competence, in the sense that they have reconstructed the same competence in grammar. But we know what it means that a social rule or norm is the same for two or more speakers ... We merely have to study their practice.

It is easy to see how the focus on social consensus and group membership with regard to the native/non-native distinction is allied to the us vs. them distinction and is sometimes directly linked with national culture in the legal sense.

Coppieters, studying perceived competence differences between native and near-native speakers of French, came to the conclusion that 'a speaker of French is someone who is *accepted as such by the community* referred to as that of French speakers, not someone who is endowed with a specific formal underlying linguistic system' (Coppieters 1987:565). As one of Paikeday's scholars says: 'If some group thinks you are a native speaker, then you are one' within the context of that group (Paikeday 1985:24). It is not enough to have intuitions about grammaticality or acceptability, and to display individual fluency and full communicative competence, one must be recognised as a native speaker by the relevant speech community. One may ask, however: How homogeneous must the speech community be to emit such judgements, or is native speaker recognition a matter of political clout? Two examples, taken from English, will illustrate the political dimension of such a question.

The first example raises issues of national linguistic sovereignty. Given the varieties of standard and non-standard English spoken by English speakers, scholars like Braj Kachru have classified several circles of membership to English speech communities (Kachru 1985). Kachru identifies an inner circle of countries like the United Kingdom, the United States, Australia and New Zealand. These special communities he calls 'norm-providing', because their speakers are recognised as models of standard English. Then there is an outer circle of countries like India or Singapore. These he calls 'norm-developing', because they are developing their own English native speaker norms. Finally there is an expanding circle whose speakers are 'norm dependent', because they depend on external norms and don't yet generate their own. Of course, one could argue that the inner circle itself includes a host of more or less prestigious, more or less stigmatised varieties of English. As Max Weinrich remarked 'A language is a dialect with an army and a navy' (cited in Paikeday p. 26). Even though the United States has an army and a navy, some French parents still prefer to send their children to study English in the UK rather than in the US, because they perceive American English to be a less authoritative version of the genuine article.

The second example raises questions of national loyalty. Using another language than the one you grew up with is not just a linguistic exercise, it raises questions of allegiance that very much depend on the tolerance of the speech community to diversity among its members. For example, the arguments made by the advocates of the English Language Amendment in the United States (see Judd 1987), who want to make the exclusive use of English compulsory in public life, claim that competent and exclusive use of English is necessary to ensure social and political integration into American society. But their goal is not merely a question of learning the correct grammatical and lexical usage of English. They view the use of English as a sign of allegiance, the use of any other language as a sign of disloyalty to the mainstream speech community. It is not uncommon to see members of the mainstream speech community discriminate against anyone who by choice flouts the social conventions of mainstream language use.

In this light, the question that has occupied linguists and language teachers alike, namely: 'Can a non-native speaker *become* a native speaker?' loses much of its relevance if one looks at the problem not in a nativistic nor in an educational perspective, but in a sociocultural one. The question has to be rephrased as: What prevents potentially bilingual outsiders from becoming integrated into a group? What is the authority of the speech community based on? This is a crucial question, but one that goes well beyond the mere acquisition of linguistic and cultural competence. I address this question indirectly in the next section.

An outdated myth?

Recent historical developments have made it more difficult to ascertain who is and who is not a native speaker. Let us take again the case of English. The rise of English as the international language of research, business and industry, has dissociated native speakership of English from its traditional geographic locations. English has become the *lingua franca* between people who don't speak each other's national languages; Japanese and Koreans, French and Germans, Finns and Swedes speak English with one another to fulfil their local needs and purposes. Moreover, English is now attached to business cultures that do not always reflect traditional Anglo-Saxon practices, but that ply the English language to make it fit a variety of local values and traditions.

In addition to increased geographical variety among non-native speakers, we are witnessing an increased diversification in language use among native speakers themselves. Not every native speaker of English speaks like white male upper middle class Anglos. And not everyone agrees with Davies (1994) that standard English should be the only target for non-native speakers of English. Native varieties of English now include the English spoken and written in Singapore and New Delhi, Nigeria and South Africa, where syntax and vocabulary can sometimes vary considerably from so-called standard English. Goldstein argued recently that non-native speakers might be interested in learning Black English Vernacular in order to communicate with the large number of Americans in the United States who, after all, have had no other language than English for fifteen to twenty consecutive generations (Goldstein 1987).

Thus, standard structures have to be differentiated from authentic language use. While there is such a thing as standardised or conventionalised English usage (a linguistic concept), there can be no such thing as standardised language use (a social concept). This is where, ironically, advocates of linguistic human rights (Skutnabb-Kangas and Phillipson 1994) and advocates of communicative language teaching converge. For, it is the desire for authenticity that is now making foreign language educators pause and wonder whether a pedagogy of the authentic should not better be replaced by a pedagogy of the appropriate, which attempts to counteract the nefarious consequences of 'linguistic imperialism' (Phillipson 1992) and respect the authenticity of local varieties of language use (Widdowson 1994). Following Thomas's distinction (1983), learners would need to develop the pragmalinguistic competence of native speakers, i.e. assign to linguistic structures the same pragmatic force as native speakers would, but they should be free to adopt or not native speakers' sociopragmatic competence, i.e. share the native speakers' judgement concerning 'the size of imposition, cost/ benefit, social distance, and relative rights and obligations' entailed by the use of such phrases (Thomas 1983:104).

The dilemma that this poses for non-native speakers is well illustrated by current efforts to revive heritage languages in officially monoglossic societies, as, for instance, the attempts made in California to revive native American indigenous languages (Hinton 1994). In master/ apprentice teams, tribe elders teach their ancestral language (e.g. Yurok, Karuk, Wintu, Hupa, Mojave) to their grandchildren, nieces or nephews, who in turn attempt to use the language with their children in activities of everyday life. But, as soon as these learners want to go beyond the acquisition of isolated words and sentences and actually communicate in the language, they face the reality of the divergent social values that were traditionally conveyed by these words. For instance, whereas a Karuk native speaker, raised and living within a close-knit community of like-minded people in close proximity to one another, with clearly defined social roles and statuses, rarely needed to make compliments, express thanks or explicitly extend invitations, present-day Native American learners of Karuk are under social pressure to accomplish these speech acts much more frequently than their elders. These young people, schooled and working in environments where distance and mobility make human relations less predictable, feel the need, through the use of language, to signal solidarity and bridge the social distance characteristic of a complex industrial society (Wolfson 1988). This extreme case of non-native speakership starkly dramatises the dilemma of language learners who have to understand the socio-pragmatic values of their teachers, but decide whether to enact them, with whom, and in which circumstances.

The revival or maintenance of heritage languages and the reconstruction of a social context for languages that have sometimes only 10 or 15 native speakers left in the world, raise an important question that learners of national languages have to ask themselves also: which social variety should be taken as the model of language use or is the notion of model itself in need of rethinking? In the case of the French spoken in France, Valdman (1992) has showed that when setting a native speaker norm, we have to distinguish between what native speakers actually say, and what native speakers like to believe they say. For example, the French have at least three ways of asking a friend where he is headed for: the regular 'Où vas-tu?' (Where are you going?), the informal 'Tu vas où?' (You're going where?) and the really familiar 'Où tu vas?' (Where you're going?). According to Valdman's survey, French native speakers use the informal 'Tu vas où?' or even the sloppy 'Où tu vas?' as much as 80 per cent of the time in informal standard French situations, but they believe they say it only 30 per cent of the time. By contrast, they believe they use the more highly valued inversion form 'Où vas-tu?' as much as 35 per cent of the time in informal standard situations, where in actuality they only use that form 5 per cent of the time in these situations. So which of these two native speaker norms should we teach non-native speakers of French? Or should there be a special pedagogic norm for non-native speakers, as Valdman advocates and as the Japanese are proud of having developed for foreign learners of Japanese? (Siegal 1994). Now that instant access to real-life interactions in far-away countries is made possible via such electronic technologies as satellite, internet, multimedia or world wide web, questions of the representativity of language forms and language use become more crucial than ever.

Finally, there is one general phenomenon that is contributing to the erosion of the native speaker norm. Immigrant language learners are increasingly disinclined to ignore, let alone buy into the values and beliefs that underpin native speaker language use in their respective speech communities (Phillipson 1992). This claim to the respect of difference prompted by the large scale migrations of the last decade, corresponds to general postmodern trends in recent cultural theory. These are best expressed by Kristeva who writes about the language learning immigrant: 'The absorption of foreignness proposed by our societies turns out to be inacceptable for modern day individuals, who cherish their national and ethnic identity and their intrinsically subjective, irreducible difference' (Kristeva 1988:10). The same can apply in more subtle ways to language learners in developing countries like Vietnam. Vietnamese pupils are eager to learn English in order to be integrated into the larger world market of information and services, but their Vietnamese teachers are sometimes reluctant to teach them also what they perceive as English native speaker ideology. A typical case arose recently in an English class in Hanoi that used an American textbook. When the text called for reading aloud and translating the sentence 'A healthy diet increases the quality of life and even prolongs it', the teacher smiled and said softly, 'A healthy diet will increase your quality of life. Yes. As for prolonging it, that is for fate to decide, isn't it?' and he turned to the grammatical exercises instead (Sullivan, forthcoming).

All these developments problematise what is meant by native speaker standards (Goldstein 1987), and what is meant by appropriate language use. They put in question the native speaker's 'ownership' of language, to use Widdowson's phrase (Widdowson 1994). The temptation is great to infer automatically from someone's language to his/her membership into a monolithic, unidimensional culture and society. This has been the Achilles' heel of cross-cultural pragmatics and speech act realisation research, as well as of contrastive rhetoric. It is tempting to extrapolate from a linguistic to a cultural perspective, as Hatch did recently: 'While English stories tend to center on actions, Japanese stories are much more concerned with the development of characters, motives and relationships between characters' (Hatch 1992:172). But surely not all stories written in the English language tend to centre on actions, nor do all writers of the Japanese language show a concern for characters.

The notion: one native speaker, one language, one national culture is, of course, a fallacy. The utopia of membership in a national or multinational community of like-spoken and like-minded speakers has led critics like Paikeday to suggest that the ideal native speaker/hearer is really a monolingual who has been exposed to one and only one language during his entire life (Paikeday 1985:48). This idealised monolingual native speaker/hearer, representative of one monolingual discourse community, might still exist in people's imaginations, but has never corresponded to reality. Most people in the world belong to more than one discourse community, as Grosjean remarks (1982). They know and use more than one language: the language of the home and the language of the school, the language at work and the language of the foreign spouse, the language of the immigrant colleague and that of the foreign business partner. In fact if, as Garfinkel has claimed, 'the basis of culture is not shared knowledge, but shared rules of interpretation' (Garfinkel 1972:304), it would make more sense to view speakers acquiring over their lifetime a whole range of rules of interpretation that they use knowingly and judiciously according to the various social contexts in which they live and with which they make sense of the world around them. That, one could argue, is the characteristic of a 'competent language user': not the ability to speak and write according to the rules of the academy and the social etiquette of one social group, but the adaptability to select those forms of accuracy and those forms of appropriateness that are called for in a given social context of use. This form of competence is precisely the competence of the 'intercultural' speaker, operating at the border between several languages or language varieties, manoeuvring his/her way through the troubled waters of cross-cultural misunderstandings (Le Page and Tabouret-Keller 1985). That, not the untroubled mythical native speaker, then, should be our model.

The intercultural speaker

In the increasingly grey zones of our multilingual, multicultural societies, the dichotomy between native versus non-native speakers has outlived its use. Both native speakers and non-native speakers potentially belong to several speech communities of which they are the more or less recognised, more or less unrecognised members. Instead of a pedagogy oriented toward the native speaker, then, we may want to devise a pedagogy oriented toward the intercultural speaker.

Current efforts in Europe to develop language learners' 'intercultural' (Buttjes and Byram 1991) or 'transnational' (Baumgratz 1987) communicative competence strive to increase the quantity and quality of contacts between learners across national borders and through student exchanges. Their aim is to help learners analyse, reflect upon and interpret foreign cultural phenomena when using the language in contact with foreign nationals. Byram and others have proposed linking foreign language education and cultural studies, broadly defined (Byram 1989a, Roberts 1993). In countries like the United States, where the majority of language students do not go abroad, but where multiculturalism has become the hallmark of American classrooms, a pedagogy of the intercultural speaker is taking the form of efforts to make classroom discourse itself more explicitly intercultural. It suggests in particular viewing students' linguistic productions as cultural products in their own right. Various activities have been proposed in this regard. For example, Kramsch (1996a, 1996b) suggests using the summary as a way of having students, after reading a short story, express in their own words what they believe the story is about. An open comparison of all the summaries, pinned to the wall or written on the blackboard, gives students the opportunity to interpret their choices as to what to write and how to write it, and to reflect on why their choices differ from those of others. What students discover, like the teachers in the Leipzig seminar, is how much each one of them has constructed the meaning of the story according to their life experiences, ethnicity, social and economic background, attitudes and beliefs. In composition classes, Cazden (1992) has the students explore the different voices that can be heard within one and the same student text, for example by having students 'script' their own texts or perform others' through variations of Readers Theatre. In addition to identifying explicitly the social and cultural voices present in class, some scholars suggest capitalising on the multiple languages present in the foreign language classroom. Because in the United States so many learners of French or German are not monolingual monocultural Anglo-Americans, but are, for example, Mexican or Chinese-American bilingual speakers of Spanish or Chinese, and English, the suggestion has been made to consider the foreign language classroom as a multilingual discourse community (Blyth 1995) and to adopt a bilingual norm of communicative competence (see for example, Preston 1981, Ellis 1994:213, Valdes 1995). Here too, intercultural awareness is fostered by the systematic confrontation of various styles and language choices, and their respective cultural associations.

Traditional pedagogies based on the native speaker model usually define language learners in terms of what they are *not*, or at least *not yet*: they don't have the right French accent, they have 'not yet' acquired the French subjunctive, they 'still' don't master the French past tenses. If the *Bon Marché* advert were to figure in a foreign language textbook, it would probably be glossed with such marginal notes as 'le privilège = the privilege', 'rive gauche = the Left Bank' and 'abolir = to abolish'. It may even give the learners some cultural information about the French Revolution, the abolition of privileges and the history of the Left Bank.

But it would be less likely to engage the learners in discovering how they, as learners, respond to the way the grammar of the caption, the composition of the image, attempt to shape their cultural imagination. If students have been encouraged to identify, through contrast with others, the social and cultural voices in their own texts, they are better able to evaluate the choices that were made in the *Bon Marché* poster, by speculating on the choices that were not made, and by, extension, those they would have made themselves, had they had to design a poster for the *Bon Marché.*

After all, the caption could have started with: 'Au *Bon Marché*' rather than with 'Rive Gauche'. By fronting the simple locative 'Rive Gauche', the caption directs the attention of the reader to the icon of the leftist left bank of the Seine. The fonts chosen could have all been the same; instead, the rather aristocratic or right-wing font used for the R of Rive Gauche clashes with the more democratic fonts of the rest of the clause. The text could have used the informal expression '*personne ne veut*' that would have matched a simple vernacular '*il y a* encore des privilèges'. Instead, the choice of the more formal phrase 'nul ne souhaite', matched with the more formal register 'il existe encore des privilèges', places the second half of the caption into a higher, more upper-class, register, that even beginners can be sensitised to. The credit card itself, in the name of 'Mme Sophie Aubert' is both rather uppity in its choice of first name, but not too uppity since it refrains from using an aristocratic last name starting with 'de'. As Fairclough remarks: 'In order to interpret the features which are actually present in a text, it is generally necessary to take account of what other choices might have been made, i.e. of the systems of options in the discourse types which actual features come from' (Fairclough 1989:110).

When the *Bon Marché* advert is used to teach French in the United States or in Germany, the world of the ad and the world of its readers come into contact. Kress reminds us that texts attempt to position their readers in quite specific ways by evoking worlds, mental representations or schemata that they assume are shared between them and their readers (Kress 1988:107). Confronted with this poster, learners of French must not only learn the relevant 'cultural information' but acquire the 'cultural knowledge' necessary to structure and make sense of the world evoked by the poster (Byram 1989:121). This knowledge or 'savoir interprétatif' (Zarate 1993:118) can help them understand how the poster's cultural codes position them as readers. In the process, they will have to confront their own frame of reference, which is likely to be different from that of the readers targeted by the ad. For example, American learners might start questioning the ideal of equal opportunity propagated by American political rhetoric, and admit that there are also in American society some privileges that even money can't buy. Similarly, for East German learners of French this ad may be a reminder that not all privileges are the result of merit, as West Germans would have it, and that most are indeed just a matter of money or of having been born in the proper half of Germany.

Conclusion

In our days of frequent border crossings, and of multilingual multicultural foreign language classrooms, it is appropriate to rethink the monolingual native speaker norm as the target of foreign language education. As we revisit the marked and unmarked forms of language usership, I propose that we make the intercultural speaker the unmarked form, the infinite of language use, and the monolingual monocultural speaker a slowly disappearing species or a nationalistic myth.

Such a proposal entails the development of an intercultural competence that should be promoted both in the field and in the classroom. Foreign language learners are in a unique position to notice the gaps, the ruptures of expectation in the foreign cultural phenomena they encounter. As Zarate notes, they are able to offer a 're-reading' of habitual signs, a new perception of the familiar and the unfamiliar. 'The first glance [of the non-native speaker] decodes foreign reality with shattering innocence; at times in total rupture with the surface appearance of things, it points to anomalies, reveals clusters of significations that have never yet been described before by those very [native speakers] who have never seen them because they have integrated them [in their daily lives]' (Zarate 1993:117, my translation). As intercultural speakers, learners are likely to engage their teachers in a voyage of discovery that they had not always anticipated and for which they don't always feel prepared. Allowing students to become intercultural speakers, therefore, means encouraging teachers to see themselves, too, as brokers between cultures of all kinds.

We should not be unaware of the difficulties inherent in a true pedagogy of the intercultural speaker (see Kramsch, Cain and Murphy 1996). It is one thing to encourage students and teachers to become aware of others' and their own national identity; quite another to ask them to speak openly in class about their own ethnic, gender-related, race-related, or class-related particularities. Both approaches can easily fall prey to reductionism, essentialism and stereotyping. Teachers are rightly reluctant to reduce their students to representative samples of one or the other social group.

But language teachers are not called upon to be amateur psychoanalysts or social psychologists. As educators who teach *language* in the full sense of the word, their obligation is to confront students with the meanings associated with the specific uses of words, not with disembodied ideas and beliefs. People are not what we believe they are, but what they say they are. The responsibility of the language teacher is to teach culture *as it is mediated through language*, not as it is studied by social scientists and anthropologists (Kramsch 1996a). The privilege of the intercultural speaker must be accompanied by an increased sense of personal and individual responsibility in the use of words and in the ownership of their meanings. Adrienne Rich captures beautifully this mandate of the language learner:

> It doesn't matter what you think
> Words are found responsible
> all you can do is choose them
> or choose
> to remain silent.   Or, you never had a choice,
> which is why the words that do stand
> are responsible
> and this is verbal privilege. (1986:34)

The privilege of the intercultural speaker is an eminently verbal privilege indeed.

Note:
This chapter is a revised version of the James Alatis plenary delivered April 1, 1995 at the Annual TESOL Conference in Long Beach, CA, and of a keynote address November 11, 1995 at the Annual TESOL-Italy meeting in Rome, Italy.

2 *Civilisation*/Cultural Studies: an experiment in French and English schools

Michael Byram and Albane Cain

Introduction

The research presented here is the result of the work of a British and a French co-operative venture. The project, initiated by two researchers, Michael Byram (Durham University, School of Education) and Albane Cain (Institut National de Recherche Pédagogique, Paris), brought together academics and school teachers as a single team.

In the two countries, both researchers were eager to promote cultural learning in foreign language teaching at secondary level, and both researchers were at the concluding stages of different research projects that could be termed descriptive, investigating the effects of existing teaching practices on students' perceptions of and attitudes towards other countries (Cain and Briane 1994; Byram *et al.* 1991). They felt that the next stage should be a move to an interventionist style of research that could lead on to curriculum development.

This chapter provides, first, a description of the contexts within which the research was carried out, identifying the shared concerns and differences in emphasis between the English and French teams. This is followed by a brief account of the theoretical background derived from the descriptive research. Finally, after an analysis of the specific aims and objectives of the project, a description is given of the curriculum materials developed for use with English and French students.

Context

As far as the respective teaching contexts were concerned, there was in both countries a need for change. Although there was a common aim to develop better intercultural competence among the secondary school population, the teaching contexts prevailing in each country were entirely different.

In England, two general points need to be taken into account:

- the necessity of setting up conditions such that learning a foreign language would be well received by students who do not always perceive this as a necessarily worthwhile objective;
- the fact that the prevailing focus in upper secondary teaching has hitherto been literature; in other words there was a tendency to equate culture with literature.

In France, the conditions are different:

- there is no hostility towards the English language, as most French students and their parents are utterly convinced of its usefulness; this creates a different kind of problem: English is considered to be a sort of international Esperanto not connected in any way to any cultural matters;
- another element to be taken into account is the gap between the 11–15 year old group and the 15–18 year old group: for the former, language itself is the main objective, one could almost say the only aim pursued, the prevailing idea being that cultural matters can always be dealt with later on, in the *lycée*. However, language mastery is still the overwhelming issue during the first two years of *lycée*, and although the last year is traditionally devoted to the study of the United States, British culture is often never dealt with.

The consequent lack of understanding of Britain is evident from the enquiry carried out by the INRP team from 1989 to 1992 concerning the perceptions students have of the countries whose languages they learn. It involved students from all over France, and their impressions of Great Britain can be summarised as follows:

> It is a rainy country, deprived of industry, with no historical past, ruled by a queen, where people drink tea, beer or whisky, where men are still carrying umbrellas and wearing bowler hats, where the countryside is green. The country is also famous for its rock groups or singers, when they are not confused with American ones. It is inhabited by people of phlegmatic temperament and will soon be connected to the continent by a tunnel. (Cain 1990a)

A similar enquiry, based on a case study of two English schools, revealed a stereotype-dominated image of France among children learning French in lower secondary education. The teaching process seemed to have little impact and relatively minor influence, and we concluded as follows:

> In our view, the effect of language teaching on pupils' views is, in short, disappointing. Despite the fact that teachers and

> educational policy-makers subscribe to the belief that foreign language teaching should encourage positive attitudes and further pupils' understanding of cultures other than their own, and despite the genuine efforts of teachers in our study to realise these aims, the outcome seems to be no more than an acquisition of separate and largely decontextualised information which does not amount to an understanding or an insight into another people's way of living and thinking. (Byram *et al.* 1991:380)

We argued that there needs to be a more clearly structured and articulated methodology if the situation is to improve. The joint INRP–Durham project was an attempt to develop such an approach.

Thus the main concerns of the two teams may be summarised as follows:

- for the English, setting up and promoting favourable attitudes to the foreign country and people, and developing knowledge and understanding rather than stereotyped 'information';
- for the French, remedying the students' almost total lack of knowledge about the country whose language they were studying; it was also very important to introduce the teaching of cultural studies during students' *collège* years, i.e. 11–15.

Thus, although there was a common concern with developing appropriate knowledge in students, the starting point was different for each team. Secondly, the English team put more emphasis on attitude change than the French team, some of whom thought this was not a proper domain of influence.

In this approach, the French team were conforming with the *Instructions Officielles* (the official ministry guidelines), which assign three aims to the teaching of a foreign language: linguistic, cultural and conceptual, all destined to stimulate reflexion. The *Instructions Officielles* recommended the establishment of cultural references (*repères*) which might result in students acquiring frameworks of understanding and encourage cross-curricular co-operation through teachers being aware that these cultural 'landmarks' might appear in several subjects. Above all, the French team were fulfilling one of the goals of the traditional concept and philosophy of *l'école laïque*, the education of citizens, in a period focused on the building of a new Europe. It was therefore seen as an essential part of the work of the *collège*, and not just of the *lycée*. Moreover, a great number of students aged 11–15 pursue their education in *lycées professionels* (vocational training *lycées*) in which their contacts with a foreign language are restricted to language for specific purposes (required by their future trade) and the cultural dimension is the least of their concerns.

The English team did not, at the time, have national guidelines, but there were available various statements of aims, including the one for the General Certificate of Secondary Education, which is an examination taken at the end of compulsory education at age 16. This statement refers to the development of favourable attitudes to language learning and speakers of other languages, and secondly to the creation of insights into other cultures and civilisations. The statement was subsequently transferred into the National Curriculum for England and Wales and supplemented with a further aim: to create in learners a better understanding of themselves and their own culture.

For technical reasons, even though the project was originally intended to involve both upper and lower secondary age groups, this was only possible in France, where the experiment took place with 13–14 year old students (*quatrième*) and 17–18 year old students (*première*, one year before the *baccalauréat*). In England, the project involved 17–18 year old students in lower sixth (one year before GCE A-level).

Both teams had a roughly equal number of people working on the project: five teachers and one research assistant for the British team (or seven including the researcher), nine teachers for the French team (or ten including the researcher).

Theoretical framework and research focus

In the first instance, we had to delineate our area of research. Among the numerous existing definitions of *civilisation*, we opted for the following, given by François Poirier:

> By *civilisation* we mean the study of all the cultural features whether cultural, ethnographic, religious, technical or aesthetic, which during the course of history have marked the societies whose language we study. (Poirier 1990)

Secondly, we had to clarify and agree our views on the learning theories on which we would found our proposals for development materials and teaching methods. Preliminary work had been introduced in an earlier publication (Byram 1989a:102–119), in which it was argued that through exposure to the language and cultural concepts of another society, learners acquire new or modified schemata through which they understand the world. Every person born into a society has built up systems of perception and interpretation which are grounded in their native context, and which, being unconscious and non-verbalised, escape their control and interfere with their perception of other cultural systems. In the course of foreign language and culture learning, learners construct their knowledge of other cultures and countries, and during the process, partial learning will necessarily take place, involving the construction of intermediary systems.

The first focus of the research was the choice of themes. The theoretical background developed from the previous descriptive research, at the INRP (Cain and Briane 1994), had led to the identification of two different types or forms of knowledge:

- firstly, there are 'privileged areas', that is areas of particular importance, in which perceptions tend to congregate. These form a limited range of areas mainly connected to the activities of the senses, particularly sight, taste and, to a lesser degree, hearing. There are also areas linked to the students' affective life, where perceptions are not of a rational kind and betray the part played by the emotions;
- secondly, there are 'blank areas', which show a total absence of, or the existence of gaps in, knowledge about history, social and political organisation, and literature. These findings guided the choice of themes, but other parameters must also be taken into account, such as the interests of the students and their degree of cognitive and affective development.

The second research focus was the issue of the criteria for selecting teaching material. As we are dealing with young students, the problem of the selection of documents was a major one. In order to ensure that even younger students aged 13–14, no longer resort only to stereotyping and learn to relativise their perceptions, the following criteria for materials selection were adopted:

- a document has to involve a 'gap in content' (*écart de contenu*) by which we mean a significant difference between the implicit references inherent in (a part of) the students' native cultural system and the information included in the document,
- there has to be a problem of cultural understanding requiring an intellectual effort involving the learners in a process of 'de-centring',
- the various documents have to be presented in a specific thematic order (*un fil conducteur*),
- the choice of topics has to ensure that they are within the intellectual grasp of learners and that they deal with significant, fundamental areas of cultural life and practices.

The English team thus made their choice for Lower Sixth by consulting several syllabuses for teaching sociology at GCE A-level, narrowing the choice by identifying common themes. It was argued that this reflects the intellectual level expected of students at this stage of secondary education, and represents what they would be studying in their own society if they were to take sociology as part of their upper secondary course. The choice made by the English team was also taken into consideration by the French team.

The third research focus was assessment. This was dealt with particularly by the English team, because in the English education system there is no nationally determined curriculum in upper secondary, and the 'backwash effect' of examinations is particularly strong. However, we would argue that the development of teaching methods for the cultural dimension will be closely related in any educational system to the efficacy of assessment methods, and we shall return to the issue of assessment below.

Aims, objectives and methods

The overall aims and specific teaching objectives of our project, for both English and French students, were:

- to foster the acquisition of a cultural competence, that is the ability to interpret social phenomena which the students may encounter in the course of their contacts with another culture, these contacts being either direct or mediated during the language class;
- to develop such flexibility in the students that they can accept other interpretative systems and relate them to their own.

These general principles were translated in terms of more specific teaching objectives:

- to allow learners to reconsider the position of their own culture and cultural practices in comparison with that of another community;
- to take the students' own society and its cultural practices as a focus of the teaching;
- to provide learners with a body of knowledge about some aspects of another country and its cultural practices.

Methods differed in the two teams as a function of the constraints of the teaching context, but also as a consequence of the disciplines upon which they drew. The French team, as will be seen below, introduced a stronger historical dimension to their materials and methods, influenced in part by the demands of the *Instructions Officielles* for cross-curricular co-operation. The English team took their starting point in sociology, social anthropology and ethnography. In spite of the specific choices made by the two teams, a common ground was found which consisted in:

- the use of a comparative approach;
- the special place allocated to the native culture;
- the stress placed on the varied nature of the documents, the variety of tasks proposed, and the variety of skills demanded in the learners' approaches to the materials.

The French dossiers

The French course consisted of six dossiers, or units of work, with a maximum of 10 lessons of one hour each devoted to each dossier, with one exception, one dossier lasting nearly five weeks instead of two or three weeks. The topics and titles for the dossiers were:

- Housing in Great Britain and in France: beyond appearances;
- Education in France and Great Britain: two ways of achieving citizenship;
- Monarchy and Republic: two views of democracy;
- British Political Institutions;
- An example of a multiethnic society: Great Britain;
- Sports.

The first three dossiers were written for the 11–15 age group and the last three for the 15–18 age group. The factors which presided over the choice of topics included:

- the need to provide the rational information which is lacking in certain 'blank areas';
- the need to show that a cultural phenomenon can only be understood when positioned in an economic or historical perspective;
- the desire to show that young students can work on topics even when they are abstract;
- the desire to stay as close as possible to the choices made by the British team.

The common approach adopted by both lower and upper secondary groups was the following:

- Stage 1: Assessing students' knowledge and perceptions.

This involved establishing an inventory of students' knowledge from a comparativist perspective. It was designed to assess the students' knowledge, bring to light their way of seeing things, and show up gaps.

- Stage 2: Analysing the perceptions/stereotypes uncovered during the previous stage.
- Stage 3: Providing information and juxtaposing the two cultural systems so that the native system is no longer the ruling force.

It will be evident that we put considerable emphasis on a body of knowledge we thought students should acquire, an emphasis which was not the original intention of the French team. There was one telling incident which might clarify our reasoning. The very first dossier on housing originated from the opinion expressed by a French student about English houses, after a stay in England: 'They're awful!' When asked to justify his opinion, he said: 'In England, all the houses look the same.' This perception of uniformity, whether correct or not, was accompanied by a derogatory value judgement. That judgement was held as specifically defining the foreign country. So there are here all the elements necessary to provide the student with sufficient reasons to settle comfortably into the role of a conscious opponent of that which is foreign, who will find it quite pointless to study the foreign language. It was this analysis which gradually brought the French team to share the preoccupations of the British team. Our hypothesis was that if students are made to understand *why* there is some similarity among houses and to see that a comparable similarity exists in France, then maybe they will avoid complete rejection, which will otherwise not only create a dismissive evaluation of English housing but also affect the whole process of language learning.

One of the centres of interest of the project was the issue of adapting themes and methods to different levels of linguistic proficiency and to different age groups and levels of cognitive development. This was evident in two dossiers which dealt with the same theme for lower and upper secondary students. The theme of the two dossiers was that of power and politics. 'Monarchy and Republic' was designed for the 13–14 age group and 'British Political Institutions' for the 16–17 age group. The data on which both dossiers were based included election results, statistics, political speeches and interviews with politicians. For example, the issues in 'Monarchy and Republic' include:

- The sovereign (the work consists in determining the role of the Queen in British society from the clues given by her picture on stamps, coins and similar public objects, and bringing students to an awareness of the hereditary nature of monarchy);
- The degree to which the Church and State are or are not separate (using a comparison of images on banknotes in France and Britain, and a speech given by the Queen for Christmas 1991, in which references to 'God' and 'prayers' appear);

- The distinction between Queen and Prime Minister (UK);
- The electoral systems (UK and France);
- The anthems and the part God plays, or does not play, in each (UK and France). (For a description of sample lessons see Byram, Morgan *et al.* 1994:82–88.)

The second dossier relies almost exclusively on a historical approach, and involves four stages:

- factual data concerning the British political system;
- work on the ideological programme of political parties, and on the potential contradictions and surprises these positions at times imply;
- a study of the profile of the British electorate on the basis of statistical data;
- an analysis of the symbolic role of the monarch through the study of a range of interviews with members of the British electorate.

In general, the materials and methods involved in almost all of the dossiers combined ethnographic and historical approaches, and were thus an indication of the ways in which a joint, international project brought new ideas. For instance, as far as the dossier entitled 'Housing in Great Britain and France: beyond appearances' is concerned, the starting point of the work was based on an ethnographic approach. It originated in the words of a student quoted earlier from an interview aimed at assessing the effects of a trip to Britain on school children aged 14. The uniformity they perceived and revealed provided the topic for further interviews of British natives discussing the student's judgement and expressing their own opinion. This notion of uniformity was then considered from a historical point of view and seen to have been brought about by the industrial revolution. The students were gradually made to perceive the correlation between the location of industrial ideas and the demographic growth of some specific cities. As a consequence of this sudden increase of population, a logical response was the development of the type of housing known as 'back to backs'.

The English units of work

As indicated above, the choice of topics for the units of work was based on parallel courses in sociology. It was important that the experimental work should be related to students' existing syllabus, so that they would not perceive the course as wasting valuable time. Five topics were chosen, and each unit was designed for approximately ten hours of work. The first three focused on stages of socialisation and on the values inherent in the process of acquiring various social identities. The first is 'The Family', and themes within the unit include: name-giving, ceremonies (of name-days, birthdays, Christmas, etc.), meal-times (as a location for the creation of a family and its values) and differing family structures, including links with extended families.

Secondary socialisation takes place largely through schooling and the second topic was 'Education'. Here the specific nature of French schooling and its historical origins was the starting point. Students also learnt about the structures and experiences of being in upper secondary education through interviews with French students, and compared them with their own.

The third topic was 'Work'. Here students studied working patterns, questions of the prestige of different jobs, the ways in which people acquire particular jobs and the process of their socialisation into them, and the relationship between 'work' and 'leisure'. Although the students had only limited experience of work, through part-time jobs, for example, they recognised this as a third stage of the life-cycle and had friends who had already left full-time education for the world of work – here again, they could compare.

The fourth topic was 'Regional Identity'. This was chosen as a particular illustration of the concept of social identity, attempting to demonstrate to students that we have multiple identities, each linked with a particular culture and cultural practices. This fourth unit focused on Britanny, since the study of the economy, geography and history of Britanny was part of the normal syllabus. The innovative dimension of our work was, however, to move away from the disciplines of history, economics and geography, for which language teachers are in any case seldom well prepared, and to draw upon another discipline, as we shall see below.

The specificity of the English units was their attempt to draw upon ethnographic methods of data collection and analysis. In addition to the common aims of the French and English projects outlined above, the English team put emphasis on the aim of encouraging 'empathy with French people and some feeling of what it is like to be French', as it was stated in the team's declaration of aims and objectives. We attempted to develop an insider perspective on aspects of French life based on the ethnographic methods of participant observation, even though this had to be done vicariously in the classroom, rather than in the immediacy of fieldwork. We thus also included in our specific aims the acquisition of 'ethnographic techniques with which to approach other cultures and the curiosity, openness and independence to do so'.

This aim was linked with the comparative method, in order to turn students' attention onto their own cultural practices and environment. Students were asked to carry out small-scale investigations and observations of the world around them and then studied corresponding data, previously collected by the research team 'in the field' in France. This approach was most effective in the units on the family and education. For example, learners devised sociograms of relationships among students and teachers in their class and school, and compared them with sociograms collected from *lycée* students. They listened to ethnographic, in-depth interviews with French people of their own age who described their family life, their school and particular events within them. They also attended a day-school where the focus was on learning techniques of questionnaire production, of interviewing and of observation, and they tried out their skills with native speakers or with video-recordings.

It will be evident from this that the English team put less emphasis on the historical than did the French team. It was decided that a historical dimension should be pursued when it reflected what native speakers might be expected to know about their own cultural history. This of course begs the question of what 'native-speaker knowledge' might mean. It is related, too, to the question of which materials should be selected as examples of particular cultural practices. In other words, it is necessary to have a view on what 'body of knowledge' should be made available to students. Our response was to think in terms of what their French peers at a similar level of education might be expected to know about their own society, but augmented by the insights of the outsider and 'participant observer' who has the benefit of a comparative perspective.

In all these issues there is a danger that students will over-generalise and acquire new stereotypes to substitute for or complement those discovered in our earlier research. The use of specific historical or contemporary illustrations – interviews with particular people from particular places, for example – was an attempt to overcome this problem, as was the emphasis on acquiring skills and techniques of enquiry. The intention was to ensure that students recognised the diversity in both their own and the foreign society, whilst realising that there are some values, shared meanings and traditions of which every member of a social group is aware, even if they do not subscribe to them.

Evidence from assessment suggested that the English team were not always successful in overcoming the problem of over-generalisation, and the issue of assessment becomes all the more significant.

Assessment

The issue of assessment is not untilled ground. In the English education system, examination boards have introduced new syllabuses in which knowledge about a foreign country and its *civilisation* are tested. However, a closer analysis of these tests and the processes of marking scripts showed that this knowledge is allocated only a small percentage of marks, the larger percentage being allocated to issues such as fluent and accurate use of the foreign language, analytical skill, good organisation and control of the material (Byram, Morgan *et al.* 1994:144).

In our project we identified various aspects of the testing of cultural learning:

- the 'content' to be tested: knowledge, attitudes, behavioural skill with respect to the non-verbal dimensions of social exchange;
- the ability to investigate: since we had focused on ethnographic techniques, these should in principle also be tested;
- the techniques for testing: oral and/or written assessment, using role-play, using the essay;
- the criteria for assessment and the determination of levels of competence.

We experimented with a number of techniques where the main aim was to explore students' ability to analyse and relate different cultures to each other. These included asking them to comment on and explain the reactions of some French people to living in an English environment. They were expected to draw upon their knowledge of French cultural practices – in the home and family or at school – to suggest what might be the underlying conflict of perspectives causing the interviewees to complain or criticise. Another technique involved role play where students had to mediate in a clash of English and French practices with respect to school uniforms. Further details can be found elsewhere (Byram, Morgan *et al.* 1994:147–68), but the issue of criteria to establish differentiated levels of competence remained unresolved. (For a more recent attempt to define cultural competence and suggest approaches to assessment, see Byram and Zarate 1994.)

Conclusion

Although our project focused on specific topics taught to specific groups of learners, it was our intention to develop some generalisable principles. These involve issues of content and the representation of (part of) another culture, of methodology and the reference disciplines, and of assessment. The production of particular materials was not the main concern, although many teachers have asked us for copies of materials. In fact many of the materials used were taken from published sources, from textbooks or video materials, and it was rather in the development of aims, objectives and methods that the project was innovative. Nonetheless, the French team has published its materials (Cain 1996) in order to facilitate the dissemination of the methods and ideas which underpin them.

As for the development of linguistic competence, it is important to stress that the units of work and the dossiers were taught in parallel with other lessons which focused on the acquisition of linguistic skills and knowledge of the foreign language. Nonetheless, we would argue that linguistic and cultural learning are integrated. The study of the structures and semantics of a language raise students' awareness of its relationship to the cultures it expresses. Secondly, the specific tasks in the dossiers and units, which were all carried out in the foreign language, ensured that language activities – which are often empty of any content, with an exclusive emphasis on communicative objectives – are instead recharged with meaning and purpose.

The value of such a project resides in cross-cultural collaboration and for teachers and researchers the benefits lie in the awareness that language teaching is enriched by the contribution from other disciplines. New disciplines are worth exploring, in our case ethnography and history, and a new balance may be struck between the disciplines. The scope of the project and of the topics being taught made teachers realise that they should accept that they are no longer the only sources of knowledge. It is essential in this kind of work to let students play their part, and plan for experiential learning. The experiments in assessment, though inconclusive, ensured that we recognise that assessment should deal not only with knowledge, but also with flexibility and openness to other cultures, the affective and the cognitive should both be part of the teaching/learning and assessment objectives.

Many of these insights and experiences would not have developed in the same ways without international co-operation and the confrontation with other traditions of teaching and research which it brought. Such co-operation is, however, not always easy, since it challenges the taken-for-granted modes of working, and submits teachers and researchers to precisely those experiences of otherness which are the aims and methods of the course developed for students (see Morgan this volume). It is a salutary reminder of the demands involved.

3 Evolving intercultural perceptions among university language learners in Europe

James A. Coleman

Introduction

Every year, around twelve thousand students from the British Isles undertake extended residence abroad in the context of a degree programme which includes one or more foreign languages (Coleman 1995a). The majority go to study at a university in the target country, although the exact proportion following a study placement depends on the target language. A quarter of students of French, 20 per cent of students of German, and 10 per cent of students of Spanish go as English language assistants, and the remainder on work placements or in a combination of roles (Coleman 1996a).

The intuition that immersion in the target language community would bring linguistic benefits to the learner, combined with the advantage to the host country of having native-speaker input in language classes in secondary schools led to the establishment of a programme of exchanges between the United Kingdom and France in 1904, and numbers of students spending what is generally known as a 'year abroad' grew as an increasing proportion of British universities made such a stay mandatory. For other European countries, residence abroad for language students has been the exception rather than the rule, but European Union programmes such as ERASMUS, LINGUA and SOCRATES have further increased the flow of students, although the EU objective of 10 per cent of students following part of their degree programme in a different member state has not yet been achieved. Outside Europe, attendance at a foreign university is the norm, and the common title is 'study abroad programs'. It has been suggested that worldwide over a million students each year take part in immersion programmes (Furnham 1993).

Where the objectives of the programme are explicitly stated (which is often not the case for UK universities), they typically fall into three domains: personal maturity and independence, cultural insight, and improved foreign language proficiency. A close link is to be assumed between enhanced linguistic competence and enhanced cultural competence. Not only do most definitions of foreign language proficiency include a sociocultural/sociolinguistic competence (Canale and Swain 1980; Canale 1983; Bachman 1990), but additionally a sympathetic attitude to speakers of the target language which cultural insight might provide has been associated, within several influential models of second language acquisition (SLA), with above-average proficiency levels (Gardner and Lambert 1972; Schumann 1978; 1986).

Studies of the motivation of university language learners (Ely 1986; Evans 1988; Roberts 1992; Singleton and Singleton 1992; Oxford and Shearin 1994; Meara 1994; Coleman 1994; 1995b; 1996a) invariably show the importance of an interest in the foreign people and their culture. The topic is explored more fully in Coleman (1996a) and in other chapters of the present volume.

Underpinning many of the often tacit assumptions concerning student residence abroad is the belief that 'to know them is to love them': that residence will inevitably lead to cultural understanding and that this in turn will lead to more positive attitudes, which will feed into improved language acquisition in a virtuous spiral. One of the objectives of the European Language Proficiency Survey was to test this assumption.

The method (subjects, procedure, materials) have been fully described in Coleman (1996a), and are merely summarised here. The European Language Proficiency Survey, a quantitative, repeated measured cross-sectional study of over twenty-five thousand language learners, has been conducted since 1993 by the University of Portsmouth, with the cooperation of the Universities of Duisburg and Bochum, and with additional funding from the British Council and Deutscher Akademischer Austauschdienst under their Academic Research Collaboration programme, and from the Commission of the European Communities under its LINGUA programme. Data elicitation, in the two administrations here described (autumn 1993, autumn 1994) has relied on a target language C-Test and an evolving questionnaire. The C-Test (see Grotjahn, Klein-Braley and Raatz 1997: Klein-Braley 1997) is an economical, integrative, semi-direct, objective test of reduced redundancy which intensive research has shown to have very high reliability and criterion-referenced validity. C-Tests were administered in French Spanish, German, Russian and English to students in eight European countries. While the survey as a whole explored proficiency, progress, background, attitudes, motivations and skills, the questionnaire item considered in the present article sought data on the attitudes of respondents in the British Isles to members of the target language community and of their own community, and on how these attitudes evolve. The question has its origins in an unpublished MA thesis by

Lorraine Pickett (Pickett 1993), which was in turn based on a semantic differential technique using adjectives which have figured in many earlier studies. In the version of the questionnaire administered in the pilot survey in October 1993, respondents were asked:

> **22. In your opinion, which of the following adjectives best describe:**
> **(a) People of your own nationality (b) People who speak the language you are being tested on? Please use the following scale:**
>
> 1 = not at all 2 = rarely 3 = sometimes 4 = frequently 5 = very much

	(a)	(b)
Emotional		
Arrogant		
Serious		
Friendly		
Confident		
Logical		
Generous		
Calm		
Lazy		
Helpful		
Efficient		
Impatient		
Stubborn		
Honourable		
Competent		
Good-humoured		
Shy		
Honest		

Hard-working
Patient
Loud
Tolerant
Thrifty

In the full survey, the list of adjectives was reduced by the elimination of 'honourable', 'honest' and 'thrifty', and the accidental omission by the printer of 'generous' from the L2landers' table.[1] The two halves of the question were physically separated on different pages of the questionnaire, with the adjectives presented in a different order in each. The scale was reduced from five to four in order to accentuate any movement from positive to negative or negative to positive (Coleman 1995c). In each case, there was a far higher non-response rate on this question than on any other in the questionnaire, with annotations indicating some students' unwillingness to stereotype nationalities. The non-response rate varied according to whether a quality was positive or negative, and how closely it fitted a recognisable stereotype; rates were in the range 8–10 per cent in the pilot, 7–13 per cent in the full survey, with up to 18 per cent non-responses from Russianists.

Previous residence abroad

One factor which might be predicted to influence attitudes to native speakers of the target language is previous first-hand experience of them, and this will depend on the circumstances of contact with them. As Tables[2] 1, 2 and 3 show, students going on placement are by no means inexperienced travellers, whether measured in absolute terms, by the number of visits, or by the total time spent in L2land (and the data exclude travel to other destinations). Nine out of ten students who are just beginning their university career have already made the acquaintance of L2land; many have made multiple visits and stayed for at least a month. Compulsory residence abroad is therefore not, in the vast

[1] In common with other published reports on the European Language Proficiency Survey, which already encompasses five target languages and eight countries of origin, this article adopts the convention of referring to the target foreign language as the L2, to a country or countries where the L2 is spoken as L2land, and to its inhabitants as L2landers. The native language, country and compatriots are L1, L1land and L1landers.

[2] All tables are to be found at the end of this chapter.

majority of cases, their first acquaintance with a target language community. Amalgamating data from the two survey stages, we can say that fewer than one in twenty Year 2 respondents in French and German had *not* already visited L2land: the figures are 4.31 per cent and 4.36 per cent respectively.

The circumstances of previous visits to L2land varied according to target language. Table 4 gives data for all years of study. For French, holidays precede school trips and exchanges, with visits to friends or relations next. For German, exchanges are more significant than the other three main options. For Spanish, holidays dominate and school trips are relatively unimportant. About one in five students of these three languages will have worked in L2land, the same proportion as have been there to meet a course requirement. Russianists' experiences of L2land tend to be more academic than social, with course requirements and language courses the principal reasons for travel.

It should be noted that the samples of Year 1 students of Russian and Spanish are anomalous: the C-Test being too difficult for beginners, *ab initio* learners are excluded from the Year 1 sample, but they are present in the Year 2 group, which, as a result, is on average younger and less proficient than the Year 1 sample. Thus in Tables 5, 6, 7 and 8, where the data are broken down by year of study, responses for Year 1 Russian are anomalous in columns relating to exchanges and university requirements.

The tables show that figures concerning previous L2land residence are relatively stable across years of study for most categories, although students in German, Spanish and Russian may take a language course during their university career, and there is a modest rise in holidays taken in Germany, France and Russia. The major difference, as might be expected, comes from meeting university residential requirements per se, or from employment, including assistantships, undertaken to meet such requirements.

It is clear, then, that the vast majority of British Isles language students undertaking compulsory residence abroad already know the country they are going to, often from frequent and extended visits, but that the role played in L2land – holiday-maker, exchange student, employee, au pair or whatever – will vary with the language being studied.

Findings of the pilot survey

In an earlier article describing the findings of the pilot study on attitudes to L2landers (Coleman 1996b), I summarised some theoretical work and other research on attitudes and stereotypes in relation to second language acquisition (SLA). In particular, I reported the results of a study of 108 study placements in France and Germany. Willis *et al.* (1977) found changes in the attitudes of University of Bradford students towards the British, the French and the Germans on a range of qualities, though by no means all, after residence abroad. However, perhaps in part because of the modest scope of the survey, no pattern of change emerges, and it is unclear what students' original attitudes were and what stereotyped notions they may have had.

My analysis of the European Language Proficiency Survey pilot data (Coleman 1996b) confirmed the existence of national stereotypes among approximately 3,000 respondents. In summary, on *emotionality*, the Spaniards outscore the French, British and Germans respectively, while the French and Germans are far more *arrogant* than the British or Spanish. The Germans are most *serious*, *competent* and *efficient*, the Spanish least so, with roles exactly reversed on *friendly*. Germans win on *logicality*, followed by Britons, French and Spanish, but the latter win on *generosity*. On *calmness* the Mediterranean temperament counts against the French and Spanish, but the French are perceived as somewhat less *lazy* than the British, with the Spanish and Germans at opposite extremes. Spaniards are more *helpful* and *good-humoured* than the British, who marginally outscore both French and Germans. The British are the only *patient* nation, the Germans by far the most *hard-working*. The Spanish are most *loud*, the British least. But Britons are more *tolerant* than the French or Germans. No nation is *shy* – but especially not foreigners – while all foreigners are more *confident* than the British. This last judgment probably reflects the insecurity of the language learner. The conclusion on stereotypes is a comparative one:

> Compared to the British, the French are arrogant, emotional, impatient, ill-tempered, loud, confident, intolerant, not at all calm or shy, and relatively stubborn, unserious, illogical and lazy. Compared to the British, the Germans are serious, unemotional, logical, efficient, hard-working, competent, not lazy or shy in the slightest, arrogant, confident, impatient, intolerant, ill-tempered, loud and relatively unfriendly and ungenerous. Compared to the British, the Spanish are loud, emotional, unserious, illogical, inefficient, incompetent, and sometimes impatient, but at the same time friendly, confident, helpful, good-humoured and generous to a fault. (Coleman 1996b: 166–7)

Judgments of the British are relatively homogeneous across students of different L2s, but it is noticeable that in some instances the British rating is affected by conscious or unconscious comparison with the

L2lander rating. For instance, students of German, whose target language community rates as very unemotional and very logical, score the British higher on *emotional* and lower on *logical* than do students of other languages.

The same article (Coleman 1996b) notes that these stereotypes are remarkably stable, surviving L2land residence wholly unscathed. However, it also notes some evidence of change in attitudes in part of the sample, nearly always in the same direction, i.e. to the detriment of L2landers. Thus returners from a sojourn abroad, as compared to first-year students of the same language, find the French less friendly, less efficient, less good-humoured and rather less helpful (but also less loud). They find the Germans more competent, more hard-working, rather more efficient, less emotional, less lazy, more impatient, less patient, and at the same time less friendly, less helpful, less honourable, less tolerant and rather less good-humoured. They find the Spanish more emotional, less serious, more tolerant, and rather less efficient, hard-working, competent and logical. In the case of both Germans and Spaniards, the stereotypes are actually reinforced by contact.

The sample of students of Russian were too small to allow generalisations, but responses suggested that the effect on student attitudes of residence in Russia was even more dramatically negative than living in France, Germany or Spain.

Comparisons with groups of students of French and English from Germany and Austria showed that national stereotypes of one's own and other cultures are not confined to the British Isles.

The pilot survey thus suggested that UK students of foreign languages hold clear, differentiated stereotypes of other European nationalities, and that residence in L2land has served, if anything, to reinforce the stereotype, while diminishing students' rating of L2landers on non-stereotypical qualities.

Findings of the full survey

Respondents delivered generally favourable judgments of all nationalities: this should be borne in mind during the following analysis, which concentrates on differentiated stereotypes and on diachronic changes in attitudes.

Table 9 is reproduced from Coleman (1996a). Responses for the total sample, including all years of study, give an idea of the qualities most strongly associated with particular nationalities, especially by comparison with the British.

Comparison between the two adjacent columns, 'L1landers' and

'L2landers', for each language group will give the differences between the stereotypes students have of their compatriots and of their target language community. Students of French, for instance, find the British markedly more good-humoured than they do the French, markedly less confident, but equally hard-working.

Comparing the successive 'L1lander' columns will show the stability of Britons' views of themselves, for example on competence, across students of the four target languages. Any variations would appear to be motivated by contrast – unconscious in this case – with particular L2landers: see for example the difference between how *serious* the British are viewed by Germanists (whose L2landers are very serious) and Hispanists (whose L2landers are not) or a similar effect with regard to *efficient*.

Comparing successive 'L2lander' columns reveals the distinct images our students have of speakers of the different foreign languages. On *logical*, for example, one could establish a hierarchy: Germans lead the French and British, ahead of the Spanish and finally the Russians.

Looking across all eight rows shows which qualities are not associated with any particular nationality: stubbornness, for instance.

Vertical comparisons reveal the strength of association between the country and the quality. Anything over 3.0 or under 2.0 is distinctive: the Germans' 3.591 for *hard-working* or the Spaniards' 1.730 for *shy* are exceptional. The Russians, to take an example from the middle of the final column, are seen as more emotional than stubborn or competent.

These data, drawn from a huge sample of some seventeen thousand students, thus confirmed the pilot study's finding that foreign language students in the British Isles hold firm stereotypes of other European nations whose language they are learning.

Evolution of perceptions

Our first attempt to identify movement in students' perceptions of L2landers took the form of comparative mean ratings on the three-point scale (Coleman 1996b), but as the chart for learners of French in the full survey shows (Table 10), this approach did not identify any substantial, statistically significant differences.

And yet a comparison of Year 1 mean ratings, to three decimal points, with ratings from Year 4 students, if only differences of 0.1 and above were retained, *did* suggest that a non-random change was present, however slight (Table 11).

It will be noted that while the changes are modest, they are all in the same direction, i.e. towards a lower rating for L2landers on positive qualities and a higher rating on negative qualities (with the exception of *loud* and *serious*). As in the pilot study, views on L1landers remained comparatively stable, but where they did move, the direction was always opposite to that observed with regard to L2landers, as if experience of the other had increased appreciation of one's compatriots. It should be remembered here that, in the revised questionnaire as opposed to the pilot questionnaire, the two questionnaire items were physically separated and the order of qualities scrambled to make consciously comparative ratings all but impossible.

With the pilot data, we were able to show movement by totalling those making positive judgments and those making negative judgments, and expressing one as a proportion of the other, or the changing ratio between the two (Coleman 1996a). Having excluded the neutral choice from the revised questionnaire, we are better able to express the shift from positive to negative and vice versa with regard to the findings of the full survey (Tables 12 to 19: only differences of 8 percentage points or more are retained).

Between one-twelfth and one-fifth of students returning from France or *Francophonie* have a less favourable opinion of their hosts on seven positive and two negative qualities than do students at an earlier stage of their course (Table 12); this is entirely consistent with the findings of the pilot survey (Coleman 1996b). Table 13 suggests that the unconscious comparison of L2landers and L1landers operates diachronically as well as synchronically: whereas views of the home community are far more stable – after all, the respondents know that community far more intimately – the changes in perception of the impatience, patience and calm of the British are a mirror image of the new perception of French speakers.

In other words, 12–15 per cent *more* of post-residence-abroad students than of pre-residence-abroad students find the French arrogant and impatient, and 8–15 *fewer* of them find the French good-humoured, logical, patient, friendly, tolerant, helpful or efficient; while 8–12 per cent *fewer* of the post-residence-abroad group rate the British emotional or impatient, and a similar proportion *more* find them patient and calm. Extended residence abroad tends to increase the ethnocentricity of some students of French.

Intimate experience of German speakers appears from Table 14 to bring similar disillusion. L2landers are marked down by returning sojourners on positive characteristics – patient, good-humoured, helpful, tolerant, friendly – and marked up on negative ones (arrogant and impatient). The change on *emotional* is from a low level to a still lower one, reflecting a strengthening of the national stereotype.

Table 15 again shows a corresponding change in returners' opinions of their compatriots, with revised judgments on patience, seriousness and generosity. Although the changes on other qualities are lower than eight percentage points and therefore not shown in the Table, L2landers for Year 4 do score markedly higher on *hard-working* and *serious*, while L1landers are marked down by Year 4 students on *logical*, *efficient*, and *competent* (but also *stubborn*), and up on *good-humoured* and *tolerant*. It is hard to conclude other than that students are re-evaluating their own community in the light of their experience of the other. This re-evaluation is usually but not always to the benefit of the home community, and almost invariably by contradistinction to the L2land community.

It is interesting to note that, for learners of French and German, who represent the vast majority of UK and Irish students abroad, nearly all the major changes in perception are on *inter-personal* variables and not *personal* variables, i.e. those qualities which reflect social psychology rather than the psychology of personality, and which are likely to reflect personal experiences rather than observation, subjective responses rather than objective ones. It is tempting to speculate that student attitudes are more influenced by *interactions* while abroad than by mere *observations*. The topic would reward further research.

For learners of Spanish, however (Table 16), the experience of living abroad leads returners to downgrade their hosts on both personal and inter-personal qualities: efficiency, logicality, hard work, calmness, competence, laziness, patience, seriousness, arrogance and tolerance. There is very little evidence here (Table 17) of compensatory re-evaluation of the British or Irish.

The greatest disillusionment (Table 18) seems reserved for students of Russian. There is scarcely a quality on which finalists do not judge Russian speakers more harshly than first-year students. Not only are the Russians marked down on nearly every characteristic, but it is also in this chart that the largest percentage swings are found – up to 31 per cent. One possible explanation is that the Russian people are the least known by our students before they go to live there. Another is that the smaller sample might be less representative. It may also be that the Year 1 population, having opted for an unusual subject at A-level, has an exceptional commitment to it which encompasses unrealistically rosy views of the target population, views which are not shared by the *ab initio* students who join the sample from Year 2 onwards and are therefore reflected in the Year 4 figures.

Nonetheless, and although a majority will often have a positive attitude to both their own and the foreign culture, it seems to be demonstrated that, whatever the target language, the experience of residence abroad for language students will not enhance their view of the target culture, and may well diminish it.

From Tables 12 to 19 it is clear that not every change in perception of L2landers sees a corresponding shift in the opposite direction, in the perception of L1landers. But, with a single exception (*emotional* for French speakers), there is no shift in the latter without a corresponding and opposite shift in the former. In other words, all changes in students' perception of their compatriots seem to have their origin in a changed perception of foreigners: the perception of the degree to which the British lack a negative quality or possess a good one is influenced by students' disillusionment with the degree to which their target language community display that quality.

These findings are counter-intuitive: would UK universities send twelve thousand students abroad each year if they expected a substantial proportion to come back with a more negative view of the culture whose language they are studying? Since the study was cross-sectional rather than longitudinal, it is important to establish whether the findings can be further replicated, and in particular to establish to what extent the pilot study, with parallel, albeit smaller, samples, confirms the findings on changing views as it confirmed those on stereotypes.

It is unfortunately not possible to establish a direct comparison between the pilot study and the full study, since the former used a five-point scale and the latter a four-point scale. However, the trends (cf. Coleman 1996b) are very clear. For students of French there is an identical movement on most qualities, and no movements which contradict the results of the full survey. The German findings exactly replicate the pilot study, with movement in the same direction on the same variables. The pilot Spanish sample comprised two different and relatively small groups whose views sometimes differed, but as with French most changes are replicated, and none are inconsistent, with the exception of one group's showing an increased appreciation of Spanish speakers' tolerance. All the many shifts in perception by students of Russian reflect similar shifts in the pilot study, except for a reversed trend on *confident*, which may be explained by the small pilot sample (N = 42 of this item). Thus, as regards changed perceptions of foreigners among students returning from mandatory residence abroad, the very large numbers of the full survey replicate in virtually every respect the findings of the pilot survey: for a significant minority of students ranging from 8 per cent to over 30 per cent, living in the target language community results in less favourable views of the inter-personal and personal qualities of that community.

Possible explanations

We have already discussed (Coleman 1996a) factors which may have influenced student responses. These include a reactivity effect (attitudes form or solidify *because* the questionnaire elicits them), the suggestion that students all have unrealistically optimistic views of L2landers until they live with them, and the timing of the administration of the questionnaire very early in the final year – although this last explanation was explored by re-administration of the questionnaire eight months later and found inadequate. A single explanation is in any case unlikely, given that the changes in perception relate to different factors in different target countries. Perhaps students have discovered the truth, and that stereotypes do correspond to a nation's reality. Perhaps culture shock has frozen students' perception at an early stage of acclimatisation.

In investigating such phenomena from cross-sectional data alone, one can either start from similar attitudes and try to find common factors in respondents' background, or compare students with different backgrounds to see how they assess L2landers. The first approach showed only that the typical profile of those giving highest ratings on at least two adjectives which are either positive or negative does not differ from the norm. The second found, not surprisingly, that those who judge harshly on certain qualities are more likely than others to judge harshly on other qualities. Table 20 gives Pearson product moment correlations for key qualities as assessed by learners of French ($n > 11000$, $p < .001$ in every case). Correlations were still stronger among those who had spent time in L2land as a mandatory part of their degree course.

But for the global sample there was no correlation between judgments and visits abroad, their number or duration.

Among students of French who had spent a compulsory period of residence abroad, however, some patterns did begin to emerge, although in relation to type of residence only and not to its duration. After those selecting 'other' or a combination of roles were excluded, a significance level of .05 or better was obtained in an Analysis of Variance (ANOVA) on the following factors: helpful, good-humoured, hard-working, serious, emotional, patient, arrogant, tolerant, friendly and efficient. In other words, the type of study placement the students had previously undertaken was likely to influence the judgment they made on French speakers with regard to these qualities.

The relationship is not a straightforward one (see Table 21). Britons studying at a French-language university are less likely to find French speakers helpful, good-humoured, tolerant and friendly than are assistants or those on work placements, but are more likely to find them hard-working and serious – and arrogant. Assistants are most likely to find them emotional and inefficient, while those on work placements are most likely to find them patient and tolerant and least likely to find them arrogant.

It is a common student misapprehension that, because French students with whom they share the *Cité universitaire* study hard between Monday lunchtime and Friday lunchtime, they must be hard-working by nature and have no social life. This anecdotal observation now receives statistical support, and underlines more firmly than ever the necessity for providing our students with a preparation for residence abroad which is not only material and practical, but also psychological and, perhaps most importantly of all, intercultural.

The data also suggest that, not unexpectedly, students' attitudes will be influenced by the circumstances of their placement abroad, with students apparently more isolated from their native-speaker peers and *stagiaires* finding most support from their hosts.

Are attitudes sex-linked?

Byram *et al.* (1991) and Cain (1990) found that females were more generous in their verdicts on foreigners. To explore whether the same was true of our own data, we carried out an analysis of variance (ANOVA) on judgments on the six characteristics on which judgments tended to vary most, three positive and three negative: *helpful*, *good-humoured*, *impatient*, *stubborn*, *arrogant* and *friendly*.

For Year 4 students, there was a statistically significant (sig.$<.05$) difference between the verdict of around 500 men and that of over 1,500 women on L2landers (French speakers) in the case of *helpful*, *good-humoured*, and *impatient* – but given the large numbers almost any difference would be statistically significant: it does not mean they are very meaningful. When only those Year 4 students who have spent a compulsory period of residence in L2land are considered, the numbers are about 15 per cent lower for men and 10 per cent lower for women, and only on *impatient* does the difference remain significant. For Year 2 students, there was a significant difference on all qualities but *friendly*, and in Year 1 on all qualities, but differences remained small.

As far as judgments on L1landers are concerned, there were significant differences by sex on *helpful* and *friendly* only in Years 1 and 2, with the addition of *arrogant* for Year 4 returners. In conclusion, we can say there is a measurable but marginal difference in mean judgments made by male and female students on L1landers and L2landers, but that it is not a matter of xenophilia or ethnocentricity: in every case, whoever is being judged, the female students' verdict is more generous. In any event, sex-related differences are far less significant than differences related to year level.

Extreme views

Only a longitudinal study can explore the factors which correlate with falling esteem for L2landers, but our data do allow us to identify extreme views, taking students of German as an example. Enthusiastic pro-Germans in Year 4 can be identified by positive responses (high ratings) on positive qualities, or negative responses (low ratings) on negative qualities, and anti-Germans by negative responses (low ratings) on positive qualities, or positive responses (high ratings) on negative qualities. In fact, the two low-rating groups are very small: only seven respondents rate the Germans not at all *arrogant* or *stubborn*, and only four rate them not at all *friendly* or *helpful*. But the views of these extremists are consistent: the first group unanimously finds Germans 'frequently' or 'very much' *good-humoured* and *friendly*, and five out of seven also rate their *helpfulness* in the same categories. All four anti-Germans opt for similarly high ratings on *arrogant* and *stubborn*, and three of them on *impatient*.

The positively positive and positively negative groups are rather larger. Those with a positive view of Germans (i.e. rating 'very much' on *helpful* and *good-humoured*) number 18, 15 of them women, with an average age of 21.6 years and a mean C-Test score of 57.61 per cent. But their enthusiasm does not stop them from finding fault: 29.4 per cent of them positively associate the Germans with *impatience*, and 43.8 per cent *stubbornness* and *arrogance*.

The 74 respondents with a very negative view of Germans (i.e. rating 'very much' on *stubborn* and *arrogant*) remain nonetheless still more open-minded, with 41.9 per cent positively associating *good humour* with the Germans, 62.1 *friendliness*, and 66.3 per cent *helpfulness*. The mean age of this larger group is comparable at 21.7 per cent but, intriguingly, their mean C-Test score is higher at 64.3 per cent and much closer to the mean for all fourth-year students of German at 65.5 per cent. Further analysis is clearly required – but it would be a surprise were it to be confirmed that the most enthusiastic pro-Germans were under-achieving women. Rather, there are no consistent extremists. From the data analysed to date and in light of the correlations found between judgments on related qualities, it appears that students are judging individual characteristics and not on the basis of affective responses to the nation as a whole.

Conclusion

The study found, firstly, that language students have clear national stereotypes; secondly, that extended residence in the target language community will not influence these stereotypes except to reinforce them; and thirdly, that on many qualities a proportion of students, up to 30 per cent of the total, will return from residence abroad with a more negative view of the target language community than is held by those who have not yet undertaken residence abroad. In each respect, the findings of the pilot 1993 study were replicated in the far larger 1994 study.

The existence of national stereotypes is already well attested: the near-identical findings of the two stages of the European Language Proficiency Survey merely confirm their existence among a group which might be expected to attach less credence to them: university students of foreign languages. Since residence abroad confirms and in some cases strengthens the stereotypical perception, rather than diluting it, the implication for university language departments may well be that students must be alerted before residence abroad to the existence of – and their own acceptance of – socially-constructed cultural stereotypes. Perhaps a similar pre-emptive sensitisation to the way intercultural judgments are formed, especially under the influence of language and culture shock, might alleviate the negative impact which L2land residence has on the way a minority of students perceive the target language community.

We have noted that although students tended to make similar judgments on related qualities, they did not judge the target language community globally but on individual criteria. Nonetheless, it was found that a work placement might be linked to more favourable judgments, and a studentship to less favourable judgments, with significant differences on individual qualities. Female students tended to judge both their own and the target language community somewhat less harshly than males.

The European Language Proficiency Survey is the first to demonstrate the sometimes negative outcome of student residence abroad on intercultural perceptions. The finding is both counter-intuitive and disturbing, given the resources presently devoted to exchange and study-abroad schemes and the number of students undertaking part of their degree course in a country whose language is not their own – 170,000 on the European Union ERASMUS scheme alone in 1995–96.

There appears to be an urgent need to initiate further research to explore the variables – including the extent and circumstances of previous L2land visits, and the type of student placement undertaken –

which may diminish the esteem in which our students hold the communities whose language they are learning, and thereby impair the experience of L2land residence, an experience which should bring the individual nothing but benefits on the personal, professional, linguistic and cultural planes.

Appendix: Statistical tables

The total number of respondents to a particular questionnaire item varies as individual respondents, intentionally or otherwise, miss an item or enter an ambiguous or unintelligible response. Percentages given here are valid percentages, i.e. disregarding absent or invalid responses.

Table 1. *Percentage of students reporting previous visits to L2land*

	Pilot study				Full survey			
	French	German	Span.1	Span. 2	French	German	Spanish	Russian
Year 1	96.6% n = 709	93.2% n = 44	91.8% n = 85	92.1% n = 63	93.7% n = 5107	87.8% n = 1504	88.1% n = 704	66.2% n = 65
Year 2	99.7% n = 307	100.0% n = 35	100.0% n = 60	100.0% n = 33	99.6% n = 2308	99.0% n = 797	95.4% n = 496	97.7% n = 213

Table 2. *Percentage of respondents who have been to L2land at least six times*

	Pilot study				Full survey			
	French	German	Span.1*	Span. 2*	French	German	Spanish	Russian
Year 1	49.9% n = 682	40.0% n = 40	34.6% n = 78	26.8% n = 56	43.3% n = 4786	19.6% n = 1318	41.3% n = 618	7.0% n = 43
Year 2	67.3% n = 303	40.0% n = 35	37.3% n = 59	45.5% n = 33	58.7% n = 2295	31.9% n = 792	37.0% n = 473	3.4% n = 208

* Span. 1 students spend Year 2 in a Hispanophone country, Span. 2 spend Year 3: the two groups have been separated in all reports on the survey.

Table 3. *Percentage of respondents who have spent more than a month in L2land*

	Pilot study				Full survey			
	French	German	Span. 1	Span. 2	French	German	Spanish	Russian
Year 1	55.7% n=682	39.0% n=43	56.4% n=78	50.9% n=55	54.5% n=4762	38.5% n=1314	58.0% n=615	20.9% n=43
Year 2	92.4% n=303	97.1% n=35	95.0% n=60	93.9% n=33	95.9% n=2276	94.7% n=790	88.2% n=468	96.2% n=208

Table 4. *Circumstances of visits to L2land (multiple responses possible)*

	French	German	Spanish	Russian
holiday	71.6%	36.6%	61.1%	9.5%
school trip	50.6%	31.2%	12.2%	16.2%
exchange	45.8%	47.8%	21.2%	12.0%
stay with friends or relations	32.5%	30.0%	26.2%	10.7%
university requirement	20.6%	22.6%	21.2%	44.7%
work	19.7%	21.5%	15.6%	10.2%
au pair	9.4%	5.2%	5.2%	0.2%
language course	9.1%	6.9%	14.9%	26.0%
other	7.6%	7.9%	7.8%	3.6%

Table 5. *Circumstances of L2land visits by year of study, students of French*

	School	Exch.	Lang. C'rse	Friend or rel.	Au pair	Hols.	Work	Univ. Req't.	Other
Year 1	51.6%	45.7%	7.2%	29.5%	6.3%	69.8%	12.9%	0.4%	7.5%
Year 2	51.9%	47.0%	7.5%	32.8%	9.1%	73.2%	16.7%	3.2%	8.2%
Year 4	51.6%	48.4%	14.4%	39.3%	14.6%	74.0%	37.0%	87.6%	6.2%

Table 6. *Circumstances of L2land visits by year of study, students of German*

	School	Exch.	Lang. C'rse	Friend or rel.	Au pair	Hols.	Work	Univ. Req't.	Other
Year 1	30.2%	50.4%	4.8%	28.9%	3.4%	33.3%	15.3%	0.6%	8.6%
Year 2	32.2%	47.8%	5.7%	30.8%	5.2%	37.4%	17.2%	3.3%	8.5%
Year 4	34.7%	50.3%	11.4%	34.2%	8.0%	42.6%	36.0%	85.0%	6.0%

Table 7. *Circumstances of L2land visits by year of study, students of Spanish*

	School	Exch.	Lang. C'rse	Friend or rel.	Au pair	Hols.	Work	Univ. Req't.	Other
Year 1	16.3%	29.8%	9.7%	29.4%	3.8%	60.8%	13.2%	1.3%	9.4%
Year 2	10.8%	18.6%	15.4%	23.4%	4.1%	64.2%	10.3%	5.3%	6.0%
Year 4	12.5%	21.4%	22.4%	32.1%	6.7%	61.5%	25.0%	72.8%	7.1%

Table 8. *Circumstances of L2land visits by year of study, students of Russian*

	School	Exch.	Lang. C'rse	Friend or rel.	Au pair	Hols.	Work	Univ. Req't.	Other
Year 1	26.2%	24.6%	10.8%	12.3%	0	7.7%	4.6%	15.4%	4.6%
Year 2	17.7%	9.1%	16.0%	7.4%	0	5.7%	8.6%	9.7%	4.0%
Year 4	16.4%	9.9%	35.7%	10.8%	0	11.3%	13.6%	85.9%	1.9%

Table 9. *Attitudes to L2landers and L2landers*

	Students of French		Students of German		Students of Spanish		Students of Russian	
	L1-landers	L2-landers	L1-landers	L2-landers	L1-landers	L2-landers	L1-landers	L2-landers
helpful	3.073	2.844	3.148	3.023	2.945	3.157	2.967	2.832
good-humoured	3.277	2.863	3.416	2.694	3.106	3.296	3.252	2.814
impatient	2.605	2.761	2.590	2.546	2.710	2.563	2.665	2.462
confident	2.815	3.360	2.800	3.479	2.853	3.257	2.836	2.842
hard-working	2.994	3.056	2.908	3.591	3.087	2.729	2.950	2.911
loud	2.605	2.770	2.654	2.804	2.472	3.286	2.598	2.506
serious	2.867	2.924	2.696	3.264	3.013	2.418	2.830	3.181
calm	2.861	2.373	2.795	2.776	2.855	2.313	2.885	2.500
stubborn	2.751	2.831	2.698	2.741	2.782	2.613	2.806	2.854
emotional	2.435	3.083	2.625	2.172	2.439	3.301	2.385	3.105
competent	3.019	3.051	2.980	3.410	3.093	2.913	2.983	2.719
shy	2.537	1.876	2.518	1.899	2.571	1.730	2.525	2.101
patient	2.740	2.357	2.767	2.592	2.689	2.514	2.678	2.650
arrogant	2.518	2.836	2.453	2.757	2.627	2.390	2.729	2.180
tolerant	2.772	2.522	2.825	2.669	2.737	2.759	2.694	2.602
lazy	2.572	2.124	2.620	1.728	2.394	2.442	2.576	2.234
friendly	3.165	3.103	3.232	3.137	3.009	3.617	2.996	3.231
efficient	2.820	2.904	2.691	3.533	3.010	2.580	2.841	2.237
logical	2.817	2.758	2.684	3.342	2.986	2.605	2.766	2.410

Table 10. *Evolving attitudes to L2landers*

Quality	Students of French Year 1	Students of French Year 2	Students of French Year 4
helpful	2.9	2.9	2.7
good-humoured	2.9	2.9	2.8
impatient	2.7	2.8	2.9
confident	3.4	3.4	3.3
hard-working	3.1	3.0	3.1
loud	2.8	2.8	2.7
serious	2.9	2.9	3.0
calm	2.4	2.4	2.3
stubborn	2.8	2.8	2.9
emotional	3.1	3.1	3.0
competent	3.1	3.0	3.0
shy	1.9	1.9	1.9
patient	2.4	2.4	2.2
arrogant	2.7	2.8	3.0
tolerant	2.6	2.5	2.4
lazy	2.1	2.1	2.1
friendly	3.2	3.1	3.0
efficient	3.0	2.9	2.8
logical	2.8	2.8	2.7

Table 11. *Change in ratings of L1landers (French speakers) and L2landers between Year 1 (n = 4619–4780) and Year 4 (n = 2096–2185)*

Quality	Change in rating of L2landers	Change in rating of L1landers
helpful	minus .193	
good-humoured	minus .113	
impatient	plus .160	minus .135
confident		
hard-working		
loud	minus .164	
serious	plus .122	
calm	minus .099	plus .166
stubborn	plus .114	
emotional		minus .152
competent	minus .103	
shy		plus .118
patient	minus .163	plus .108
arrogant	plus .290	
tolerant	minus .185	
lazy		
friendly	minus .207	
efficient	minus .203	
logical	minus .116	

Table 12. *Change in ratings of L2landers between Years 1 and 4: full survey, learners of French*

		Not at all	Rarely	Frequently	Very much	Positive (frequently + very much)	Difference Year 1 – Year 4
Good-humoured	Year 1	1.7%	18.9%	67.8%	11.5%	79.3%	8.0%
	Year 4	2.1%	26.3%	63.3%	8.0%	71.3%	
Logical	Year 1	2.9%	24.1%	64.4%	8.4%	72.8%	9.5%
	Year 4	4.4%	32.3%	55.3%	8.0%	63.3%	
Patient	Year 1	10.4%	44.8%	39.7%	4.9%	44.6%	10.0%
	Year 4	13.9%	51.4%	31.5%	3.1%	34.6%	
Friendly	Year 1	1.2%	10.5%	59.0%	29.1%	88.1%	10.1%
	Year 4	2.1%	19.6%	58.4%	19.8%	78.2%	
Tolerant	Year 1	4.9%	39.1%	50.3%	5.4%	55.7%	12.4%
	Year 4	7.9%	48.7%	40.2%	3.1%	43.3%	
Helpful	Year 1	1.0%	18.4%	69.9%	10.6%	80.5%	14.7%
	Year 4	2.4%	31.7%	58.7%	7.1%	65.8%	
Efficient	Year 1	1.2%	15.5%	70.0%	13.2%	83.2%	14.9%
	Year 4	4.1%	27.4%	57.0%	11.3%	68.3%	
Arrogant	Year 1	6.5%	31.5%	43.5%	18.4%	61.9%	15.4%
	Year 4	3.0%	19.4%	48.7%	28.6%	77.3%	
Impatient	Year 1	3.9%	37.4%	43.1%	15.3%	58.4%	11.8%
	Year 4	2.5%	27.2%	50.4%	19.8%	70.2%	

Table 13. *Change in ratings of L2landers between Years 1 and 4: full survey, learners of French (Year 1 n>4562, Year 4 n>1975)*

		Not at all	Rarely	Frequently	Very much	Positive (frequently + very much)	Difference Year 1 – Year 4
Impatient	Year 1	2.8%	38.9%	50.3%	7.9%	58.2%	11.5%
	Year 4	2.8%	50.5%	41.1%	5.6%	46.7%	
Emotional*	Year 1	3.7%	51.9%	37.3%	7.1%	44.4%	11.2%
	Year 4	4.8%	61.9%	28.9%	4.3%	33.2%	
Calm*	Year 1	2.8%	26.2%	57.8%	13.0%	70.8%	9.5%
	Year 4	1.8%	17.7%	62.1%	18.2%	80.3%	
Patient	Year 1	2.1%	32.8%	57.2%	7.7%	64.9%	8.6%
	Year 4	1.5%	24.9%	64.0%	9.5%	73.5%	

* Although 'calm' and 'emotional' do not figure in Table 12, since the change was less than 8 percentage points, there was in fact a move from positive to negative on 'calm' from 42.8% to 37.7%, which would reinforce a notion of counterbalance. However, on 'emotional' the change was also from negative to positive, albeit slight (78.7% to 76.9%).

Table 14. *Change in ratings of L2landers between Years 1 and 4: full survey, learners of German (Year 1 n>1316, Year 4 n>684)*

		Not at all	Rarely	Frequently	Very much	Positive (frequently + very much)	Difference Year 1 – Year 4
Arrogant	Year 1	7.0%	35.4%	42.0%	15.5%	57.5%	14.3%
	Year 4	2.9%	24.3%	46.6%	26.2%	72.8%	
Impatient	Year 1	5.0%	51.0%	35.1%	8.7%	43.8%	13.7%
	Year 4	4.1%	38.3%	42.0%	15.5%	57.5%	
Patient	Year 1	5.2%	33.4%	54.5%	6.9%	61.4%	12.4%
	Year 4	6.7%	44.1%	44.9%	4.1%	49.0%	
Good-humoured	Year 1	3.6%	25.3%	62.5%	8.4%	70.9%	12.3%
	Year 4	4.2%	36.9%	53.2%	5.4%	58.6%	
Helpful	Year 1	1.1%	10.0%	70.0%	18.9%	88.9%	10.3%
	Year 4	1.1%	20.3%	64.6%	14.0%	78.6%	
Emotional	Year 1	9.7%	61.3%	25.2%	3.6%	28.8%	9.7%
	Year 4	12.0%	68.8%	17.6%	1.5%	19.1%	
Tolerant	Year 1	3.0%	29.3%	61.0%	6.7%	67.7%	9.5%
	Year 4	5.2%	36.7%	51.6%	6.5%	58.2%	
Friendly	Year 1	0.8%	8.1%	60.5%	30.6%	91.1%	9.0%
	Year 4	1.3%	16.4%	60.5%	21.6%	82.1%	

Table 15. *Change in ratings of L2landers between Years 1 and 4: full survey, learners of German*

		Not at all	Rarely	Frequently	Very much	Positive (frequently + very much)	Difference Year 1 – Year 4
Patient	Year 1	1.8%	33.1%	56.7%	8.2%	64.9%	11.8%
	Year 4	1.7%	21.4%	65.1%	11.6%	76.7%	
Impatient	Year 1	2.9%	38.8%	51.0%	7.1%	58.1%	11.2%
	Year 4	3.7%	49.4%	43.2%	3.7%	46.9%	
Serious	Year 1	1.9%	30.2%	61.9%	6.0%	67.9%	9.6%
	Year 4	2.0%	39.7%	54.6%	3.7%	58.3%	
Generous*	Year 1	1.5%	25.4%	56.3%	16.8%	73.1%	8.3%
	Year 4	1.0%	17.6%	64.4%	17.0%	81.4%	

* 'Generous' was omitted by mistake from the list of qualities applying to L2landers.

Table 16. *Change in ratings of L2landers between Years 1 and 4: full survey, learners of Spanish (Year 1 n>644, Year 4 n>437)*

		Not at all	Rarely	Frequently	Very much	Positive (frequently + very much)	Difference Year 1 – Year 4
Efficient	Year 1	2.6%	32.7%	56.6%	8.1%	64.7%	24.7%
	Year 4	12.5%	47.3%	36.9%	3.1%	40.0%	
Logical	Year 1	2.5%	32.0%	60.5%	4.6%	65.1%	18.9%
	Year 4	6.6%	47.2%	44.2%	2.0%	46.2%	
Hard-working	Year 1	3.5%	22.1%	58.2%	16.2%	74.4%	18.3%
	Year 4	7.8%	40.1%	44.0%	8.1%	52.1%	
Calm	Year 1	12.0%	45.0%	36.9%	5.6%	42.5%	15.7%
	Year 4	15.9%	57.1%	23.7%	3.1%	26.8%	
Competent	Year 1	0.3%	12.2%	72.6%	14.5%	87.1%	15.4%
	Year 4	2.0%	26.3%	64.7%	7.0%	71.7%	
Lazy	Year 1	12.3%	48.6%	31.9%	7.1%	39.0%	14.9%
	Year 4	5.1%	40.5%	42.1%	11.8%	53.9%	
Patient	Year 1	6.3%	37.6%	49.6%	6.4%	56.0%	14.5%
	Year 4	11.1%	47.2%	36.4%	5.1%	41.5%	
Serious	Year 1	5.0%	47.5%	43.2%	4.1%	47.3%	9.6%
	Year 4	8.3%	57.0%	32.5%	2.2%	37.7%	
Arrogant	Year 1	12.9%	47.2%	32.2%	7.7%	39.9%	8.7%
	Year 4	9.1%	42.1%	39.5%	9.1%	48.6%	
Tolerant	Year 1	3.0%	26.1%	60.1%	10.5%	70.6%	8.1%
	Year 4	3.8%	33.7%	56.3%	6.2%	62.5%	

Table 17. *Change in ratings of L2landers between Years 1 and 4: full survey, learners of Spanish*

		Not at all	Rarely	Frequently	Very much	Positive (frequently + very much)	Difference Year 1 – Year 4
Loud	Year 1	6.1%	43.4%	39.2%	11.1%	50.3%	14.5%
	Year 4	7.7%	58.3%	28.1%	5.7%	35.8%	
Lazy	Year 1	7.2%	51.0%	34.5%	7.1%	41.6%	11.3%
	Year 4	9.7%	60.0%	29.2%	1.1%	30.3%	

Table 18. *Change in ratings of L2landers between Years 1 and 4: full survey, learners of Russian (Year 1 n>179, Year 4 n>51)*

		Not at all	Rarely	Frequently	Very much	Positive (frequently + very much)	Difference Year 1 – Year 4
Efficient	Year 1	11.1%	35.2%	44.4%	9.3%	53.7%	31.0%
	Year 4	30.3%	47.0%	20.0%	2.7%	22.7%	
Tolerant	Year 1	1.9%	24.1%	59.3%	14.8%	74.1%	30.2%
	Year 4	15.5%	40.6%	35.3%	8.6%	43.9%	
Lazy	Year 1	30.2%	45.3%	15.1%	9.4%	24.5%	23.3%
	Year 4	13.7%	38.5%	36.8%	11.0%	47.8%	
Logical	Year 1	7.7%	34.6%	44.2%	13.5%	57.7%	22.8%
	Year 4	30.3%	47.0%	20.0%	2.7%	22.7%	
Emotional	Year 1	5.5%	34.5%	30.9%	29.1%	60.0%	22.6%
	Year 4	2.6%	14.3%	36.0%	46.6%	82.6%	
Patient	Year 1	5.6%	22.2%	57.4%	14.8%	72.2%	22.2%
	Year 4	10.6%	38.9%	41.1%	8.9%	50.0%	

Table 18 *continued*

Stubborn	Year 1	11.5%	32.7%	40.4%	15.4%	55.8%	19.9%
	Year 4	4.3%	20.0%	47.6%	28.1%	75.7%	
Hard-working	Year 1	3.7%	16.7%	35.2%	44.4%	79.6%	19.5%
	Year 4	12.8%	27.1%	38.3%	21.8%	60.1%	
Arrogant	Year 1	25.0%	51.9%	21.2%	1.9%	23.1%	16.4%
	Year 4	13.7%	46.7%	33.5%	6.0%	39.5%	
Helpful	Year 1	5.2%	20.7%	46.6%	27.6%	74.2%	15.7%
	Year 4	5.2%	35.8%	46.6%	11.9%	58.5%	
Good-humoured	Year 1	7.0%	17.5%	56.1%	19.3%	75.4%	15.5%
	Year 4	4.2%	35.9%	50.0%	9.9%	59.9%	
Competent	Year 1	3.7%	27.8%	46.3%	22.2%	68.5%	10.7%
	Year 4	6.7%	35.6%	46.7%	11.1%	57.8%	
Calm	Year 1	5.7%	39.6%	47.2%	7.5%	54.7%	10.6%
	Year 4	11.4%	44.6%	37.0%	7.1%	44.1%	
Friendly	Year 1	1.8%	5.3%	50.9%	42.1%	93.0%	10.6%
	Year 4	1.0%	16.1%	56.5%	25.9%	82.4%	
Impatient	Year 1	15.8%	43.9%	29.8%	10.5%	40.3%	10.2%
	Year 4	9.5%	39.5%	38.4%	12.1%	50.5%	
Confident	Year 1	–	24.1%	51.9%	24.1%	76.0%	9.7%
	Year 4	3.3%	29.9%	54.3%	12.0%	66.3%	
Loud	Year 1	7.7%	48.1%	34.6%	9.6%	44.2%	9.1%
	Year 4	10.2%	36.0%	40.9%	12.4%	53.3%	

Table 19. *Change in ratings of L1landers between Years 1 and 4: full survey, learners of Russian*

		Not at all	Rarely	Frequently	Very much	Positive (frequently + very much)	Difference Year 1 – Year 4
Hard-working	Year 1	1.7%	20.7%	58.6%	19.0%	77.6%	11.6%
	Year 4	–	10.8%	74.6%	14.6%	89.2%	
Tolerant	Year 1	5.6%	33.3%	50.0%	9.3%	59.3%	11.4%
	Year 4	6.4%	22.9%	61.7%	9.0%	70.7%	
Shy*	Year 1	1.8%	56.4%	38.2%	3.6%	41.8%	9.8%
	Year 4	7.2%	41.1%	44.4%	7.2%	51.6%	
Lazy	Year 1	11.1%	35.2%	40.7%	11.1%	51.8%	9.2%
	Year 4	8.8%	48.6%	37.6%	5.0%	42.6%	
Loud	Year 1	5.4%	37.5%	39.3%	17.9%	57.2%	8.9%
	Year 4	5.4%	46.2%	35.3%	13.0%	48.3%	

* 'Shy', in Table 19, has no counterpart in Table 18, but its exclusion is marginal: the shift in numbers of students of Russian who see the Russians as 'shy' goes from 24.6% in Year 1 to 17.0% in Year 4, a change of 7.6%.

Table 20. *Bivariate correlations among judgments of L2landers*

	Loud	Arrogant	Helpful	Good-humoured	Friendly
Impatient	.1952	.3329	−.2234	−.1308	−.1958
Loud		.1957	NS	NS	NS
Arrogant			−.3084	−.2234	−.3060
Helpful				.3734	.4306
Good-humoured					.3868

Table 21. *Relationships between type of residence abroad and judgments of L2landers. Mean ratings on a four-point scale ('not at all' to 'very much')*

Quality	Assistants	Work placement	Students	Significance
Helpful	2.8249 SD .67 n = 651	2.8000 SD .66 n = 275	2.6190 SD .60 n = 1260	F 26.36 Sig <.0001
Good-humoured	2.9256 SD .6432 n = 645	2.8400 SD .68 n = 275	2.6946 SD .69 n = 1254	F 26.01 Sig <.0001
Hard-working	3.0577 SD .66 n = 641	3.0688 SD .64 n = 276	3.1604 SD .71 n = 1241	F 5.50 Sig .0042
Serious	2.9732 SD .60 n = 635	2.9091 SD .72 n = 275	3.1029 SD .64 n = 1244	F 15.37 Sig <.0001
Emotional	3.1260 SD .79 n = 643	3.0073 SD .78 n = 273	2.9679 SD .77 n = 1245	F 8.79 Sig .0002
Patient	2.2720 SD .78 n = 636	2.3619 SD .69 n = 268	2.2265 SD .80 n = 1214	F 3.47 Sig .0313
Arrogant	3.0296 SD .81 n = 642	2.9015 SD .81 n = 274	3.0681 SD .81 n = 1249	F 4.74 Sig .0088
Tolerant	2.4107 SD .78 n = 633	2.5055 SD .67 n = 271	2.3653 SD .73 n = 1221	F 4.19 Sig .0153
Friendly	3.0923 SD .66 n = 650	3.0982 SD .66 n = 275	2.8739 SD .78 n = 1253	F 24.13 Sig <.0001
Efficient	2.6792 SD .72 n = 639	2.8095 SD .6533 n = 273	2.7728 SD .73 n = 1228	F 4.64 Sig .0097

4 Cultural practice in everyday life: the language learner as ethnographer

Ana Barro, Shirley Jordan and Celia Roberts

The anthropologist Del Hymes believes that we are born as ethnographers but lose the ethnographic habit as we grow older. From our earliest days, we are busy making sense of the world around us through observation, listening and eventually talking. Everything is strange until it becomes familiar and taken for granted. We learn to function within our particular social world, we learn to become communicatively competent. Ironically, the notion of 'communicative competence' lost its anthropological moorings as it became assimilated into the thinking of foreign language education. It came to be interpreted rather narrowly as appropriate language use rather than a competence in the social and cultural practices of a community of which language is a central part.

The notion of the language learner as ethnographer revisits 'communicative competence', and its roots in the ethnography of communication, in order to provide a framework and set of activities for cultural and intercultural learning within foreign language pedagogy. It uses the idea of learners undertaking an ethnographic project as a means of linking language development and cultural learning.

Ethnography is loosely defined as the study of 'other' people and the social and cultural patterns that give meaning to their lives. Ethnography is both a method and a written account. Ethnographic methods are drawn from the extended period of fieldwork which characterise this approach and which include living with a group, participating in their lives and simultaneously collecting data and analysing it. The ethnography is the writing up of this process, 'translating' the lived experience of intercultural contact into an account – a version of this group's lives mediated through the writer's own cultural understandings. Ethnographic approaches, therefore, offer language learners an opportunity to link cultural knowledge and awareness with their own developing communicative competence.

This chapter is based on a research and development project around the year abroad in modern languages degree courses run at Thames Valley University, Ealing. It takes as its central theme the fact that language learners have a unique opportunity to use the period abroad as a site for field research on the analogy with anthropologists who go out into the field to study a particular community while at the same time being participants in it. As such, this field experience combines developing and using language with a systematic approach to cultural learning.

Language learning and cultural studies

Linking language learning and cultural studies together is neither easy nor comfortable. There are several reasons for this. Firstly applied linguistics and language education generally have tended to look to linguistics and psychology for their theoretical and conceptual frames, whereas anthropology, which can claim to be the discipline most closely associated with studying cultures, has been pushed to the margins. The result has been that 'culture' has not been debated in the language pedagogy literature, but has simply been inserted into language textbooks. Cultural references tend to take the form of essentialist and unreflexive statements with little sense of individual agency; for example, 'The French *are* more family orientated than the English'. Quite what the word 'are' is meant to stand for is never questioned despite the fact that Greenwood has suggested that 'is' is the most dangerous word in the English language (quoted in Herzfeld 1992).

This assertion about the 'French family' scoops up the entire population of France and stereotypes French people by comparing them with the English. The statement by implication also stereotypes the English. But the comparison leaves the latter as the norm, the unmarked group and, if spoken by a member of that group, there is an unspoken let-out clause. This says that it is fine to use generalisations about ourselves when we compare ourselves with others but that our own experiences, the 'felt reality' of our everyday lives can be set alongside such generalisations turning them into rhetoric rather than positive knowledge. In other words, we may take for granted that we are family orientated, as are most people in our community, but may still feel comfortable with a generalisation that 'we' (the English) are less family orientated than people in other countries.

Cultural analysis as practised by anthropologists would ask questions about the 'felt reality' of our family life and about how we represent ourselves to others (Cohen 1982). In attempting to answer these questions, the idea of 'family' as an aspect of 'culture' becomes both richer and more grounded in everyday practices, taking us a long way from those simple statements in textbooks and somewhat closer to an understanding of what 'family' might mean to one or a group of families in a particular French community. This understanding will involve us in what Geertz calls a 'thick description' (1975). Whereas a thin description is a relatively undetailed observation of some aspect of behaviour (e.g. French children are not allowed to leave the dinner table early), a 'thick' description combines detailed observation with interpretation. For example, such a description might include answers to questions like: 'How do meals "end"?' 'Do meals at different times of the day end in different ways?' 'What is the home context within which these meals were observed?' 'Is there a notion of "getting down from the table?"' and so on.

'Culture' has tended to be dealt with superficially in textbooks, as 'thin description', but superficiality in textbooks is not the only problem. In the discourses of everyday life, 'culture' is often invoked to explain difference and justify exclusion. Anthropologists have shown how language and culture linked together have been used as the tool in the construction of the nation state, and the ideologies that support it, and so in the symbolic construction of difference and exclusion (Anderson 1983; Herzfeld 1992). This is particularly evident in the treatment of ethnic and linguistic minorities in Europe. For example the 'Gastarbeiter' in Germany are 'guests' who are excluded by their cultural differences from being part of the nation conceptualised as family or as home. Herzfeld and others have shown how bureaucrats and other representatives of the state use the rhetoric of 'cultural difference' to stigmatise and exclude. 'Culture' becomes an excuse for racism.

So whether 'culture' is presented benignly as interesting difference, as in foreign language textbooks, or much less so in the discourses of racism and exclusion in the multilingual societies of Western Europe, the likelihood is that students will have a superficial and unproblematised model of what it is.

Anthropological studies have always offered an antidote to this model but in the last twenty years anthropology has taken a more critical turn, re-evaluating its traditional descriptions of how other groups make meaning out of their lives and starting to ask 'How do these meanings come to be produced?' (Asad 1980; Street 1993; Thornton 1988). It also takes a much more self-conscious stance, reflecting on the relationship between researcher and researched and the problems of 'translating the other' (Asad and Dixon 1984) when anthropologists write up their field experience for an academic audience.

These new approaches have great potential in reconceptualising 'culture' in language learning. Firstly, they highlight the importance of understanding how certain cultural practices and discourses come to be dominant in a given society. The social behaviour of a particular group is not in any sense natural but is constructed out of relationships of power. These approaches also illuminate the process of travelling between two 'cultures', of understanding one and of belonging to another. This has in some respects always been the linguistic translator's dilemma – how to find a means of conveying the rich associations and subtle emphases of one language into another. Anthropologists, however, do not have a given text to work from, but are fashioning their own out of the recorded experiences in the field. So the process of comparison and translation begins with their first encounters.

Anthropology is, therefore, an essential source in constructing programmes of cultural learning. It offers a set of conceptual tools and an ethnographic method. However most anthropological research is still based on rural communities (Delamont 1995), and outside the traditions of linguistic anthropology and the ethnography of communication, does not engage with the detailed use of language as cultural practice.

As well as looking to anthropology, the language educator can turn to the vastly influential multi-disciplinary Cultural Studies (Hall *et al.* 1980; Grossberg, Nelson and Treichler 1992) movement and its particular focus on the media and popular culture (Fiske 1989; McRobbie 1994). Unlike traditional anthropology, Cultural Studies has turned its gaze on the ordinary and everyday in the researchers' own social and cultural worlds and specifically on urban culture. The result has been a vast outpouring of highly sophisticated and theoretical interpretations of both ethnographic studies and media and other texts, although media texts and a more semiotically based approach have come to dominate.

There are, however, also some difficulties and limitations of the Cultural Studies approach as Byram has pointed out (Byram 1997a). It is presented to students as a series of texts to be analysed. Within foreign language pedagogy this means that the learner is still presented with 'the other' albeit mediated through a much richer set of interpretative tools than were previously available. This presentation of the other inevitably reifies people and practices and students cannot easily make connections between their own experienced cultures and those of the groups being studied. There is still the gap between learning *about* another set of cultural practices and learning *with* and *through* those practices. In other words there is a distance between text and experience, between the cognitive and palpable, between reading about and living which no amount of textual analysis can close. Cultural Studies has become 'schooled culture' rather than 'everyday culture' despite its origins in the popular and the ordinary.

Cultural Studies also lacks a detailed account of language practices, a coming together of language and culture which Agar calls

'Languaculture' (Agar 1994). To find this, it is necessary to return to anthropology, specifically the American tradition of linguistic anthropology and the ethnography of communication.

The ethnography of communication brings together language and cultural practice by looking at *speaking* as a cultural system (Bauman and Sherzer 1989; Gumperz and Hymes 1972; Saville-Troike 1989). Bridging the gap between grammar and ethnography it looks at the way in which speaking gets done as part of a community's culture. So, for example, the way in which stories are told, religious practices and aspects of political life are carried out or greetings are made are part of the wider cultural system but are also significant in themselves and an important focus of study:

> ... the unifying principle is that society and culture are communicatively constituted, and that *no* sphere of social and cultural life is fully comprehensible apart from speaking as an instrument of its constitution. (Bauman and Sherzer 1989:xi)

Studies in the ethnography of communication either start from a particular aspect of speaking and consider its ramifications for social life or they start with a theme such as marriage or role conflict and examine how these themes are illuminated through communication. Either way, they require linking cultural concepts to a close scrutiny of speaking practices and as such are particularly relevant to language learners in search of cultural understanding. These studies have remained almost entirely within the tradition of American anthropology but there is no reason why this should continue to be the case. Language learners as ethnographers are well placed to participate in speech events in the field and to use this experience to develop both their own communicative competence and their capacity to understand the organisation, functions and symbolic value of culturally specific ways of speaking.

To sum up, therefore, the link between language learning and cultural studies is a combination of the intellectual and the experiential. Both anthropology and cultural studies can provide conceptual frameworks and interpretative tools for the former but structuring *experience* so that it links systematically with the *intellectual* endeavour is not so straightforward. The notion of the language learner as ethnographer aims to combine the experience of the ethnographer in the field and a set of conceptual frameworks for cultural analysis with the best practice from communicative and immersion language learning.

Malinowski, the 'father' of modern anthropology, its first ethnographer and someone who believed that you could only understand language in its context of situation, asserts the necessary connection between experience and academic learning:

> Meaning ... does not come ... from contemplation of things, or analysis of occurrences, but in practical and active acquaintance with relevant situations. (Malinowski 1923:325)

He does not cast aside reflection and analysis, far from it, but he emphasises the active participation in events in order to understand them. Ethnographic participation in the field involves language learners in taking part in the day to day practices which surround them, in creating more opportunities to communicate through working with informants and developing a reflective and critical habit of mind.

We have suggested some of the sources to which the language educator can turn in order to combine language and cultural learning. From these, we can draw out some of the conditions for such learning:

- working in the field;
- developing a palpable sense of being with a group, rubbing shoulders with them as cultural beings;
- the opportunity for the gradual accretion of ideas, values and interactional knowledge which are necessary to make someone a culturally competent member of that group;
- a holistic approach which tries to account for the contexts in which action takes place and is interpreted;
- the habit of comparison (which is both an experiential and intellectual habit) which is, on the analogy of Geertz's 'thick description', a 'thick comparison'. Differences are not simply read off from behaviour and compared within one's own surface memory of a similar event in one's home country, but as far as possible are interpreted thickly and then compared with a detailed analysis of one's own cultural world.

Ethnography as the link

The method of ethnography provides the link between the experiential and the intellectual and the year abroad provides the opportunity to undertake an ethnographic project.

The Ealing Ethnography programme was developed spanning three years and had the following aims:

1. Develop some innovative methods of teaching and learning cultural studies for advanced language learners.
2. Explore the transfer of other methods of teaching from other disciplines (particularly anthropology).
3. Develop methods of assessing cultural learning as a result of the year abroad.

4. Establish greater integration of the year abroad into the undergraduate curriculum.

The programme consisted of three parts:

- one semester-long module in the second year of the BA called 'Introduction to Ethnography';
- an ethnographic study during the year abroad;
- writing up the ethnography in the foreign language on the students' return in the final year.

The ethnographic project forms part of the degree assessment and was also examined through an oral examination.

The most obvious support that students needed was in the area of ethnographic method. They had little or no experience of doing participant observation, ethnographic interviewing or interpretive data analysis. However, it was soon clear that learning method without a conceptual framework drawn from anthropology would offer skills without intellectual content, encouragement to collect data without the understandings to analyse it and draw patterns out of it.

The contents of the second year course 'Introduction to Ethnography' are, therefore, a mix of method units and conceptual units:

1 Preparing for fieldwork
2 What is an ethnographic approach?
3 Non-verbal communication and social space
4 Shared cultural knowledge
5 Families and households
6 Gender relations
7 Ethnography of education
8 Participant observation
9 Ethnographic conversations
10 Ethnographic interviewing
11 From data collection to analysis
12 Recording and analysing naturally occurring events
13 National identity and local boundaries
14 Language and social identities
15 Local level politics
16 Belief and action – 1: symbolic classification
17 Belief and action – 2: discourse and power
18 Writing an ethnographic project

The students at the outset of the course see themselves as 'language people' (Evans 1988), technical people learning the skills to become interpreters and translators. On many applied languages courses there is little tradition of intellectual discovery and debate. Apart from language classes and translation work, there is a programme of area studies which tends to take a transmission mode of teaching with overview lectures on broad topics.

The ethnography course challenges students' identity, their expectations about content and their assumptions about learning. Indeed, the course itself is something of a culture shock long before students arrive in the new country. The course assumes as axiomatic that learning to understand a different set of cultural practices entails first studying the practices of your own socially constructed world. So students begin to question their own social identity and to develop analytical and conceptual ways of thinking which are quite new to them.

They are also expected to work in new ways. The anthropological concepts and ethnographic methods are taught largely experientially. Each week students are given a mini field work assignment which is then exploited in the teaching sessions through group work, presentations, discussion and so on. Initially students often feel confused and disturbed because of the highly experiential and participative nature of the course and the lack of hard facts or detailed code-cracking linguistic exercises. The great majority are, in the end, excited to discover that the mix of intellectual and experiential learning gives them important insights into, and resources for, questioning their own and others' cultural practices; that culture is not something prone, waiting to be discovered but an active meaning-making system of experiences which enters into and is constructed within every act of communication.

The ethnography course is designed so that the teaching and learning themselves run on ethnographic principles. This means that students are encouraged to be reflective about their own learning and to engage in the course as active participants in a community. An important part of the course is the requirement to undertake a 'home ethnography'. This is a short project exploring some aspects of their own cultural world while in Britain, both to develop their skills and as an opportunity to reflect on their own socially constructed identities. The language teachers also undertake home ethnographies as part of their personal and staff development and to give them insider experience of carrying out a small ethnographic project as their students will have to do.

At the beginning of the course, students usually have no idea what ethnography is. They usually opt for this module because they have heard from other students that it is interesting and something different. Their experience of area studies means that they are used to facts – information about political, social and economic institutions – not to the idea that 'family', or 'doing business' or the politics of a particular party are socially and culturally constructed.

Early on in the course, students begin the process of looking at their own worlds as social constructs. This involves encouraging them to see meaning and significance in the most ordinary and routine aspects of their everyday lives. One of their first exercises is to describe their daily journey to university as if they were complete strangers to the experience. This idea of 'making the familiar strange' is central to the ethnographic process and it involves making explicit all the social knowledge required to manage even the most ordinary activity or the most routine social relationship. So, for example, students have to observe how they manage the space between themselves and others on a crowded train or bus. Later, this theme is taken up in the unit on social space.

The next stage is to move from detailed observation and description to analysis and interpretation. Here the students begin to look for patterns in the behaviour and meanings of everyday life. This involves more extensive periods of 'hanging around with a purpose', observing the fine-grained detail of social actions and beginning to question the basis on which inferences from these observations are made. For example, a student who comments that 'a man was rude to a woman in a pub' has to question on what basis she can categorise the behaviour she saw in this way; what constitutes 'rude' behaviour? What evidence does she have that both interactants interpreted what happened as rude and so on? The habit of interrogating one's own taken-for-granted assumptions, developed during the 'home ethnography' period, is then in place when students go abroad.

The process of finding patterns in the data collected in these early exercises is related to some basic concepts in anthropology. We have already mentioned the notion of social space as a way of looking at how people manage relations in public places. Another concept introduced early on is that of gendered identity. Students are asked to record a female/male conversation and to analyse some of the ways in which female and male identity are acted out or accomplished in everyday conversations. In this way, they develop an understanding of how the moment by moment cues and interpretations in an interaction can be related to wider concepts. These concepts, or ways of looking at social life, can then be used to illuminate similar interactions so that a more general picture can be built up, but one which remains grounded in the local and the particular.

Once in the field, abroad, the course takes on a new significance. Unlike their 'non-ethnography' peers, these students feel they have a specific purpose for being there and can immediately put to use the ethnographic methods learnt, as well as drawing on their newly acquired habits of reflection and reflexivity in locating themselves in relation to the new community. Their ethnographic projects help to establish patterns of relationships within this community, whether with, for example, transsexual prostitutes in Cadiz, Catholic families in Seville, *carnavaliers* in Nice or blind students in Marburg. By contrast, the non-ethnographers tend to make their projects book-based. One of the strongest responses from the ethnography group was the sense of ownership of their projects; the feeling that the data collected and analysed is all theirs and not driven by the authority of books and lectures.

Local level politics: an example from the ethnography programme

An overview of one of the units from the second year course will allow us to illustrate some of the materials used and the approach adopted in the classroom. We will also discuss the ways in which students have subsequently built on the concepts introduced in the session when carrying out their own ethnographic research and exploring cultural processes either at home or during the period of residence abroad.

The unit we have selected is that on local level politics. This unit is placed in the later stages of the course since it is more abstract and conceptually challenging than some of the earlier ones, whilst allowing students to refer back to concepts with which they are by now familiar such as 'boundaries', 'hierarchies' and 'identities'. Here the focus is primarily on the symbolic aspects of gift exchange and the interpretation of messages involving rights and obligations as a framework for understanding the cultural patterning of local level politics.

We will describe how students begin to interrogate their own practices of gift exchange through an assignment in data collection, then go on to explore the relationship of their data to anthropological concepts, and to consider how such concepts may also underpin everyday processes in very different societies. The range of materials allows us to draw connections between practices of exchange as apparently diverse as the extravagant ceremony of the Moka in New Guinea, and the ostensibly 'homely' practice of buying a round of drinks in the student bar. Both these processes can be related to the anthropological and sociological literature on exchange; both involve issues of obligation, reciprocity, reputation, power and influence which are the essentials of micro-politics.

Students who have studied, for example, French or German politics as part of a traditional area studies course will generally be accustomed to a macro approach to politics, and a rather top-down, factual way of learning. In such courses a 'body of knowledge' will typically be transmitted about political institutions, parties, national and local elections, etc. Students will rarely look at the more local, interpersonal manoeuvrings behind the scenes of elections (e.g. at the mechanisms whereby the local leader of the village council does favours for others in exchange for gifts or votes) or at the fine-grained detail of day-to-day interactions outside the arena of what they commonly understand as 'politics'. They will probably think of the political processes discussed in the media and in textbooks as quite separate from the minutiae of their everyday lives. But it is precisely these everyday communicative experiences which are such an obvious target for the language learner. As students gradually build up a description of the routine interactions of a particular community, so they begin to understand what it means to be communicatively competent in this local context.

In this unit, students are encouraged to think through politics at work in smaller, more private units such as the family, the workplace or the classroom, and to explore the continuum which exists between the public and the local, the explicit and the implicit. What are the tacit understandings we have about where we stand in relation to others, and how do we routinely manage social relations with them on the micro level? And how do these relations feed into and reflect the more explicit politics of the party system and local and national government? Although the processes involved in local level politics may not be intrinsically the same as those involved in politics with a capital 'P', as the anthropologist Bailey points out, 'small activities can reveal patterns of behaviour no less useful than the actions of statesmen' (Bailey 1971:3).

Broadly speaking then, this unit focuses on the management of interpersonal negotiations which are illustrative of how communities maintain equilibrium. In one of the student readings, Bailey gives a good example of the political and emotional consequences of everyday interactions, which alerts students to the importance of shared cultural knowledge, laconic cues and the large repercussions of small practices: how would an outsider know that housewives in Valloire are telling people something specific when they wear their apron on the way to the shops (Bailey 1971)? During this trip to buy provisions they will almost certainly encounter neighbours. If they stop to chat, they will more than likely be assumed to be indulging in *mauvaise langue* (gossip); if they fail to do so they may be branded as *fière* (haughty). The apron they wear has become a powerful signifier telling people that they are politically offstage and not available for exchanges, thus allowing them to emerge from their shopping trip with their reputation intact.

The students draw on several readings to help prepare them for the session and to assist them in the analysis of their own data. These involve studies of local patronage systems (Delamont 1995); concepts of exchange and gift-giving (Bailey 1971; Beattie 1962; Davis 1992); the importance of role and reputation in different types of community and the idea of a 'moral community' (Bailey 1971). In connection with these concepts students are introduced to the notion of high and low density community networks (Milroy 1980), and to some of the sociolinguistic work on face (Goffman 1967).

There are a good many anthropological studies of local patronage systems, in Mediterranean Europe in particular, which students can compare with their own experiences in complex urban environments which may be less 'gift oriented'. The reading from Delamont (1995: ch. 7) gives plenty of examples of local dealings between patrons and leaders on the one hand, and clients and followers on the other, pointing out that here people's reputations are in part measured by their ability to 'fix' things, or to know the appropriate 'fixers' (people of higher status such as doctors or school teachers) who can deal on their behalf with channels of bureaucracy, or pull strings. One of the studies she cites looks at the patronage system in a French village in the Hautes Alpes and, for example, the role of the former village secretary to the Mayor, Mme. Belier, who is used to sorting out pensions. In exchange, people offer her deference, accompany her to church or choir practice, or patronise her nephew's grocery shop. Delamont points out that this is typical of how a local patron is rewarded.

The role and function of exchange within different societies has been widely studied by sociologists and anthropologists. Students cannot be introduced to all the theory, but there are fundamental issues raised in the unit which they can then follow up through readings suggested in the bibliography. The description we give here will be limited to the main points which guide students through the session. The most important of these is the fundamental notion that exchange constitutes the 'social glue' which keeps a society together, since 'society exists in that men give each other deference, challenge, pieces of information, money, tribute, service' (Bailey 1971:10). Investigating this notion involves students in making distinctions between the various levels of exchange relationships people routinely engage in, from the impersonal ones we briefly enter into when purchasing or selling, or in our relationships with bureaucracy rather than with known individuals (e.g. when we pay the council tax in return for local services), to our face-to-face dealings with family, friends and colleagues.

We look at how in our culture we are careful to keep the two systems of trade and gifts separate (Barley 1989) and at the serious taboos which may be involved in giving money as a gift, or associating money with sexual relations. This of course can be compared with other cultural practices not subject to the same taboos (where bride prices or dowries are customary). We consider how the commodification of modern society means we are less and less involved with people in face-to-face relations of mutual interest and interdependence, and how our relationships with institutions are an increasingly vital part of the way we organise our lives.

From the broader notion of exchange, the focus shifts to one aspect: that of gift giving as a way of managing social relations, and the notions of obligation and reciprocity this entails. This aspect of the exchange system creates and maintains interpersonal relationships. As Bailey puts it, 'Gifts are the channels along which social relations run' (Bailey 1971:2). Beattie also makes this point, distinguishing between gifts (which create social relations) and purchases (which create only economic ones). Gift giving, says Beattie (and here we include favours, compliments, greetings, even the gift of courtesy) takes place because people 'want to be indebted to one another' (Beattie 1962:22). In this Beattie is not unlike Mauss, who suggests in his *Essai sur le don* that gifts are a part of the self and are therefore potent, symbolic as much as material, and dangerous to possess unless a return gift is made. The original gift must somehow find its way back to the giver (Mauss 1954).

The dynamics of giving and receiving, typically discussed by students through references to positive experiences, may also have a negative symbolic weight. This is what Bailey stresses in his connection of gifts with contamination, and his reference to 'the poisoning of human relationships' (Bailey 1971:2). By connecting the terms 'gift' and 'poison', he is referring to the complex system of obligations encoded in all our gift giving, whereby gifts become symbols with identifiable consequences, both political and moral. There is generally a conceptual leap to be made by students in applying this idea to their own practices, and Bailey's thesis in particular sometimes meets with initial resistance.

Gift giving, then, may seem like a very small manifestation of social and economic life, but a gift, like a pebble dropped in a pond, creates a series of ripples. As Davis suggests in his discussion of the important political and emotional consequences of gifts: 'A simple gift has meanings which can involve class, social mobility, matrimony, patronage, employment, manufacturing processes, issues of style and of changing rituals or conventions of gift giving' (Davis 1992). It is these kinds of ramifications we encourage our students to follow up as they begin to 'make strange' their own familiar practices and to explore the idea that gift giving in their own lives can be something more than arbitrary or altruistic, often invoking powerful obligations of reciprocity.

To draw on an example raised by the students, one could look at buying a round of drinks in the student bar and, through thick description, analyse the shared cultural knowledge at work. How is the event managed? What are the discourses surrounding the activity of social drinking? What kinds of things are at stake? Our actions here may frame us as 'generous' or 'nice' and hence enhance our reputation. Buying a round also creates an obligation and leaves others indebted to us. To dip out of the round-buying game requires careful prior establishment of our exclusion on some mutually acceptable grounds. An individual from a cultural group where round buying was not a feature of social life would have to observe very carefully how it is done and elicit a lot of information about the practice in order to participate successfully. (An early example from the ethnography of communication on 'How to ask for a drink in Subanun' (Frake 1964) is a classic illustration of how a thick description of drinking practices illuminates fundamental social and cultural practices.)

Engaging in exchanges is, as the example above suggests, also a confirmation of one's belonging in a community, being known in it and so having a reputation. Here we introduce Milroy's (1980) ideas on social networks, which she defines as either 'high density' (e.g. a small rural community where everyone knows everyone else – and everyone else's business) and 'low density' (e.g. a larger urban community). We discuss more explicitly how reputation – our own and that of others – is negotiated in all exchanges, and explore the idea that a reputation is both more crucial and more difficult to maintain in a high density community. In turn, the concept of a 'moral community' is raised, which may be defined as a group of people with shared values and beliefs for interpreting behaviour, who are prepared to make moral judgements on others in their group.

Indeed, one question which often arises in student projects is that of boundary maintenance: how are belonging and exclusion achieved and what is the social glue, the shared cultural knowledge which makes groups cohere? One aspect of group cohesion is the network of exchange, obligation and reputation management which goes by the name of 'local level politics'. Even where exchange is not taken as the explicit focus for a project, some of the issues discussed here are likely to provide students with guidance during their participant observation. For example, one student who studied the place of foreign students in a German university, was interested in the discourses around cleanliness in the student kitchens. Assumptions about rights and obligations in tidying up and cleaning the kitchens caused both individuals and groups to be ascribed a certain reputation.

What we are attempting to do in this unit, then, is to get students to see all levels of politics as connected rather than as separate categories, to show how people's management of politics is culturally patterned, both on the micro and the macro levels, and, as in all the units, to give students practice in moving from the descriptive to the analytical as they use their own naturally occurring data to exemplify or test theoretical claims.

Description of a class session

Given that, as Bailey remarked, local politics are largely implicit, taken for granted and only 'fleetingly seen', how do we get students to begin talking about these cultural patterns in behaviour and language? As often happens in the units, we begin with their own experiences – with what seems obvious. Prior to the session they undertake some reading and an assignment where they record favours or exchanges in which they have recently been involved (see chart p. 91). At this stage, their examples may remain at a rather anecdotal level, and much of the analysis of their raw data takes place during the session.

The session proper begins with a video extract from *Ongka's Big Moka*, a documentary from the Granada TV *Disappearing World* series broadcast in 1974. The setting is the Western Highlands of Papua New Guinea, which has a non-capitalist economy. The eponymous Ongka is the leader or 'big-man', an honorific title given to the head of a community of some 1,000 people. The film is an account of a huge gift-giving ceremony, known as a Moka, orchestrated by Ongka, and the excerpt shown to students describes his lengthy preparations to get the Moka off the ground.

Ongka derives a lot of status and benefits for his community and for himself by this ritual gift giving, which entails accumulating a huge number of pigs. Indeed, pigs are the main commodity for exchange in this community. As Ongka himself puts it, 'If you don't have pigs, you are rubbish'. It emerges, in fact, that the Moka is the only means Ongka has of securing his status and maintaining his reputation as big-man. This is why it is worth all the years of preparation, negotiation and fixing.

The word *Moka* actually means 'accumulated interest'. In a previous ceremony, Ongka received fewer pigs from the donor than he is actually going to return; his own gift will be far in excess of what is really owed. The recipient of Ongka's gift is the leader of a neighbouring tribe who is also a local government official and who will owe all sorts of favours in return for such an impressive Moka. The Moka, then, involves a complex example of reciprocity, its principal object being to humiliate with generosity, and thus to create a burden of obligation.

This is not the kind of cultural scene our students are likely to encounter as participant observers, but it is the kind of example we would expect them to refer back to and use as a point of comparison. In the session they are asked to think about two main points while watching the video: firstly, what differences or parallels they can see with gift-giving practices in their own cultural environment, and secondly what issues or difficulties may be involved in interpreting unfamiliar practices such as these.

Issues which often arise in class discussion include: the delicate nature of persuasion (Ongka has no actual authority so he cannot push too hard for the cooperation of his community); the effort involved in maintaining the status quo; the notion of gifts and poisons, which is neatly encapsulated here, since the Moka is a fine illustration of the ambivalence of gifts, and of the familiar saying 'to be overwhelmed with gratitude'; the idea of being locked into a system of exchange (the Delamont reading students are given is a useful reference here since it shows the lack of incentives on the part of either patrons or clients to change the system); and finally the vulnerability of those in power.

Local level politics: Gift giving

Gift/Favour/ Exchange	Relationship symbolised	Obligations	Wider implications
Information regarding possibilities for work in TEFL, and offer of 'recommendation' to a contact who controls such posts	Teacher–student Guide – looking Experienced – learning Insider – outsider (vis-à-vis TEFL)	Thanks for information Thanks for offer of help Reply/decision whether to take up the offer Follow-up by teacher (either positive of negative) Owing a 'favour' back/wanting to give a favour back	Teacher's assessment of compatibility of student (i.e. me) and language school: must be suitable I must believe this and trust judgement No immediate exchange is evident What gain for teacher? Favour in return stored for future 'collection'? Satisfaction in arranging a mutually beneficial exchange (beneficial for school and for me)

Lending £1.00 to a student who needs change to pay somebody else what he owes them	Friendship Trust Fellow sufferer from change-related problems at times Sympathy	To try to help (me) To say thank you for that help (him) To say (sometimes) when it will be returned To pay back (sometimes) To say that it doesn't matter – either today or tomorrow will do Prompt reimbursement and thanks Accept thanks	Shared conception of value (symbolic) of money, despite nominal amount Confirmation/ realignment regarding degree of friendship/trust/ sympathy Do you need to say it will be paid back by a certain time? Depends on relationship How much 'dare' one borrow? What explanation need be given? When is it okay to remind someone about an outstanding debt?

After looking at something that is so anthropologically and culturally strange, students are required to examine their own idea of gift giving, moving rapidly between cultures, which can help them to 'make strange' and see their own practices as culturally determined.

For their pre-session assignment students are given a chart to complete. This entails looking back over the previous week to think of several examples of gift giving in which they have been involved. They are then asked to try to think about the wider implications of these interactions, to interpret any messages involving rights and obligations and to look beyond the immediate gift or favour to the moral and symbolic aspects. In the session this data is analysed in small groups where students pool their findings and then report back to the class. The ensuing discussion generally focuses on notions of reciprocity and obligation, which students often find difficult. Some of the most telling examples they have raised include the student who had felt suspicious and embarrassed about a gift she had received; the student who had subverted the obligation to receive by refusing food from a host; and the student who had returned a gift. Analysing such naturally occurring examples is an important way of drawing out the concept of moral expectations and symbolic messages embedded in gift giving.

Further impetus is given to the discussion by handing out the British

Repertoire of Exchange (Davis 1992). This list of terms for exchange ranges from the apparently altruistic (e.g. donations or alms giving) to the self-interested and non-reciprocal (e.g. bribery, burglary or mugging). Students are asked to consider the associations of some of these and how they can be interpreted in cultural terms.

This discussion of the linguistic repertoire helps to focus on more sociolinguistic and pragmatic issues. The literature on face (Goffman 1967) and politeness (Brown and Levinson 1987; Scollon and Scollon 1983, 1995) is drawn on to alert students to the ways in which politeness is linguistically realised. The notions of 'negative face' to indicate deference and 'positive face' to indicate solidarity are managed through a series of politeness strategies which themselves are rooted in the principle of exchange. One good example and one that has been well studied in the literature on cross-cultural pragmatics is that of compliments (Manes 1983; Wolfson 1989). A study of the conditions under which they are given, to whom and how they are received is a good example of how 'small activities' are a microcosm of much larger patterns of obligation and control.

Projects

Using exchange as an entry to local level politics opens up new possibilities for our language students. In the project which they undertake during the period abroad, they often want to base their research on the political/economic matters introduced in area studies. Looking at the broader and all-pervasive notion of exchange gives a conceptually richer and more focused opportunity for their research. It implies a more rigorous set of methodological and conceptual considerations as well as providing a framework for analysing and understanding some of the intercultural situations they will encounter. The challenge for them is to focus their project work and to link the small-scale to local, national or cultural values and perspectives.

A number of students have drawn very successfully on the concepts of exchange introduced in the unit on local level politics, either for their 'home ethnography' project (assessed as part of the course) or for the more extensive and challenging project they undertake abroad. In one 'home ethnography' project the student explored the ways in which employees of a major high street store accomplished the complex range of exchanges at the Customer Service Desk. These usually involved the reversal of a purchase (e.g. refunds or exchanges of one item for another). Here the interpersonal dimension was crucial, and the student recorded the carefully managed verbal exchanges which took place with the customers at this sensitive part of the store. In this way, the student combined some of the conceptual work on local level politics with the ethnography of communication. Issues of staff hierarchy, control, customer relations, politeness and reputation (that of the store, the members of staff, and also of the customer) were seen to underpin interactions in specific ways. The student and her colleagues had to operate in situations where they were caught between personal decisions and judgements and statutory policy of the store. The public's perception of the store and the employees' duty as its ambassadors provided a very specific set of tensions and an interesting frame for this localised study of exchange at work. A detailed scrutiny of the way in which the interactions were managed, using methods from the ethnography of communication, revealed the ground rules for such a speech event and the patterns of interactional behaviour which serve to constitute it.

A second and quite different home project was undertaken by a Spanish student in a family context. It involved him examining the ritual and discourses surrounding a major gift-giving ceremony, *Reyes* or *Twelfth Night*. Far from being a simple exchange of gifts, his research led him to the persuasive conclusion that it was one of the very powerful ways his family re-confirmed its identity as a family, and through notions of reciprocity, re-confirmed hierarchical relationships within it.

A lot of Spanish ethnography in recent decades has focused on patron/client relations, especially in rural areas, and 'honour and shame' is a vital dimension, e.g. family honour and shame is a more important asset than material wealth, (Davis 1977; Gilmore 1987). By contrast, the students on the Ealing Ethnography programme always go to cities and so have to do an urban ethnography. In complex urban environments, it is much more difficult to focus down on a particular theme and so one option is to choose a particular locality or group who tend to live or hang out in a relatively bounded area of the city.

For example, one student whose placement was in Cadiz initially chose to do his ethnographic project on the relationships between the American navy presence and the local community. He soon found that this was both too broad and too politically sensitive. So he turned instead to studying a less controversial group: transsexual prostitutes! He concentrated on a few bars in a particular location where he had come across some of the prostitutes and gradually became friendly with a small group of them. He found that exchange was an important element in the conversations he had with his informants, and a crucial part of their value system. They defined themselves largely as different from mainstream culture in their more honest and up-front management of sexual exchange and in transferring the values of the marketplace to transform sex into an economic activity in a very explicit way. The student derived many insights not just into the systems of meaning they had developed and into those they were reacting against and subverting, but also into his own values and attitudes.

Another project took a more sociolinguistic direction and examined compliments in Las Palmas. This student also stumbled across her project following a series of cultural misunderstandings when she first arrived. In Spain there are two terms for compliments, with different functions and norms of appropriacy. The first, *piropo*, is almost exclusively sexual, used in the street generally by men and directed at women, and non-reciprocal. The second, *cumplido*, is broader and almost always requires a response. These she documented and analysed. Some of the categories that emerged from her research included:

Cumplido categories

a) about an object
b) about a person
c) to affirm belonging to a group
d) to seek reassurance
e) gender differences – often used in conjunction with what Tannen calls one-downmanship
f) power differences (e.g. student/tutor)
g) compliments used for 'hunting', courtship skills as a way of starting relationships

Many of her informants saw the *cumplido* compliments as essentially insincere or hypocritical. For example, one conventional *cumplido* is the daughter-in-law's compliment about her mother-in-law's cooking. Such compliments are so expected, so much a part of the patterns of everyday life, that they are not invested with any significance. Yet their conventionalised and institutionalised role is an important element in managing social relationships. This project was another example of combining more linguistically orientated work (in this case sociolinguistic and pragmatic studies of politeness) with the anthropological notions of exchange and gift giving.

On their return from the year abroad, students write up their ethnographic projects with tutorial support. The writing up is particularly daunting because of the fact that it has to be in the foreign language and there are relatively few ethnographic studies in French, German or Spanish which are relevant and suitable models for the students. The process of analysing the mass of data and searching for cultural patterns which are thoroughly grounded in it, brings together the intellectual and the experiential. This process of writing up can be exemplified from the experience of one student whose project was on the *carnavaliers* of Nice.

After starting her observations with a wide-angled lens, she finally focused down on the tension between maintaining the traditions of the carnival and the fact that those very traditions were causing the event and the practices that surrounded it to break down. In particular, she looked at the means of excluding all women from becoming *carnavaliers* and yet it was the women who were keenest to maintain the event.

So she investigated gender relations not in some general way but as they were embedded in the particular and local context of the rituals of the carnival. In the process of doing this, she had constantly to question the source of her knowledge. For example, on what basis could she say that women wished to be involved? Had she observed this? Who had told her? On what basis had they told her? This is an epistemological activity – in which she had to work on what kinds of knowledge come to be constructed. Finally, she had to learn the art of relativising, of seeing one's own and others' worlds as socially and culturally constructed and not natural. This involved a comparative technique in which she had to think of comparable events within her own society, to see that they too did not just happen but were the product of particular social pressures and that they were sustained or eroded by the need to make meanings, or question the significance of those meanings.

The capacity to relativise, to interrogate the meanings of her data and to write about the specific and the detailed were all challenges for her. There was a tendency to leave out much of the descriptive life of the carnival, to hide the palpable excitement behind safe and prosaic statements. She also had to work hard on drawing out the patterns of gender relationships from the data itself. The skill and tenacity to move from the very specific to the more abstract patterns and to analyse interview data rather than just quoting from it are hard to achieve for many students. These skills and the imagination to rove around the data and seize on connections are not just technical requirements of a good ethnographic project, they are central to the process of cultural learning. They are part of the process of 'translating culture' and not just 'translating language', referred to above. The act of writing such a project not only pushes the writer to her limits in terms of vocabulary, metaphor and coherence in the foreign language, it can push her to struggle with how she can make meaningful her own experience abroad and in doing so apprehend something of the otherness of a different group or community.

The process that students go through in their analysis and writing up gives a much richer interpretation to the notion of 'communicative competence' with which this chapter started. Instead of being used rather narrowly and prescriptively as 'appropriate language use', it takes on its original significance as the ability to use patterns of speaking as a cultural system. Added to this, students have had the opportunity to reflect on their own and others' cultural systems and this habit of analysis and interpretation is a transferable habit which they can draw on in the future in whatever contexts they live and work in.

Conclusion: the language learner as ethnographer

The students are not intending to become specialists in social anthropology. They are language students who, we hope, will become even better language students as a result of living the ethnographic life. The method and contents reflect this, focusing on areas that will be relevant to them in complex urban environments in Western Europe and helping to develop conceptual frameworks rather than assimilate difficult theory.

The aim of the programme is also to help students inhabit a more uncertain and critical world in which their own assumptions and stereotypes are challenged by the constant questioning of the sources of evidence presented to them. As linguists, their jobs and interests are likely to involve them in multilingual worlds where their whole social being must interact with others. They need the cultural tools for making sense of new intercultural contacts and experiences rather than positivistic facts about other countries, structures and systems which are, despite the textbooks' attempts to freeze-dry them and turn them into fresh-looking digestible items of information, constantly in a process of contestation and change.

Note:
The project *Cultural Studies in Advanced Language Learning* was funded by the ESRC 1990–1993 (R000232716). It was directed by Mike Byram and Celia Roberts. The project consultant was Brian Street and the language staff were Ana Barro and Hanns Grimm. The team was later joined by Shirley Jordan and Marc Bergman.

5 The culture the learner brings: a bridge or a barrier?

Lixian Jin and Martin Cortazzi

It is commonplace to think of foreign language teaching as bringing a target culture to learners. This is culture as content. The aim is that students should acquire knowledge of a target culture. The learning of intercultural skills in relation to target culture peoples is less often emphasised. It is less usual to consider the culture learners bring to the foreign language classroom and its relationship to the target culture. This is, we argue, more than simply a background influence. It has a deep effect on classroom processes because it is a significant factor in how teachers and students perceive language learning and how they evaluate each other's roles and classroom performance.

Learning a foreign language implies a degree of intercultural learning: students may be led to become more aware of their own culture in the process of learning about another and hence may be in a better position to develop intercultural skills. A further step – developed in this chapter – is to consider the situation in which the teacher and students come from different cultural backgrounds, e.g. when the teacher is a 'native speaker' of the target language and is teaching foreign language students. In such cases, teacher and students bring different cultural experiences and expectations with them, not only as content, but also as medium since there are cultural ways of learning all subjects, including foreign languages. As these ways are practised in the classroom they mediate learning, often unconsciously. Such intercultural situations, now very common around the world, might be viewed as bridges for the learning of intercultural skills or alternatively as barriers to intercultural communication and foreign language learning.

In this chapter, we use the term 'culture' to refer to socially transmitted patterns of behaviour and interaction. We stress the interpretive aspect of culture: the frameworks of expectations and norms of interpretation through which cultures mediate learning and classroom communication. We take the case of 'Western' teachers (i.e. from core English-speaking countries such as the USA, Canada, the UK, Australia or New Zealand, usually teaching at university level, often teaching oral

English) and Chinese learners of English, probably the largest national group of foreign language students in the world. Drawing on data gathered in universities and schools in Britain and China between 1989 and 1995, we contrast the cultural expectations of the two groups and examine some effects of these expectations on classroom interaction. Some of these expectations involve stereotypes which we would wish to challenge, but first we need to see exactly what the expectations are. The analysis of different cultures of learning which emerges from our study indicates several dilemmas. For example, classroom discourse, which could be a site for intercultural classroom learning, is often structured in a way which actually impedes the development of such skills.

We propose that a solution for such difficulties is for participants to become more aware of their own cultural presuppositions and those of others in order to build a bridge of mutual intercultural learning. The process of raising cultural awareness implies a willingness for classroom participants to challenge their own assumptions. A detailed example of this intercultural learning is given in the form of a cultural synergy model. This, in turn, gives rise to questions relating to cultural identity.

Language and culture: a framework of communication and learning

The links between language and culture are, to say the least, complex. They can be seen on several levels, as shown in Figure 1.

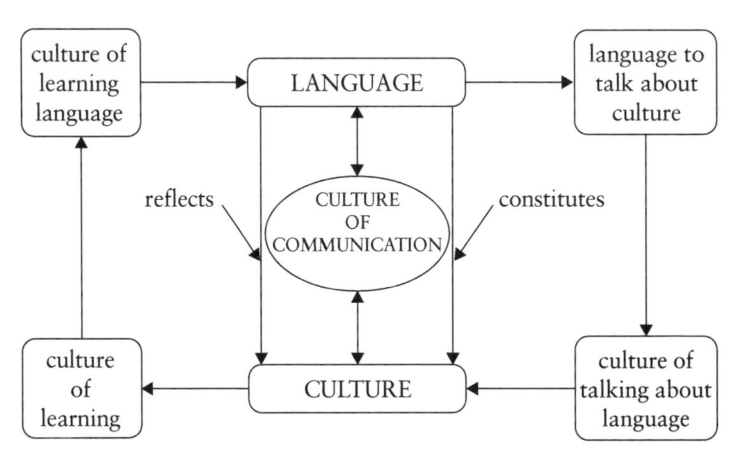

Figure 1 Complex links between language and culture: a framework of communication and learning

Nyack College Library

As every foreign language student knows, language *reflects* culture. However, language is part of culture and it also *constitutes* culture: there are very few aspects of cultural life which are comprehensible without considering cultural ways of speaking (or literacy) as being an instrument of their constitution (Bauman and Sherzer 1974; Saville-Troike 1989). Together, these aspects can be seen as making up a *culture of communication*: a systematic pattern of culturally specific emphases in ways of speaking which mediates language and culture in verbal interaction.

The cultures of communication associated with foreign languages are, or should be, part of the target in the language classroom. Students need to learn the cultural ways in which L2 speakers communicate. However, since classroom discourse – as the medium of learning – is likely to be in L2, this raises the dilemma of whether (and how) the target culture of communication should be used as the means to reach this target. For 'non-native' speaking teachers (itself a complex notion, as Kramsch shows in this volume), it may be a professional challenge to teach a foreign language using the target culture of communication. It is also a challenge to students, who will very likely find some aspects unfamiliar or uncomfortable. On the other hand, if the teacher uses the students' own culture of communication (which is difficult for the 'native' speaker teacher) this makes it easy for students, but it risks the fact that the medium may deny the message: the culture of communication may be dissonant with that of the target language. This would deprive students of the opportunity of learning intercultural skills.

There are further elements in Figure 1: in learning about target cultures, students need a set of terms, a *language to talk about culture*. This metalanguage might be in L1 or L2. It may include folk-linguistic terms used with varying degrees of accuracy or understanding. In some classes, with younger learners perhaps, it may be more student-centred, based on the learners' own expressions. Among teachers and more advanced learners there is also a *culture of talking about language*. This is likely to draw on the academic culture of linguistics or education. It includes ways of using grammar terms and talking about meanings.

Further, as shown in Figure 1, there are *cultures of learning*. These are often overlooked or taken for granted. They include culturally based ideas about teaching and learning, about appropriate ways of participating in class, about whether and how to ask questions. Cultures of learning can be seen in all classrooms. However much language teachers strive to provide a stimulating environment for language learning and cultural immersion the language classroom is still a classroom – there are always deep-rooted expectations about how to behave, and how to interpret others' behaviour. We give examples below.

The language classroom is specifically influenced by cultural notions about languages and about how to learn them. When patterns of classroom interaction in different cultural settings for learning languages are compared, it is readily apparent how a *culture of learning language* can affect teachers' or students' beliefs, classroom practices, and their interpretations of each other's classroom behaviour. These cultural notions often underlie – and sometimes constrain or contradict – the pedagogic training of teachers and efforts aimed at learner training.

The relationship shown in Figure 1 may apply fairly consistently when teachers and students come from the same cultural background, although there are still different cultural expectations arising from generational, occupational or other sub-cultures. However, greater mismatches between these complex links and the corresponding set of links between the target language and its associated cultures are more likely when teachers and students come from different cultural groups. Such gaps are more than a notional distance between a source culture (C1) and target cultures (C2). They are very real when the teacher attempts to expose students to target cultures of communication or learning as part of the means of learning. For a 'non-native' speaking teacher it can be challenging to draw on the target culture of learning while actually teaching L2.

Even more of a gap in expectations, beliefs and classroom practices may arise when students come from a culture which is relatively distinct or distant from that of the teacher. This is the case with 'Western' teachers of EFL working in China, or when Chinese students travel to the West to study. The range of challenges may include: learning to communicate in L2; using L2 for learning about C2 or for other curricular learning; learning C2; learning an academic culture associated with C2 (e.g. when a Chinese student studies management in the West and needs to understand Western cultures of management); and perhaps even using C2 and its academic cultures for learning (as when a Chinese student uses British ways of learning and the academic culture of Western management to take an advanced management course).

Western and Chinese cultures of learning

To speak of 'Western' cultures of learning is to generalise. There are, of course, enormous differences between the various core English-speaking countries and cultures. Similarly, China has a huge population with enormous social and cultural variation. Still, Chinese learners share some common cultural background, including language and clear long-standing cultural perceptions of what it means to be Chinese and of how to learn. In contrast, 'Western' cultures of learning share a different set of norms, perceptions and ideals – at least, they do so in the eyes of very many Chinese, whatever the actual differences between, say, British, American or Australian cultures. These generalisations do not, of course, mean that all individuals will conform to the cultural norms, though they will probably recognise how others do so in their group. A highly influential Chinese culture of learning a language can be analysed (Cortazzi and Jin 1996) as being fundamentally concerned with mastery of knowledge (including knowledge of skills) which is focused on achieving knowledge of grammar and vocabulary, mainly from two sources, the teacher and textbook, as shown in Figure 2.

The verb 'teach' in Chinese is 'jiao shu', literally 'teach the book'. The teacher and textbook are seen as authoritative sources of knowledge: of grammar rules, of explanations of meanings, of what to learn. This learning will take place through dedication and hard work, through close attention to texts and memorisation of vocabulary. This is largely a transmission model of learning, which has a long cultural history in China. It has its roots in the teaching of Confucius and continues to be influential today (Louie 1984).

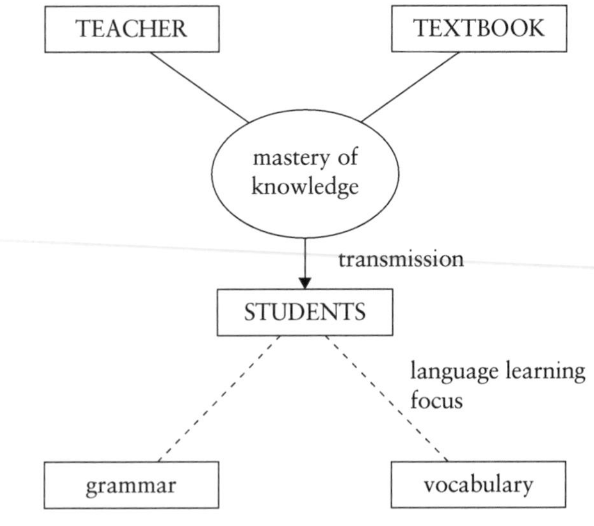

Figure 2 A Chinese cultural model of learning English

Recently, this culture of learning has been changing, partly as a result of general social and economic developments and partly under the influence of communicative approaches to language learning. For many

Chinese teachers 'jiao shu' is balanced by a more humanistic term 'yu ren', meaning 'cultivate a person'. The teacher is thus held to be a moral example, a model of learning and to be like a parent or friend, since this is considered the crucial standard of relationships which nurtures a person, as we shall see below.

The social and pedagogic relations are thought of in quite different terms in current Western cultures of learning. In many language classrooms, the major focus is on the development of skills for communication. Much attention is paid to learning contexts and students needs, to creative and appropriate expression. Classroom environments are influenced by learner-centred notions and a task-based or problem-solving approach, for both linguistic and cultural learning, as shown in Figure 3. There is a strong focus on classroom interaction and student participation as ways of learning and developing skills related to the functions and uses of language.

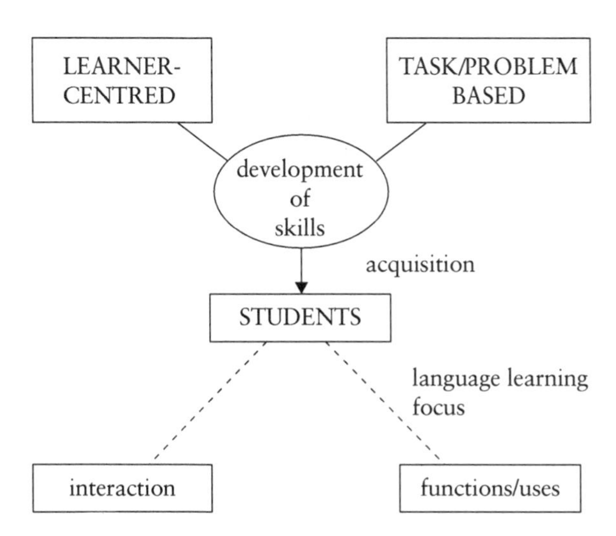

Figure 3 A Western cultural model of foreign language learning

These different cultural orientations to language learning can become barriers. There may be completely different expectations about the roles of teachers and students. There may be variant interpretations about what is effective teaching. Judgements may be made of the other party which are effectively misplaced, or stereotyped views, strongly filtered by participants' culture of learning. This is illustrated by an extensive case study in China carried out between 1993 and 1995 based on classroom observations in schools and universities, interviews, questionnaires and the analysis of students' essays (Cortazzi and Jin in press). This included a focus on Western teachers' views about Chinese learners and Chinese students' perceptions and experiences of having Western teachers (from Britain, North America, Australia and New Zealand).

Chinese students were said to be diligent, thorough, persistent and friendly. They had a strong desire to learn English well. However, when Western teachers attempted to use a range of communicative approaches they found students were 'weak' at oral communication, they were 'unwilling' to work in groups and preferred whole class work or individual work. Students were seen as 'shy' and 'passive'. Their advanced knowledge of grammar and ability to memorise many thousands of English words was rather 'quaint' or a 'misguided' barrier to actual communication. The students' mastery through memory (which students say brings confidence and a feeling of success) was interpreted as 'parrot-learning' and a 'burden'.

On the Chinese side, students saw themselves as hardworking and sociable, in that they learnt from and with others. They paid close attention and gave respect to the teacher, yet they were 'active' in class (in the sense that they mentally interacted with the teaching intensively) and 'cooperated' with teachers. Some saw themselves as 'independent' learners, who 'think for themselves' and 'overcome their puzzles and difficulties on their own'.

The students appreciated the teachers' encouragement of oral language and self-expression. Teachers were good models of pronunciation. They had the 'authority', even 'superiority' of being native speakers. They were valued for their ability to present useful knowledge about the history, cultures and customs of Western societies. Yet, as shown in Figure 4, the Chinese students had mixed views about having Western teachers compared with Chinese teachers of English.

Western teachers brought a useful cognitive dimension to the classroom: students felt they benefited from 'different thinking'. However, students were 'puzzled' when the teachers did not seem to understand their writing: a 'good' essay, (in the students' view) got a low grade, while a 'not very well written' one received a high mark and good comments. Students concluded that there were 'differences between our minds and foreign teachers' minds', but more likely they were simply drawing on different emphases in cultural patterns of rhetoric or discourse. Students found that Western teachers used 'simple' English, they 'simplified vocabulary' whereas Chinese teachers of English were seen as being systematic and effective in helping students to learn more advanced vocabulary.

Western teachers were 'very welcome' for oral classes: they were

Students' comments about:	WESTERN TEACHERS	CHINESE TEACHERS
THINKING	*students benefit and learn from different thinking*	*students don't expect to learn about culture*
WRITING	*students puzzled: teachers don't understand Ss' writing*	*teachers' judgement matches student expectations*
VOCABULARY	*simplify vocabulary*	*systematic, effective in teaching*
ORAL LANGUAGE	*friendly, help Ss to practise; encourage Ss*	*give knowledge of language*
GRAMMAR	*don't stress grammar don't know grammar don't correct errors*	*good knowledge correct errors*

Figure 4 Chinese students' views about teachers of English in China

'friendly', they helped students to practise and gave encouragement. On the other hand, Chinese teachers gave 'much more knowledge'. Western teachers were said not to pay much attention to grammar, they did not stress grammar, did not appear to know grammatical rules or to correct student errors. Chinese teachers, in contrast, did all of these and had a 'good' knowledge of grammar. Such perceptions, stereotyped or limited as they may be, can influence foreign language learning. They are partly derived from and constructed in classroom discourse.

Interpreting classroom discourse

Classroom discourse, whether in L1 or L2, is a medium of learning. How the discourse functions can be further affected by the culture brought into the classroom by learners – and teachers. What is objectively the same classroom communication pattern can be interpreted in diverse ways subjectively, as seen in the following examples.

The activity of having a group discussion in class, in which students listen and respond to each other, may be positively valued by Western teachers, as shown in Figure 3. Discussion is useful interaction and productive language practice. It embodies several aspects of student-centred learning. Many Chinese students, on the other hand, consider it 'fruitless': they thought it wasted time; they risked learning errors from their peers. As shown in Figure 2, they believed the teacher should present knowledge and a correct model. The teacher, not other learners, should practise with them. They expected to 'take something useful home' after class so that they could review and practise it later. Group language practice should be carried out between peer students after class in order to use class time with the teacher to the best advantage.

Another example is the issue of asking for help. The Western teachers expected Chinese students to request clarification if they did not understand or to express any anxiety or doubt if they needed help. They believed this was part of the normal learning process and often asked '*Does everyone understand?*' or '*Does anyone need help?*' or said '*Do ask me if you have a problem*'. For most of the Chinese students this was embarrassing: asking for help means giving a burden to others. They expect the teacher, and other students, to be sensitive to any need for help and to offer it (unasked) when it was needed. This 'caring' nature, admired by the Chinese, comes from Chinese tradition and culture. Children are trained from a very young age to develop this aspect, as can be observed in kindergartens. This is also a part of teacher training programmes in the aspect of moral education. Hence, in the intercultural classroom, Chinese students tended not to ask for help according to their cultural values, while Western teachers tended not to offer it beyond ritual statements (as above). Since the students' needs were unexpressed, they were not met; some problems passed unnoticed by teachers.

A third example is students' questions. The Western teachers believed that the students should ask questions in class. This shows that students are actively participating and learning by asking. They were puzzled, however, by the fact that this heuristic function of questions was realised in a different way: many students tended to ask questions *after* a class, at the end of the lesson. Good questions seemed 'wasted' because the answers or ensuing discussion were only heard by the individual who asked, rather than the class.

The Chinese perspective was different. Students thought of themselves as being 'active', but not necessarily verbally, even in a language class. They 'participated' by listening, by thinking (and questioning in their mind), by asking questions after class and by discussing with each other after class. The main reason why they didn't ask questions was because they were 'shy' or because they were afraid of making mistakes. If they do ask, Chinese students' questions are carefully thought out, since they do not like to waste the teacher's time. Few questions are spontaneous; rather, questions tend to be devices to elicit confirmation of students' ideas after deep reflection. Many students explained their lack of questions with reference to 'face'. They did not want to lose face by asking foolish questions, nor by asking 'smart' questions which may be interpreted by peers as showing off. To stand out in this way is not in harmony with their collective beliefs. Further, their questions might cause the teacher to lose face if the teacher was unable to answer – this would cause the student to lose face also. Since, in their view, a good teacher should predict questions and answer them unasked, the students tended to wait till later before asking.

The influence of Chinese traditional culture on present Chinese students

The contrasts between Western and Chinese cultural perceptions shown in the previous sections have presented different beliefs and values in the aspects of relationships, learning styles, classroom discourse and activities, teaching and assessment. From a Chinese point of view, this may be traced back to traditional cultural influences from Confucianism and Taoism which have had a strong impact. To understand this traditional resource is an effective way to understand Chinese students' thinking at a deeper level, a level which they themselves may not be able to talk about explicitly, but it may be the thinking that they follow in their behaviour in the language classroom.

The implications of Confucianism and Taoism on Chinese students are shown in Figures 5 (p. 108) and 6 (p. 109). The variables are found in the data of interviews and questionnaires of 101 Chinese postgraduate students in UK universities and 37 of their British supervisors (Jin 1992). These variables are further confirmed in more recent observation and interview data in recent studies (Jin and Cortazzi 1993, 1995; Cortazzi and Jin in press).

Chinese philosophies present ways of thinking which are quite different from those of Western culture (Watts 1979). Many researchers and scholars (Moore 1967; Smith 1985; Bond 1986, 1991; Li 1986) would agree that the thinking of modern Chinese people is significantly structured by Chinese traditional cultural beliefs represented mainly by Confucianism, Taosim and Buddhism, although China has been undergoing rapid modernisation. Surprisingly, these traditional values have been widely seen as a major influence on contemporary economic development and education (Louie 1984; Tu *et al.* 1991; Hofstede 1994). The traditional philosophical systems of cultural beliefs in China are very complex. Therefore the discussion here only attempts to link relevant parts of Chinese traditional culture to the current focus. This section shows how Chinese students understand these cultural concepts and how they may be influenced by their beliefs about such concepts.

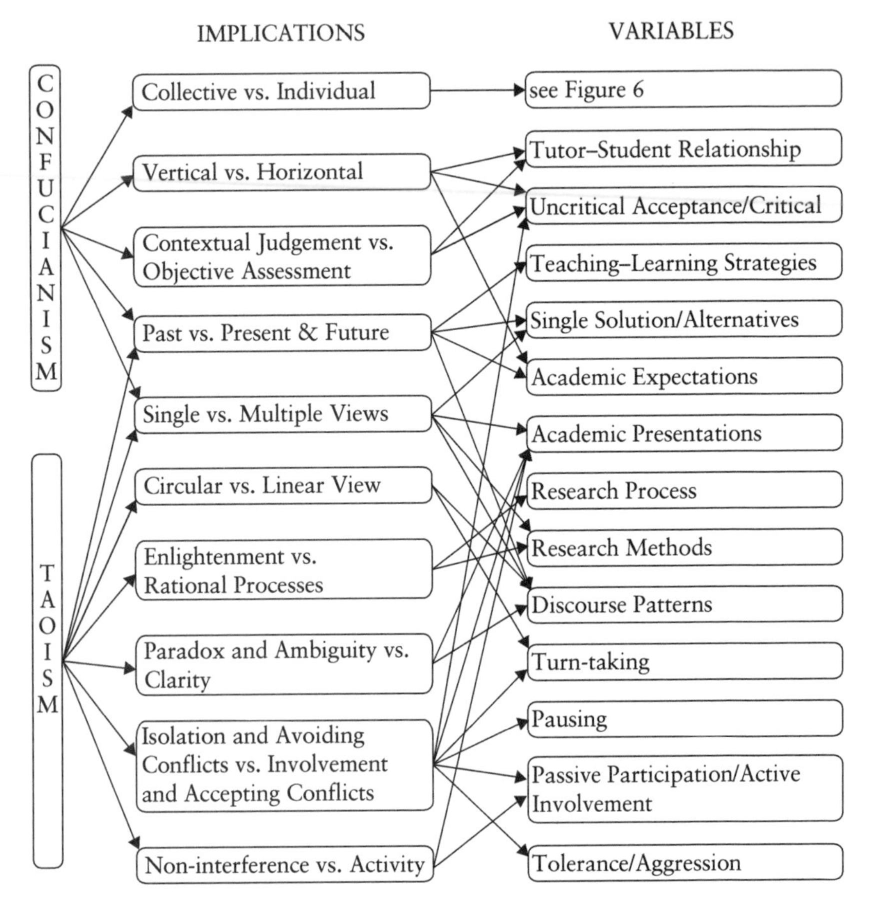

Figure 5 Confucian and Taoist implications on the variables

Further, the focus of such influences will be on Confucianism and Taoism which are considered the two main influences on Chinese intellectuals (Jin 1992).

The teachings of Confucius (551–479 BC) have been transmitted for over two thousand years of Chinese civilisation, resulting from a continual reference in education and culture to nine key books, the Five Classics and the Four Books. Confucianism has become deeply rooted in Chinese culture, it has 'moulded and shaped' Chinese thinking (Smith 1985:11). Confucius' teaching stresses the Three Bonds or Hierarchies (san gang), i.e. the relationships between the monarch and his subjects, between the father and the son and between the husband and the wife; and the Five Relations or Principles (wu chang), i.e. 'Ren', Righteousness, Rites, Intelligence and Trust. The core elements of Confucianism

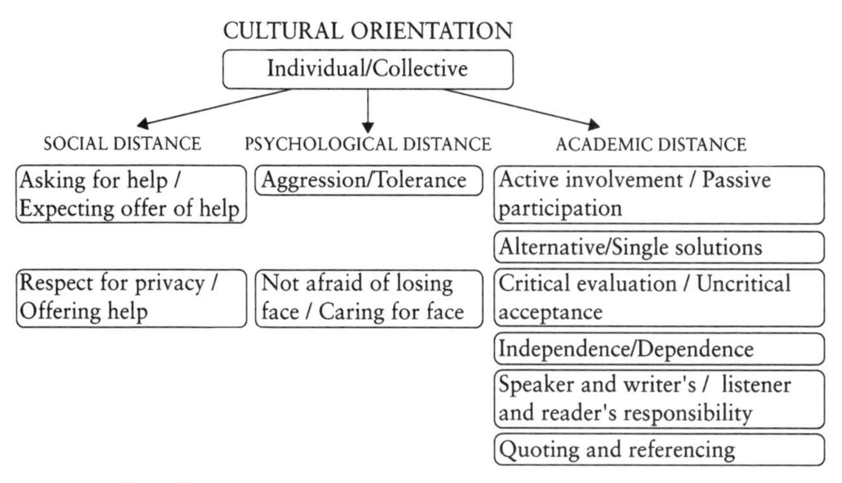

Figure 6 The cultural orientation of individualism and collectivism in the Cultural Synergy Model

contain the Zhou Rites (which refer to sets of ceremonies, institutions, regulations, and social systems in the Zhou Dynasty) and the concept of Ren. Ren has been translated as 'compassion', 'perfect virtue', 'love', 'benevolence', 'human-heartedness', 'moral character' (Mei 1967:152); it refers to the highest principle of human action. These elements emphasise:

- the human relationships of consanguinity and hierarchy;
- the moral and psychological principle which makes the Zhou Rites – the external disciplines of behaviour – into an internal moral demand to maintain consanguinity and hierarchy;
- humanitarianism which advocates love, peace, avoidance of conflicts;
- cultivating personal morality such as loyalty, altruism, righteousness.

These ideas can be seen further in Figure 7.

The ideal society	**The Zhou Rites**
	↑
The perfect human inner qualities which can make that society	**Ren** ↓
The major elements in **Ren**	Filial piety; Fraternal duty; Loyalty; Righteousness; Altruism; Governing by virtue; The middle way

Figure 7 Core concepts of Confucianism (after Jin 1992)

Ren has formed an important part of the cultural and psychological structure of Chinese people and is still a functional and pragmatic ideology in contemporary Chinese society. This is because Ren:

- is based on people's emotions and blood relationships: filial piety and fraternal duty, in the family; loyalty and righteousness and altruism in society;
- emphasises morality, kindness, humanity, non-violence, as shown in filial piety, fraternal duty, altruism, the middle way and governing by virtue;
- demands a very high spiritual life, and encourages one to endure and tolerate a hard and poor material life, so that the external world does not have much influence on the stability of the ideology itself nor on people's minds;
- emphasises self-sacrifice in order to maintain one's family or to let others be happy so that the world is not disturbed, as in righteousness and altruism. (Jin 1992:29–30)

All of these concepts 'have permeated people's thinking, behaviour, habits, customs, beliefs, ways of thinking, emotional status ..., and guidance and basic principles which people use consciously and unconsciously to deal with things, relations and everyday life' (Li 1986:34).

Taoism originated with the book Tao Te Ching written supposedly by Lao Tzu around 476 BC (Luo 1985; Li 1986). The book discusses the key concepts of Te and Tao. It is very difficult, perhaps impossible, according to Lao Tzu, to give a definition to Te and Tao: 'The Tao that can be tao-ed is not the invariable Tao' (Fung trans. 1961).

However, many scholars of Chinese philosophies agree that Tao is the natural and objective process of the universe (Luo 1985; Li 1986; Watts 1979). But it has links with people's everyday activities. Therefore some scholars argue that Tao is the principle maintaining the world (Luo 1985; Hua 1988). Te originally referred to a set of social rules in ancient ceremonies and later was understood as skills and methods of governing (Li 1986; Hua 1988).

Taoism 'is a deep fundamental trait of Chinese thinking, and of the Chinese attitude toward life and society' (Lin 1955:74). Its teaching has had a special influence on Chinese intellectuals' thinking patterns (Li 1986) leaving a strong mark on Chinese intellectual culture, see Figure 5. Major characteristics include such notions as Wu-wei (which literally means 'not doing anything'), the use of paradox or polarity, establishing harmony with nature and relationships, maintaining a balance between two extremes or in the whole system.

Wu-wei refers to 'doing nothing and nothing is left undone' (said by Chuang Tzu, a student of Lao Tzu). This is an attitude towards the whole rather than a part, because the action of 'doing' or 'having' something is limited, but 'not doing' or 'not having' a thing is equal to 'doing' or 'having' everything philosophically. This ambiguity may result in various consequences: some people may have an attitude of concern for the world as a whole, but not any particular thing, e.g. a researcher may prefer not to have hypotheses, i.e. speculations, limitations, but keeps the range of what is to be included naturally vague and loose. Others may believe that being passive, not putting oneself forward, not joining in any activities, is the essence of Wu-wei.

Paradox or polarity is another major feature which indicates that all things are relative. 'Right' and 'wrong', 'hard' and 'soft', 'strong' and 'weak' are only pairs of words which may mean the same thing, depending on which partial viewpoint they are seen from (Creel 1970). This leads to a circular, or holistic, style of thinking which differs from Western linear logic. 'One should clearly understand ... that Chinese logic is both indeterminate and synchronous, instead of determinate, exclusive and sequential, as in the West ..., (for example) cause and effect in Chinese are not sequential, but are parallel aspects of the same truth' (Lin 1955:27).

The view of life in a circular and continuous way is also shown in the belief that the world is balanced by mutual rise and conquest of basic elements, e.g. the five elements of metal, wood, water, fire and earth. Their mutual rising refers to: wood makes fire, fire produces ash/earth, earth contains metal, metal attracts water; water nourishes wood. Their mutual conquest draws attention to the complementary sequence: wood ploughs earth, earth dams water, water puts out fire, fire liquefies metal, metal cuts wood. A Taoist sees the importance of keeping one element in a correct situation, so that it balances the remaining related elements. This view only stresses the necessity of harmony in nature and relationship.

However, Taoist harmony in relationship is achieved through non-interference with people and following the course of the nature. Such naturalism has implications for resisting subjective change which would interfere with the natural order and system. Taoism also believes that emotions and desire or possession of any property (including knowledge) are the causes of conflicts and problems in human relationships and society (Luo 1985).

The variables in Figures 5 and 6 have reflected the consequences of these implications. In Chinese students' academic relationship with Western teachers, it is likely to be a vertical rather than a horizontal one in discussion, debate, expressing opinions, asking questions. To them, following and obeying a teacher's suggestions are a sign of respect, and also an avoidance of conflicts. This may not be the expectation of a British teacher who probably believes that having one's own critical opinions and evaluation is a sign of academic independence and a matter of academic process. In other words, the two sides see values and show their beliefs in different ways. Those Chinese students who are influenced by the notion that the past is proven as correct and successful may find that this affects their teaching–learning strategies in UK universities which may value a critical view towards past work. This may also influence their views on solutions to a problem, their academic expectations and discourse patterns in the sense that they see the past as older and better and therefore only need to follow such patterns of guaranteed success. This may be reflected in written discourse patterns where a lengthy background is prominently placed in the beginning of the text, because they may believe that the background part fulfils the task of indicating the direction of present and future work. To a British reader, this background part may seem irrelevant and cause ambiguity and confusion.

Chinese students who emphasise results more than process may think that it is unimportant to present a process clearly, as long as the result is right. They may have a pragmatic attitude towards 'a wordy and lengthy research review', which they believe is a waste of time and space (interview data). Their academic presentation and discourse patterns may be influenced by the belief that ambiguity is perhaps able to include everything unsaid (see Taoist implications). So further clarity is unnecessary, because it would limit the context. This may be due to an orientation to readers and listeners in which scope is designedly left for their interpretation.

The Chinese cultural value of non-interference may affect students' performance in academic presentation and participation since initiating and asking a 'smart' question is seen as 'showing off', which is regarded as an uneducated manner. The participation of British students (asking questions, interrupting or disagreeing) might be seen by the Chinese as a lack of respect for teachers.

Chinese students tend to look at their academic life in a collective way, in which they care about their relationships, harmony in their learning and in their communication with others. They are tolerant and avoid situations which may cause anybody (both themselves and others) to lose face. In contrast, British teachers and students are likely to have an individual tendency and give much less importance to such beliefs and values as Chinese students hold.

KEY FEATURE	COMMENT
Learning is valued	Students should love learning, be curious, expect to learn.
Learning is respect	Filial piety is extended to teachers. They are respected experts, parents, friends. Teachers give care, concern and help.
Learning involves reciprocal relationships	Teachers and students have duties and responsibilities to each other; both learn academically and morally.
Learning is social	Self-development occurs in a collective setting. Key relationships should achieve harmony, not disagreement.
Learning means thinking and doing	Learning is incomplete without deep reflection, practical application; therefore students focus on products and results.
Learning is an apprenticeship	Learning involves long-term strategies of hard work now for later rewards. It involves following a 'master' in word and deed.
Learning is enlightenment	Learning involves memorisation and accumulation of knowledge. What is memorised is later understood for further development and used for creation.
Learning is memorising	Memorising (even by rote) is a concession to the collected past experience and authority of others. Memorising is part of progress.

Figure 8 Key features of a Chinese culture of learning

Chinese cultures of learning and communication

Some of the chief elements in Chinese cultures of learning and communication are shown in Figures 8 and 9 (based on Moore 1967, Oliver, 1971, Smith, 1985, Chen 1990, Tu *et al.* 1991, Young 1994, Scollon and Scollon 1995, Cortazzi and Jin in press). These figures show broad trends: not every individual will follow them; many depend on contexts and circumstances. The figures derive directly from the Confucian and Taoist heritage in Chinese culture. These are cultural elements which Chinese students bring to the language classroom. They affect the kinds of perceptions of classroom events and interaction illustrated earlier.

KEY FEATURE	COMMENT
Communication produces harmony	The chief aim of communication is to bring harmonious relationships rather than mainly to share information functionally.
Communication depends on authority	Communication follows tradition and authority rather than originality or spontaneity. Speakers defer to experts, including the teacher.
Communication depends on the known	Speakers say what is known rather than regarding saying as a way of knowing.
Communication is inductive	Often inductive patterns are used – background first, main point later or reason then result, rather than vice versa.
Communication is holistic	Opposites may be part of a larger truth, so there is a tendency to think 'both – and' rather than 'either – or' as in binary thinking.
Communication is reciprocal	Both participants have responsibility for understanding. Not everything needs to be explicit – hearers/readers can work out implications.
Communication works by analogy	Proof can come from analogy, examples or indications rather than by explicit sequential links.
Silence is communication	Silence can be acceptable on ambiguous or sensitive topics. Silence can show solidarity and avoid embarrassment.

Figure 9 Key features of a Chinese culture of communication

A cultural synergy model

A cultural synergy model (Figure 10) is a proposal to bridge the different perceptions and attitudes shown in previous sections (Jin 1992, Jin and Cortazzi 1995). This model suggests the need for mutual understanding of different cultures, communication styles and academic cultures. This does not mean that diversity and variety will be merged into one, but that natural divisions exist and academic cultural practitioners should have an open mind to be aware of the operation of other styles and appreciate their emphasis. Cultural synergy here implies that there is an additional benefit from collaboration which is greater than the single benefit for each side in the intercultural context.

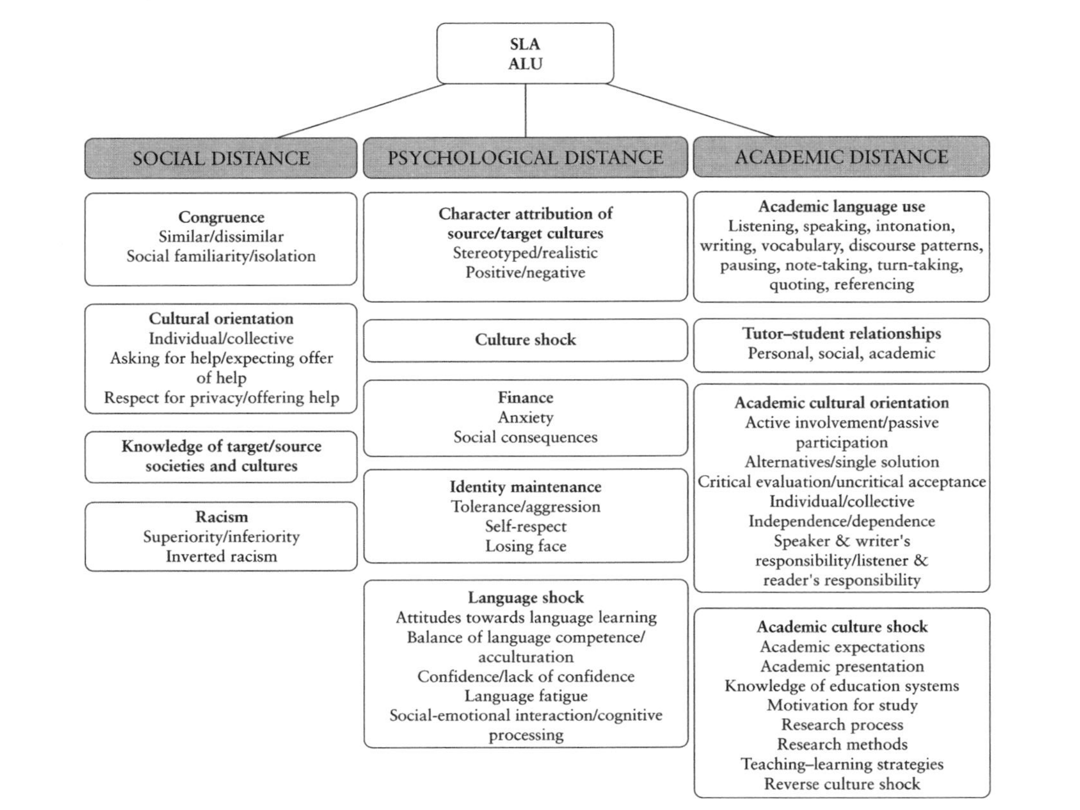

Figure 10 The cultural synergy model of second language acquisition and academic language use (Jin 1992)

Teachers and students from different cultures need to develop an attitude of being willing to learn, understand and appreciate the other's culture without loss of their own status, role or cultural identity. Mutual understanding and adaptation by choice, rather than assimilation, is stressed, for the latter may cause a psychological barrier and a fear of the loss of L1 identity (Clement 1980). The model involves the following key notions:

1. Movement towards mutual congruence

Congruence needs to be thought of as mutual congruence or a dynamic synergetic process. The emphasis is on a two-way acculturation, instead of a one-way version (which refers to the movement from source to target culture), as suggested in Schumann's acculturation model (1978) or Giles and Coupland's intergroup model (1991) or implied in Kim's model of intercultural adaptation (1989). This would mean that participants develop a mutual awareness and understanding of each other's culture: from second/foreign language learner to target language speaker and vice versa.

2. Collective/individual tendencies

Cultures emphasising the collective orientation focus more on 'in-group', though individualist cultures also have such groups. Individualist cultures have many specific in-groups and these exert less influence on individuals than the in-groups of collectivist cultures (Triandis 1995). In contrast with British teachers, Chinese students are seen to have a collective orientation socially which influences their activities and performance academically. This collectively-oriented culture is regarded as a 'high synergy society' (Moran and Harris 1991:313) which emphasises group consciousness, cooperation and mutual reciprocity. This may be why British people are seen by some Chinese students as cold, unhelpful and uncooperative; and Chinese students are seen by some British people as not sociable, but only involved with their own group.

3. Second language acquisition/academic language use and academic culture

This model is relevant to second language acquisition and academic language use, especially in instances of high language competence and low acculturation. Chinese postgraduate students in the UK have achieved a rather high level of language competence through the selection and language test procedures. Yet their understanding of L2 culture and L2 academic culture does not at all achieve the same level as their competence in the second language. The gaps have been illustrated in the variables under the topic of academic distance in the model (Figure 10).

4. Identity maintenance

The concept of synergy does not mean the merging of two cultures into one or that individuals from one culture should assimilate to another. Rather it means understanding the other culture, behaving appropriately in the other cultural environment, without losing one's original cultural identity. This requires explicitness: participants need to be aware of their own cultures of learning and communication and to be able to explain them to others. Further they should be willing to understand the views, perceptions and behaviour of people from other cultures. Preferably, they should be able to use their understanding and knowledge of different cultures and styles of learning and communication to discuss their differences and negotiate a way both sides accept.

A practical way to discuss such issues might be to use the kind of diagrams shown here (Figures 2, 3, 8, 9) in the classroom in order to help students to make explicit their own ideas and experiences. This has been found useful in EAP courses.

Intercultural competence and identity

The cultural synergy model is aimed at fostering intercultural competence, in the sense that participants will be socially – and educationally – effective across cultures, not only communicating appropriately in intercultural contexts (Martin 1993; Meyer 1991) but, further, understanding the communication patterns, expectations and interpretations of others. This could be seen as a threat to learners' cultural identity: learning the foreign language to the extent of being able to identify, even to identify with, others' intentions and cultural meanings could imply losing one's own identity. This would be, however, to take 'identity' as a single entity whereas current social-psychologists interested in intercultural communication do not do so. Rather, identity is seen in a 'mosaic sense' in which people identify themselves not only in relatively stable terms (on such dimensions as nationality, mother tongue, ethnic group, age, gender) but also in dynamic terms. In the latter, major aspects of identity are 'framed, negotiated, modified, confirmed, and challenged through communication and contact with others' (Collier and Thomas 1988:42). This intercultural situation in the language classroom can therefore be seen as offering options for effective identity negotiations vis-à-vis target culture practices and beliefs (Ting-Toomey 1993:73). Cultures are thus important resources in the foreign language classroom, brought by both teachers and students. The learners' culture is safeguarded when teachers respect it and consider that it has a key role in a system of options for identity negotiation. This negotiation can, it is argued, take place best in intercultural contexts since these are the contexts which often highlight differences within which learners can confirm their preferred identity through negotiating mutual meanings and coming to understand others' identities. Intercultural communication, in terms of synergy, is likely to stabilise learners' self-identity (Meyer 1991:137). The synergy model, because it is seen in Chinese relation terms of offering mutual benefit and requiring mutual responsibility for intercultural understanding, offers three benefits for teachers. First, it avoids any overtones of cultural imperialism or assumed predominance of C2 over C1, or vice versa. Rather, it emphasises the kind of mutual learning and negotiation which would seem to be essential in any multi-cultural society. Second, it draws attention to the discourse processes involved in interaction where cultures of learning operate, usually at a level of which teachers and students have little awareness. The model might, in fact, be presented to more advanced students in EAP contexts, to raise their consciousness of typical variables which make up a culture of learning and communication. Third, the model is useful for the professional development of teachers, to help solve some of the dilemmas of the intercultural classroom but also, perhaps more significantly, to show useful directions for teachers' own learning of the dynamics of intercultural processes. At the same time, the model offers a tool to help teachers to see how the processes of intercultural communication can help students to stabilise their self-identity.

6 Mind the gap! An ethnographic approach to cross-cultural workplace communication research

Antonia Cooper

The research project described in this chapter was designed to establish whether the ubiquitously perceived gap between employers' expectations and the English competence of a particular section of graduates entering employment in Hong Kong had a basis in reality. Such a deceptively simple brief might appear to lend itself to a conventional needs analysis by means of a company audit followed by tailor-made materials developed for further training. It will be argued, however, that an ethnographic approach provides a richer analysis of the cultural context and yields more fruitful results. Although some of the findings and implications of the research project will be reported, the central thrust of this chapter will be to argue for the value of an ethnographic approach in cross-cultural workplace communication, and to discuss the implications of the project in a wider context.

Education and training in a changed and changing world

The ability to communicate concisely and with clarity is much desired, but sorely lacking. This at least, seems to be the rather worrying opinion of UK employers, judging from recent employer satisfaction surveys on graduates entering employment (Association of Graduate Recruiters 1994; University of Central England 1994).

Moreover the issue seems to surface above all – though by no means exclusively – at the stage when young people enter employment. Surveys reveal that there are considerable mismatches between employers' communication needs and what educators and trainers are providing and similarly there are mismatches between young people's aspirations and abilities, and educational provision (London University Survey 1994, AIESEC Survey). The dissatisfaction is, however, not confined to British culture: one major study by the world's largest private testing agency (Educational Testing Service 1994) described graduate illiteracy in the USA as ranging from 'a lot less than impressive' to 'near alarming', and an internal survey at BMW AG, Germany found a lack of what they termed 'soft skills'. Nor is the phenomenon confined to Western cultures; Far Eastern cultures are not immune either:

> In Hong Kong employers find academic standards high, but language standards not, whereas other countries need improvements in both. Senior Manager Personnel, Hongkong Bank

The situation is clearly regarded as deserving serious attention throughout the region. In Hong Kong the Hongkong Bank Language Development Fund (HKLDF) was set up to fund eight major educational research and development projects – two relating to the workplace, one of which is reported on here; in Singapore an ASEAN-wide English for Business and Technology (EBT), project was recently conducted over four years and across six countries.

Whilst employers are continually canvassed as to the various competences of their young employees, opinions continue to vary as to whether their views are or should be relevant to educational concerns. One fear is that this will lead education further down the path of narrow vocationalism, and when:

> ... taken to extremes universities could become glorified training establishments. (Leader, Times Higher Educational Supplement, 13 January 1995)

Indeed, one traditional perception is that the education sector should be properly concerned with education and the workplace with training. This would at first sight place workplace research, such as is discussed in this chapter, in a position of little relevance to education. In recent decades however, the education–training divide has become much less clear-cut when Department of Education and Science publications in England as far back as 1977 state that '... industry and commerce should be involved in curriculum planning at national and local level' to make learners more effective and willing contributors to 'the creation of Britain's national wealth' (cited in Wringe 1991).

Views and statements such as the above have prompted much discussion along a number of parameters and various publications already provide discussion on the interplay of education and work (e.g. Corson 1991). Nevertheless in order to establish areas of relevance in the present research to education, a 'working' description of the purposes of education is first needed. The chapter will then go on to look at those global factors which are thought to be deeply influencing employers and education, followed by a critique of one widely used research tool, the language audit, and a discussion of an ethnographic workplace-based research project, its outcome and implications.

Corson recognises the cultural embeddedness of views on education and technology. At the same time he also distinguishes education from training by emphasising understanding over mere knowledge of facts:

> Being educated demands more than being highly trained; it involves the possession of a body of knowledge along with a conceptual scheme to raise that knowledge above the level of a collection of disjointed facts. This means some understanding of principles for the organising of facts. We need to understand the reasons behind things, an understanding that training on its own not just fails to supply, but which it can obscure. (Corson 1991:52)

Wringe insists that knowledge of the world is crucial to all aspects of life, including the vocational:

> Knowledge of the world is relevant to both the way one lives one's life and the way one does one's job ... in our work we use knowledge of a specific part of the world to make decisions of a particular kind. (Wringe 1991:42)

Wringe argues that to train is necessarily to educate and vice versa and that the two activities may take place concurrently. Like Chomsky (1991:19) though, he sees the aim of training as the production of a conforming mind, while education's aim is the development of rational autonomy with informed choice high on the agenda. Education throws further light on life choices which have to be made; it does not determine them or presuppose that they have already been made, as training does. A similar emphasis on autonomy and choice is made with respect to communication. The New London Group (1995) composed of international linguists, argues that:

> Our job is not to produce docile, compliant workers. Students need to develop the skills to speak up, to negotiate and to be able to engage critically ...

Thus, to summarise, a working description of the purposes of education is that it is concerned with knowledge and understanding of both ourselves and the world around us, as well as their interrelationship; further, that it needs reference to cultural dimensions, that the knowledge and understanding embrace aspects of technology; that it should provide a conceptual scheme to raise knowledge above the collection of mere facts; that similarly it should provide an understanding of the principles for the organising of facts, and of the reasons behind things; that it has to do with autonomy of the individual, critical engagement and communication. This view will be referred to again later in the light of the outcomes of the research described below.

Education or training for communication

Meanwhile another question should be asked and that is whether there are particular pressures on employers which might have a bearing on their communication concerns with regard to young employees. It would seem plausible for instance to argue that employer dissatisfaction and another pressing present-day concern to society, unemployment, have a common cause: massive global transformations at organisational, societal and individual level (Brownell 1992; New London Group 1995). If we can in addition accept Adent-Hoecklin's argument (1993:17) that organisations have a higher capability for change than do individuals and societies, it might go some way to explaining why the increasing pressures are first felt by employers and this subsequently leads them to voice their concerns. A glance at the broader canvas, at the unprecedented transformations which have taken place in the world since World War II, will help us to arrive at an understanding of the nature of some of the clearly powerful influences upon employers. Only then can informed decisions be taken as to whether their impact upon society and culture is of a magnitude that would justify their being addressed in an educational programme.

The problem has been formulated by Brownell (1992:44) in the context of quality in education:

> ... do we have a lapse in quality control, a design flaw, or a combination of the two? Quality control solutions improve efficiency and effectiveness of what is being done without disturbing its basic features. Design solutions, on the other hand, fundamentally alter the organization of systems themselves.

Through detailed discussion he reaches the conclusion that 'Given the extraordinary transformations which have taken place [in the world], we confront a design change.'

The following overview of the global changes, which are said to have led to new global realities and new requirements, is based on Brownell and functions as the context of change for an ethnographic approach to research; the latter approach also demands the adoption of a broader context. Brownell (op. cit.: 45–57) enumerates no fewer than twenty-two global transformations, five of which are particularly worth mentioning here, because of their implications for education, the workplace and communication. They are:

- the growth and elaboration of knowledge since the mid-twentieth century and its powerful connection to technology;
- the expansion and rapidity of worldwide communications and, it must be added, transportation;
- the growing interdependence of nations and the emergence of a global transnational economy with accelerating internationalisation as a result;
- the recent emergence of knowledge- and information-based societies and the view of knowledge as a resource;
- the move away from a mechanistic, analytic worldview to a systemic, holistic worldview, which accords a central position to the behaviour of the 'whole'.

This poses many challenges for education. The implications of all these transformations are enormous, with considerable impact on economies, societies, cultures and also on education. But they also impact upon the workplace as they do on individuals through changed and changing workplace practice, which makes it also likely that increased autonomous functioning will be expected at an international level from all employees at all levels. The formation of multicultural teams as a result of changes in society and internationalism demand cross-cultural understanding and a knowledge of languages. It has been shown that the availability of information and knowledge erodes workplace hierarchies (Rieder 1993). The research described below shows that there is indeed a demand for greater contributions and more independent functioning from even junior members of the workforce. It would seem that the new organisational requirements, which under the influence of new global realities (Drucker 1989) are increasingly focused upon organisational survival, flexibility and growth, will be more and more dependent upon the personal growth and creativity of the individual with appropriate communication skills.

In short, it seems to me that it is only through broad-based workplace research which takes account of global transformations and requirements, that we will arrive at some pointers as to what 'design changes' might be needed from a workplace perspective. Only then, and on the basis of informed debate, can a synthesis with educational perspectives take place. The workplace-based research described in this chapter aims to make a contribution in the field of cross-cultural communication and the foreign language teaching curriculum in particular. The ethnographic approach to cross-cultural communication research to be described below was developed during the extensive research project carried out at the request of the Vocational Training Council, Hong Kong.

Ethnographic research

What at first appeared to be an English language auditing project changed into cross-cultural communication research. It provides one example of primary ethnographic communication research in the workplace and demonstrates in the detail of a Hong Kong case study the effects of the global changes discussed so far.

The context will be described, a context which is very much one of change, both at a local as well as at a global level. By examining the appropriacy of a standard approach, language auditing, to the problem posed for this project, and by comparing it with an ethnographic approach and its significance, it will become clear that the situation presents a classic case for an ethnographic approach. Discussion of the results will show some of what was achieved using an ethnographic approach. The major question of how to feed the insights and knowledge gained back into learning situations will be addressed at two levels with reference to the role of culture in language teaching.

The need for an investigation was established through feedback received from Hong Kong employers, who are surveyed by the Vocational Training Council (VTC) Statistics Department on a regular basis. Statistics relating to Technical Institute (TI) graduates revealed that they were in the main satisfied with the subject competence of these graduates. They were not satisfied, however, when the subject knowledge had to be expressed in the workplace through the medium of English. This finding was confirmed by several other recent surveys in Hong Kong, such as were undertaken by the HK General Chamber of Commerce and the Chinese Manufacturing Association. The brief for our research was, therefore, deceptively succinct. The VTC wanted to establish whether the ubiquitously perceived gap between employers' needs and the English competence of this particular section of VTC graduates entering employment, had a basis in reality and, if so, to make recommendations for closing it.

This would seem a straightforward brief which, on the face of it, could be accomplished by a standard process which generally runs as follows. First there would be a needs analysis by means of company language audits, perhaps involving diagnostic testing of the four skills of the individuals concerned, to be described in an extensive report. Typically this process would then be followed up with tailor-made materials development for further training, followed by the training itself, either by the auditors or other consultants. Language auditing in industry enjoys a high profile at present and has a certain face-validity. However, this approach to establishing language needs in the workplace is not adequate for the type of research problem to be addressed here, one which ultimately would need to address curriculum issues. Auditing would confirm or disconfirm employers' need for English and other languages and might deal with a particular company's present and future strategic language needs; it would provide details of the language skills required in a particular post and whether and to what extent this need was being met adequately by the group of graduates under investigation through assessment. But auditing could not begin to explain the whole host of urgent questions that had started to present themselves (see also Lo and Lee 1993). The nature of the lack of learning, the reasons for the widely-held perceptions and assumptions mentioned below and the generally observed low levels of motivation for learning English are but a few of those questions. Motivation, for instance, is a powerful force in all successful learning and is cited in management literature as an important aspect of job performance (Jackson 1993:83). In this context it is also interesting to note that:

> Even among internationally knowledgeable companies ... there is often great difficulty recognising that the things that motivate, inspire and generate commitment depend on the culture one comes from (Adent-Hoecklin 1993:4)

Indeed, research carried out by Young (1994) in both France and the UK concluded that the socio-cultural context is of key importance in foreign language learning motivation.

At this point the reasons why a standard approach of needs analysis by means of company language audits and all it involves would not have been adequate in the Hong Kong research need to be summarised and clarified. Company language audits represent:

- A top-down approach
  Company language audits are generally carried out by an expert consultant: linguists and/or language trainers in cooperation with preferably, but in practice rarely, decision-makers within the company. The established practice of relying solely on experts and committees for systems development can lead to important data and insights being missed.
- A lack of concern with the individual and actual workplace practice: recent ethnographic studies of workplace practice show that actual workpractice differs fundamentally from the type of organisational

descriptions which audits rely upon, such as job descriptions, manuals and training programmes (Seely Brown and Duguid 1991).

- Work as a technical process
  The classical universal approach to organisational structure believed that 'work could be reviewed objectively, analysed and treated as a technical process' (Buchanan and Huczynski 1985:343), yet the last 80 years have seen a decided shift from this narrow 'technical' focus towards the principles of the Human Relations School, a perspective requiring a clear understanding of the capacities, abilities and needs of the individual.
- A static view
  Language auditing is predicated on the notion of fixed functions or posts, yet workplace reality is increasingly dynamic under the influence of the various global transformations and businesses must be prepared to respond to frequently shifting contexts, which may involve regrouping teams for different projects in lean and 'flattened' organisations.
- 'The search for the one-best-way'
  Buchanan and Huczynski (1985:360) set out different organisational cultures with their own corresponding organisational structure; with a variety of organisational cultures spanning fifteen worksectors to be investigated it would, therefore, not be adequate to do so through a research instrument which relies on fixed functions or posts, so typical of a 'role culture'.
- A lack of awareness of those psychological, social and cultural variables which affect organisational behaviour
  Brown (1995:251) sees '... increasing consensus that what matters in organisations is often "informal", "political", "ambiguous" and subject to multiple interpretations'. Perceptions, motivation, creativity, initiative and the influence of society and culture help shade behaviour in the workplace and this includes the learning and use of languages.

On the basis of the above arguments it became clear that needs analysis by means of company language audits with diagnostic testing of the four skills was not sufficient for this research. Other more adequate means of investigating the research brief had to be found and examined and we turned to an ethnographic approach.

Nunan in his discussion of ethnography in the context of language learning sets out a number of characteristics as representative of ethnographic research which contrast with those of psychometry and therefore result in very different procedures. He describes ethnography as being contextual, unobtrusive, collaborative, organic, interpretative and longitudinal (1992:56). The terms are amongst those glossed in Table 1 below. Though these characteristics are indeed present in much ethnographic research, as far as 'longitudinal' is concerned it would seem possible to consider both longitudinal and synchronic as characteristic of an ethnographic approach and discursive (or interpretive) analysis as essential but not necessarily sufficient. The research project to be described here is ethnographic in its approach, yet it is synchronic, i.e. the phenomenon was studied 'at one theoretical point in time ... disregarding whatever changes might take place during that time' (Crystal 1978:344). At the same time, it also makes use of both interpretive analysis and statistical analysis. Table 1 seeks to capture these various characteristics.

Table 1. *Characteristics of ethnographic research*

Characteristic	Gloss
Holistic approach	The researchers consider the phenomena as forming part of a broader context, one of change, a dynamic reality and they take into account behaviour.
'Thick' description and explanation	The researchers collect data on all of the factors which might impinge upon the phenomena under investigation.
Contextual	The research is carried out in the context in which the subjects normally live and work.
Unobtrusive	The researchers avoid manipulating the phenomena under investigation.
Collaborative	The research involves the participation of stakeholders other than the researchers.
Organic	The research displays interaction between the problem and data collection/interpretation.
Observational	The research makes use of participant and non-participant observation.
Grounded theory	The research displays a grounded approach to data, i.e. deriving theory from data; going beyond description to analysis, interpretation and explanation.
Interpretive	The researchers include interpretive analyses of the data.

(Based on Nunan 1992)

Further clarification of the underlying assumptions and values in ethnography is provided by Nunan (1992:71):

> Two beliefs in particular have guided the evolution of this (ethnographic) research tradition. These are the importance of context to human behaviour, and the centrality of the subjective

> belief systems of those involved in research to the processes and outcomes of research.

This project, whilst employing standard survey techniques, paid considerable attention to the two key principles of context and perceptions: the context of change is addressed at global and local level and perceptions are measured by an instrument first used in clinical psychology termed the Repertory Grid (Kelly 1955).

The Hong Kong research project; the ethnographic approach in practice

The way information is gathered following an ethnographic approach depends on a variety of factors: the setting of the fieldwork, the problem under investigation and of course, as Howard (1993:41) indicates 'the personal inclinations and theoretical biases of the researcher'. Nevertheless, he isolates some common general characteristics including probability sampling, questioning and observation. Obtaining prior information through literature searches, related research in progress and also through informants is both essential and invaluable. Gaining entry for research purposes (whether to a country or a corporation) is another important issue: some form of research permit is often required.

The project included the following procedures: setting up sampling, gathering prior information through informal questioning, observation and a literature search, designing a pilot project the findings of which are fed into the design of the main project, the main research with formal questioning and surveys, observation and collection of workplace-based data and materials and perceptual data, constant monitoring of the methodology and results, sufficient flexibility to respond to feedback where necessary and formal analysis and reporting. Below is a brief and very much simplified account of the activities.

The VTC Statistics Section provided a list, divided by discipline, of 1,151 names and addresses of employers who employed the relevant cohort of graduates, together with the names of these graduates in jobs relevant to their study. Information culled from the most up-to-date VTC 'Employment survey of technical institute graduates of full-time courses', allowed lists to be drawn up of the predominant job categories and job titles in the 15 disciplines. It soon became clear that among employers job titles vary. In other words, the same job may be described under different titles and were so listed. In order to select the representative jobs for case studies in a particular discipline a certain amount of informed discretion had to be brought into play. The two sources were collated and provided a basis from which to proceed with preliminary telephone discussions with employers. Many of these contacts eventually led to company visits by the research team, during which interviews were conducted with employers, named TI graduates and their immediate supervisors together with workplace observation.

Informal questioning (Howard 1993) prior to the start of the Hong Kong research revealed that there were several unspoken – and sometimes not quite so unspoken – assumptions and preconceptions surrounding this research project which alerted us to the need for an ethnographic approach. These included the following: falling educational standards; employers' unrealistic expectations; these young people not needing English in their employment anyway; it being more appropriate for them to be concentrating on Putonghua (Mandarin Chinese) than English; the demand for excellent English being generated by just a handful of large multinationals; a perception of this research project as a public relations exercise; and so on.

When I started working and living in Hong Kong myself I encountered to the full extent the lack of English communicative competence amongst both the young and very large sections of the adult population. I had chosen to live in a Chinese part of Hong Kong and, therefore, everyday contacts were predominantly with Chinese-staffed shops and organisations across a range of goods and services from food shops to estate agents and from department stores to resident associations and immigration offices. The findings of the surveys on inadequate English were confirmed and brought to life right in front of me, every day. This all seemed at odds with what could reasonably be expected in a territory with an estimated 97 per cent Chinese population which had it was claimed, a tradition of English as a medium of instruction, English textbooks, well-qualified teachers of English, parental support and exposure to extensive English language media and speakers if desired.

Exploratory interviews with teachers, employers and employees showed that there were various points to keep in mind:

- Many of the English lecturers, with a University degree, Diploma in Education and four years' relevant post-degree experience, had obtained this experience in secondary schools and once appointed, there was no INSET training for them. Access to suitable materials and language teaching technology seemed patchy. They reported that their students resisted attempts at Communicative Language Teaching (CLT). Many teachers felt powerless to change anything and felt that their best efforts were showing few results.
- English teachers in the Institutes often did not know the actual vocational needs of their students – though many of the subject

teachers had links with industry. There was no contact between the two sets of teachers. Information on job content and English workplace communication requirements in the broadest sense was needed.
- Preliminary interviews with employers in Small and Medium Enterprises (SMEs) showed it was not just the multinational needs that were not being met: business was at best not being run as efficiently as it might be and in worst cases business and business opportunities were being lost. In informal questioning, employers, trainers and managers reported that the supervisors of the relevant graduates were spending a lot of their valuable time having to 'cocoon' these young employees, by virtually doing their (English) work for them.
- Supervisors and employees conversely seemed much more satisfied and the latter indeed seemed to be motivated to put a lot of time into their professional studies and work. The discrepancies needed to be fully investigated.

The project was expected to investigate 15 different worksectors: from design through to accountancy, industrial technology, hotelkeeping and tourism to computer studies; any statements would need to be valid across all fifteen sectors.

Below are outlined some general considerations concerning the three main research instruments, and a broad overview of the perceptual data on the use of workplace English in particular.

Triangulation is the use of as many methodological perspectives as possible when studying some phenomena to avoid bias (Denzin 1989:234). The present research made use of triangulation in order to achieve greater reliability and a deeper level of understanding than would be possible with any one single instrument. To be fully effective it is best used at several levels, in other words, multiple triangulation. The present research made use of:

- Subject group triangulation: employers, employees, their supervisors;
- Triangulation of informants from Eastern and Western cultures: Institute teachers, teacher trainers, in-company language trainers, line-managers, Human Resource Managers, various Chambers of Commerce, present and past students;
- Triangulation of information sources: applied linguistics, the behavioural sciences (anthropology, sociology, psychology), cross-cultural studies, management and information technology;
- Methodological triangulation: the survey, workplace-based observation in case studies (observation, questioning, recording and materials collection), the repertory grid;
- Data triangulation: quantitative and qualitative, including perceptual data;

– Investigator triangulation: the use of multiple investigators from both Eastern and Western cultures and of different generations.

The main body of the research was threefold. First, case studies which consisted of visits to 26 firms across 13 work sectors (for a number of reasons reduced from the initial 15) to conduct in-depth interviews with employers, employees and supervisors and to observe and collect profiles and relevant authentic work materials. Second, some 1,066 packs of three bilingual postal questionnaires sent out to employers, employees and supervisors. Third, a perceptual instrument, the Repertory Grid, which I shall describe in more detail, administered – unusually – by post along with the questionnaires.

The Repertory Grid (Kelly 1955) was sent by post in a pack together with the questionnaires to named graduate-employees and their immediate supervisors. There are two reasons why the grids were administered by post, as opposed to on a one-to-one basis as is more usual. The first is to do with sampling and analysis: including the grid in the questionnaire pack meant that many more subjects could be addressed and different kinds of powerful computer analyses could be used to allow comparisons of grouped perceptions (employees, supervisors, per discipline, per job, etc.). The second reason is culture related: in high-context, high face-saving, diffuse cultures (Victor 1992) verbal self-disclosure is low and fear of affronting others is known to cause serious breakdowns in communication. A confidential perceptual instrument sent by post would seem to have a greater chance of getting meaningful results. The repertory grid was used in Chinese only.

The grid is a means of investigating human perceptions on topics of particular relevance to the individual or individuals concerned. The basis of a person's decisions and actions is not always immediately accessible, but the grid aims to uncover these through the charting of perceptions and expectations on these topics. The topics are termed the 'elements' in grid terminology. Identifying the topics, here the workplace language activities, and the parameters of the perceptions on these (the constructs) for the grid is thus a first step in its construction; they are derived from our observations and interviews in the workplace during fieldwork.

It is not possible to provide a full outline of the grids here and therefore examples of the constructs have not been provided. It is the grouping and content of the 'elements' that is probably of most interest and they are shown below in Figures 1 and 2. Whilst attempting various ways of grouping our workplace observations, we surveyed to see what units of organisation others in the field had generated. The work which reflected the breadth of our documented observations optimally was found in the Australian Language Levels project publications (Scarino *et al.* 1988). Their categories of activities were, however, developed with school learners in mind and, for use on the grid, they needed to be adapted so as to reflect our workplace observations. The adapted activities on which we were seeking perceptions and expectations are presented in Figures 1 and 2 below.

The vast majority of workplace activities were chained in terms of the four skills (see activities 1–5, Figure 1 for representative examples). It was clear that work required far more than interpersonal skills: handling information was a large part of the graduates' daily activities. Giving personal input was not as frequent an activity, but nevertheless important and becoming more so with their first promotion. The interpersonal skills are shown below as activities 1 and 2, Figure 1; handling information as activities 3 and 4; giving personal input as activity 5.

Figure 1

The five workplace activities using English

Activity 1. conversational activities involving clients and/or colleagues, frequently together with or followed by writing/reading/speaking;

for example:

* taking down details of customer complaints and passing these on for action
* placing an order by phone and following this up in a letter or fax
* filling in forms together with clients

Activity 2. correspondence activities involving clients and/or colleagues, frequently together with or followed by speaking/reading/writing;

for example:

* on receipt of a letter discussing a possible reply with a supervisor before replying
* on receipt of a telex reading up documentation before responding to client needs
* sending a fax to follow up a quotation received by fax earlier

Activity 3. extracting or receiving information, frequently followed by writing/speaking;

for example:

* finding out technical specifications and passing these on to a supervisor/colleague/client
* reading shipping documents received and discussing these with a supervisor
* reading documents received by mail for filing purposes or to be processed for others

Activity 4. providing information to others in written/spoken form;

for example:

* writing a software enhancement report
* giving information about company services
* writing a set of instructions

Activity 5. giving personal reactions in spoken or written form to something read/heard/viewed;

for example:

* outlining proposals for a design in response to inspiration obtained from reading
* reporting back responses to a seminar or trade fair in a personal/creative way
* writing a creative suggestion in response to a memo on the company notice board

It became equally clear that in order to process meaningfully the language they were dealing with, employees also required a knowledge of the world (see activity 6), organisational and thinking skills (activity 8) and by no means least they needed to be capable of dealing with different accents, different culture-related behaviour and to have an awareness and understanding of why their interlocutors were reacting to them as they did (activity 7). These activities were, therefore, added to the English activities in the repertory grid, so that individuals could record their perceptions on these language-related activities also. In this way their existence and relevance to workplace communication could be confirmed or disconfirmed.

Figure 2

The three workplace activities which are an important, if not *essential part of the English workplace activities.*

Activity 6. activities which involve a general knowledge of the world and the way it functions;

for example:

* knowing that Cambridge could be an address in either England or the US and addressing letters accordingly
* knowing that Americans use sorting references when talking
* understanding different life styles for product/fashion design

Activity 7. activities which include dealing with the different English accents, cultures and what is acceptable behaviour or not;

for example:

* being aware of different patterns of behaviour and expectations (e.g.

Australians tend to be more direct and therefore may appear aggressive when in fact they are not)
* knowing how to communicate politely with a person who has an accent in English which is difficult to understand
* being aware of how one's own accent and behaviour might be perceived by foreigners

Activity 8. activities which involve organisational and thinking skills;

for example:
* observing what needs to be done for a group task and making useful suggestions
* thinking through what a particular task might involve and organising details and action accordingly
* building on ideas put forward by others
* managing tasks which require problem-solving

Once the grid is constructed, printed, sent out, completed and returned, analysis and interpretation of the data follows. Analysis of a grid can be performed manually and there are also computer implementations for handling larger quantities of grids. This study used two programs available within the Grid Analysis Package: INGRID based on Principal Component Analysis (Slater 1977) and SERIES to generate various sets of analyses:

- consensus views of both groups on the work activities;
- consensus views of both groups of respondents separately and a comparison of these consensus views;
- a consensus view of the graduates as a group per study discipline;
- an analysis of individual grids to gain insight into one individual's views engaged in a particular job.

Implications of findings for Hong Kong

Taken as a whole the research project resulted in an enormous amount of data, both descriptive and statistical. Some of it was of immediate practical value to the various interested parties, some of it needs further detailed analysis, some may contribute to academic discussion.

The needs, concerns and problems mentioned earlier were addressed in the form of detailed recommendations to the VTC and included a curriculum framework so as to help close the 'gap', which was the task set for the research. The VTC has since appointed a curriculum coordinator for their implementation. On the basis of the two HKLDF workplace research projects, a Hong Kong wide Vocational English

Programme (VEP) was launched to develop, pilot and implement courses, materials and a criterion-based assessment programme.

The Company Communication profiles, the Job-type content and Job Communication profiles and the Perceptual English Workplace Needs analysed per discipline and per workplace English activity, provided a rich qualitative source of input for VTC curriculum and syllabus design. In fact, whilst the research was still in progress one new vocational course was changed considerably as new information became available: there had been too little emphasis on communication. The following information from the general survey questionnaires is Hong Kong specific also and represents but a very brief selection of employers' quantitative views:

- employers' views on certification: a preference for criterion-referencing;
- sponsorship: employers should provide it;
- recruitment criteria: English language skills rank second to technical/vocational skills followed by interpersonal skills and management skills last;
- promotion criteria: demand for English increases with job experience and steeply upon first promotion;
- English skills need improvement before entry to the workforce: listening ranked first as being in need of improvement, then reading, followed by speaking and writing, applicants lack productive skills;
- the benefits this brings to employers: increased efficiency and improved external and internal communications.

English is indeed used in Hong Kong as the principal language of international communication and virtually no other European languages are used, even for communication with Europe. Spoken in-company communication is mainly in Cantonese with English second, whereas written follow-up is usually in English. Chinese is also used for overseas communication in just over a quarter of firms surveyed, mainly with the PRC and Taiwan. Japanese for business communication is minimal. In addition to an increase in the use of Putonghua and Cantonese, employers envisage that English will not only maintain its high profile for overseas communication, but will become even more important in years to come.

The need for junior employees to engage in translation and interpreting at work is so normal a part of their everyday activities, that no one thought it worthwhile to mention until its frequency showed up in the fieldwork. This has implications for teaching programmes. Yet the repertory grid data shows that productive skills are perceived to be largely associated with seniority.

In terms of cost-benefit, the vast majority in all three groups of respondents reported that English had not only been important or very important to their career, but also *beyond* an immediate practical, work-related use. The survey also illustrates the differences between the group perceptions of English prior to entry into the workforce and once in work. A large number of all three groups (employers 71.6 per cent, supervisors 60.9 per cent and employees 61.5 per cent) wanted to see a strengthening of English as a medium of instruction. In view of recent discussions on the cultural politics of English as an international language (Pennycook 1994), this is an interesting outcome.

Wider implications: global trends within the Hong Kong study

Global economic trends and use of technology, as outlined earlier in the chapter, deeply affect communication in the workplace. The shift of certain aspects of the production processes into China, the introduction of information technology (IT) and the effects of these changes on employees, are readily observed in the workplaces of Hong Kong. The nature of the work was considered by employers and supervisors to have changed dramatically. Jobs are now less mechanical and less standardised and require more flexibility, greater personal input, cross-cultural knowledge and due also to the immediacy of IT, more independent functioning.

If Hunt and Targett's (1995:199) Japanese corporate case studies are representative, and there is an increasing awareness in business of the concept of IT as a strategic resource with the potential to gain or lose competitive advantage, the impact of IT on communication in the workplace can only be on the increase. From this research it was evident that the introduction of new technology did indeed affect the demands made on even junior personnel, particularly in terms of the need to use productive language skills when using faxes, e-mail and in direct customer contact. All this created a need for greater cross-cultural knowledge and for an ability to give personal reactions. Yet the repertory grid data shows that the young employees in this study relied heavily on their supervisors: they were unable on the whole to function independently in tasks requiring English, unless the task was standardised and involved the receptive skills. They acknowledged, however, that they would be given more communication activities if their English were better, excepting conversational activities. These they associated with seniority. Low conversational content is not necessarily a feature of the job, however, but is more likely to be a workplace response to the low standards of English communication achieved at present.

Employers, who generally have a broader perspective of their business needs, say they would like to see improvements across all four skills. They see the three associated activities (see Figure 2) as part of everyday workplace communication and would like these to be included in the curriculum. That the use of information-related technology should be addressed in classroom activity is also clearly an area of concern to employers. They would like to see in the words of one employer: 'simple things done well'. Only the simple things taught at present seem to be no longer appropriate in the workplace of the 'knowledge-information' society of today and tomorrow. More teamwork and changing structures of authority were often observed to mean that individuals at present rely on weak past practice, informally documented, and on informal consultations with others whose English competence was equally low. One firm had to abandon its newly introduced e-mail system when they became overwhelmed by messages from confused customers, and a centralised system which intercepted and monitored juniors' communications had to be set up.

Where clear line management structures are still in place, there is a much greater reliance on supervisors' editing skills for even the most simple faxes, memos and reports than had been realised. The fact that supervisors were spending a lot of their time teaching English communication skills need not necessarily imply, as is a common perception in Hong Kong, falling educational standards. Anecdotal evidence shows this to have been a common pattern in the UK in the sixties also. In the present economic climate it is often this middle management level that is removed during the 'rightsizing' of a company. Yet at the same time, and somewhat contradictory, there is a global trend in the new flatter Learning Companies, such as for instance Hewlett Packard, for mentoring schemes to be introduced for young and new employees. There is also renewed awareness emerging of 'situated learning or cognition' and 'organizational learning in communities-of-practice' (Lave 1991; Seely Brown and Duguid 1991). The observed reliance on supervisors is, on the other hand, seen by some as inefficient use of well educated and trained manpower within large firms. In Small and Medium Enterprises (SMEs) when there is no obvious line management structure the consequences of inadequate English among junior staff frequently amounted to lost business for the company.

Despite greater globalisation, young people in Hong Kong have for quite some time shown a decreased focus on the West and an increasing focus towards the East, particularly towards China. This is not altogether surprising in view of the 1997 change of sovereignty. However, China is also a vast and growing economic and political power and has considerable socio-cultural significance not least because China is the land of their ancestors. Young people's taste for more than a decade has increasingly been away from Western music, films and the media with their predominant language, English. It is interesting in this respect to consider the notion of cultural traffic: a taste for Western consumer goods, such as foods, dress, watches, cars, domestic appliances and also English as the language for international communication does not necessarily imply a Western cultural focus. These seemingly contradictory trends of cultural convergence and simultaneous divergence have been noted in management circles for some time: greater globalisation seems to lead to greater parochialism at a local level, in ways which greatly affect marketing and communication (Victor 1992:11) and, it seems, also politics: witness the various anti-European lobbies in the United Kingdom. The trend is neatly encapsulated in international management by Sony's corporate slogan 'Think global, act local'.

Yet thinking and acting both globally and locally would probably be a more appropriate aim in today's multicultural societies. Firstly there is a multiple cultural configuration with regard to English communication inside the workplace in Hong Kong. This is indicated by the different perceptual group perspectives of employers and employees and supervisors. The phenomenon of multiple cultural configuration has also been noted by Alvesson (1993) in the context of a case study of a Swedish university department as a complex corporate culture. Secondly, as indicated above, there are powerful socio-cultural and generational constraints at work in relation to English. In this research it was manifested before and after entry into the workforce, and affected a particular section of society, at a particular cycle in their lives. It is exemplified by a cohort of TI graduates in Hong Kong before and after they start work. Their initial perceptions affected their levels of motivation profoundly and ran counter to workplace requirements: English was thought to be an irrelevant optional extra by the group when still in education. Such perceptions pose an enormous dilemma once they start work, because jobs in Hong Kong demand long hours and the pressure to obtain subject qualifications is great. Once in work there is not a great deal of time to acquire or to improve English communication: employers require English as part of first promotion requirements and if employees do not measure up they will not get promoted or indeed will not continue to be employed. Employees are well aware of this: several (Chinese) employers told us about their young employees' sudden departure when they were being pressed for some outstanding task involving English, these and other 'lost' English tasks were subsequently found at the back of a desk drawer. One can only speculate on the extent to which a sense of personal inadequacy, disempowerment, culture shock and ethnocentricity are engendered as a result of these and similar experiences. The configurations which influence perceptions on English communication must be recognised and the perceptions addressed so that informed debate as to their implications can take place prior to effective action.

Implications for general and vocational education

One major question arising from this research is how to feed the findings back into learning situations. Above I have indicated some of the Hong Kong-specific findings of this research, the in-depth recommendations relating to VTC policy and curriculum issues in the research reports, and the resulting VTC action and Hong Kong VEP Programme. I have also indicated some of the wider implications of the research. Here I would like to focus on the use of language in the workplace, to return to the education-training issue highlighted at the beginning of the chapter, and to raise some of the broader socio-cultural aspects.

Within Communicative Language Teaching (CLT) the assumption has sometimes been made that adult language needs are to a large extent concerned with interpersonal communication (Council of Europe 1973:11) and more recently with increased use of IT, the transmission of information. This research confirms what many language teachers have known for a considerable time: the workplace communication situation is far more complex than some had supposed. Interpersonal, informational and creative use of language, cultural and general knowledge, and organisational and thinking skills are required even at junior levels, though in varying degrees of need depending on the worksector and the type of job. In addition it was clear that the higher up the career ladder the greater the requirement to use these aspects when using English for communication in the workplace.

The working statement of the purposes of education arrived at in the beginning of the chapter showed education as being concerned with knowledge and an understanding of ourselves and the world around us, as well as their interrelationship. Further, that it needs reference to cultural dimensions, that the knowledge and understanding embrace aspects of technology; that it should provide a conceptual scheme to raise knowledge above the collection of mere facts; that similarly it should provide an understanding of the principles for the organising of facts, and of the reasons behind things; that it has to do with autonomy of the individual, critical engagement and communication. When comparing these statements with the workplace activities analysed in the research it would seem that employees with a technical and business education, even at junior levels, are very much in need of those qualities thought of as 'educational'. It is therefore necessary for the language and communication curriculum in education (whether in a technical or general environment) to provide for and meet those needs if students are to be prepared to function in an increasingly global and multicultural workplace. Post-education training then continues this process and 'fine-tunes' in line with individual and workplace specific requirements.

Our research also demonstrates that in language teaching consideration should be given to socio-cultural aspects at two levels: at the level of the particular – a particular language and its associated culture(s) and, at the level of the universal – cross-cultural awareness and competence at a systemic level. Risager (this volume) has discussed the direction in which foreign language teaching has been and is moving in that respect. In a language teaching situation due recognition must be given to the fact that in communicating in a particular language we communicate powerful aspects of a particular culture and that these may be at odds with the learner's own culture or cultures.

To ensure that learners are disabused of the notion that '... the foreign environment differs from his/her own only in terms of the linguistic codification required to achieve a certain set of aims' (Mughan 1997), various approaches have been developed. In this volume the critical textual approach has been argued by Kramsch; culture as a lived experience is offered by the Thames Valley University team to their students abroad; the Cultural Synergy Model is put forward by Jin and Cortazzi. The latter stresses students' cultural adaptation, rather than loss of own cultural identity, considered to be a deep-seated fear in much language learning.

At the same time it must be recognised that in the reality of multicultural societies learners may themselves bring what has been called a 'hyphenated culture' to learning: e.g. the British-Asian, the Anglo-Irish. They are second generation immigrants born and brought up in one country, but who have negotiated two or more languages and cultures from birth. Many of us now have multicultural identities: indeed in many cultures women adopt different work and home identities; many of us negotiate two or more cultures through marriage or residence. This cultural hybridity is often ignored at best and seen as schizophrenic at worst, though as Risager shows in this volume, teachers are starting to meet the challenge that internationalisation brings. With this increasing local diversity, not only at linguistic, cultural and social but also at a workplace and management level, comes global connectedness (Cope and Kalantzis 1995:8). Contradictory developments have been noted which either sharpen boundaries (ethnic-led cultures) or blur them, producing phenomena such as hybridity of music (e.g. Punjabi hip-hop and France's metissage), food, fashion, media, texts, discourses, etc. Awareness of the multicultural reality around us and the need for international and multicultural functioning as shown by this research, is growing. The medical profession now teaches 'transcultural' medicine and recognises that both healthworkers and patients have '... different customs and different ways of expressing symptoms ... the problem extends way beyond language' (Collee 1996), which must be acknowledged to prevent misunderstanding and fatalities. The time has come for the language teaching profession not only to teach specific cultures, but also to investigate systematically ways in which *cross*-cultural communication competence can be achieved.

Going beyond the learning of one or more foreign languages with their associated culture(s) must start with the recognition that a culture is a learnt, internally coherent system specific to a particular group. It is a system which has been developed by its members over time to help them deal successfully with their environment. An awareness of one's own particular culturally acquired behaviour, values and perceptions and how they are expressed in language is desirable, followed by the realisation that these particular solutions are but one solution, other cultures have developed other options. In this context multicultural learners become a positive resource; Burton and Rusek (1994), for instance, propose a learning process where learners become the central culture curriculum resources and planners. Furthermore there are universal aspects to culture, there are '... major variable(s) likely to shift across cultures in a way that would affect (business) communication' (Victor 1992:14). These variables have been identified in empirical studies by Hofstede (1991), Brislin *et al.* (1986) and Trompenaars (1993). These universal aspects are taught in management within a framework. 'The underlying philosophy ... is that most people ... have the problem-solving capabilities to manage cultural factors affecting workplace communication once they are given the appropriate means for interpreting them' (Victor 1992:4). The objective is for learners of communication to acquire an understanding of how these factors work in native-to-native interaction in a context of change, in order to see how communication between individuals is affected and facilitated.

Various solutions as to how the universal aspects are best taught have been attempted in the fields of International Business Communication and Management. Some are integrated with the teaching of languages (e.g. courses sponsored by the Royal Academy of Engineering at University College London), some are free-standing units taught in the mother tongue. Mughan (1997) identifies and details two approaches: the research by Hofstede (1991) and Trompenaars (1993) leads to a kind of cross-cultural toolkit for use in multicultural work situations, whilst Brislin *et al.*'s research (1986) provides a checklist of critical incidents that expatriates encounter in various settings. Mughan lists the prime methods for present cross-cultural training as being the 'documentary' (learnt by study) and the 'interpersonal' (learnt by experience). In a comparative study Early (1987, cited in Mughan) found that neither was more markedly effective than the other, but that training in both approaches achieved the best results.

There are many more aspects to be considered if language learning and cross-cultural learning are to be united in one curriculum framework in education. Inevitably more questions are raised than can be immediately answered. What of activity 6 in Figure 2, involving general knowledge of the world and the way it functions, and activity 8, activities which involve organisational and thinking skills? To what extent is Communicative Language Teaching compatible with cross-cultural approaches such as the documentary and the interpersonal? If we believe that culture is to be seen in a context of change, how and to what extent are learners to be encouraged to negotiate their own cross-cultural roles and identities? What role do published language courses play? Burton and Rusek (1994) overcome what they see as the 'formulaicity' of courses by requiring adult learners to collect samples of their own language use in native-speaker professional settings and letting them work on the negotiation and construction of their own texts. Are cross-cultural aspects best taught to the advanced language learner who has '... the capacity to select appropriate register, to choose when to speak and when not to, to decode nuance ...' (Mughan 1997) or can a synthesis be achieved *ab initio* in an ethnographic approach?

It is crucial for the debate to continue if education is to help prepare young people to communicate in a multicultural world of work and to function with confidence and independence in an ever changing local and global context.

Note:

The HKLDF research project reported here was entitled 'TI Graduates, English and the Workplace'. The research topic was put forward by the VTC, Hong Kong; Project Leader J. R. Devereux, Deputy Executive Director VTC; Research Fellow Antonia Cooper; R and D officer L. C. Ng; secretary Y. Wong. The managing agent was the ILE, now the Hong Kong Institute of Education. The funding agent was the Hongkong Bank Language Development Fund (HKLDF). An extensive three-part report with recommendations was submitted to all three parties.

Part 2 Approaches through drama

Introduction

The writers in this section demonstrate how drama can be used in different ways to promote intercultural competence when the extent of its potential in educational contexts is fully understood and exploited. Amongst other aims, the purpose of drama has been variously described in its history as providing training in performance skills, developing personal qualities or creating contexts for practice in communication through simulation of real-life experiences. The latter aim has been particularly emphasised in the context of modern languages teaching. What the writers in this section share, however, is a conception of drama the primary purpose of which is to enable participants to make sense of their world and human behaviour through a process of active reflection. Conceived in this way, the links between drama and ethnography, which might seem at first to be somewhat disparate themes, are clearer, and the potential for using drama to enable understanding of one's own and other cultures more apparent.

Drama as an art form works paradoxically by bringing participants closer to the subject through emotional engagement but at the same time preserving a distance by virtue of the fact that the context is make-believe. The actors in the drama can be likened to 'participant observers' who are engaged in the social world and yet are distanced enough to be able to reflect on the products of that engagement. This is all the more so in drama contexts because the world has been created by the participants themselves. When properly conceived and taught, drama involves looking beyond surface actions to the values which underlie them, and as such it provides an ideal context for exploration of cultural values, both one's own and other people's.

Although the writers have a common view of the purpose of drama, the chapters which follow do not adhere to any one particular drama method but employ a variety of different approaches ranging from various forms of role play, exercises and drama strategies to full participation in theatre. The strong emphasis on concrete, practical examples drawn from the classroom illustrates the variety of approaches which are possible, depending on the experience of the participants.

The first chapter provides some broad historical background to the development of drama in education (which receives more detailed consideration in the second chapter) and explores different approaches to teaching drama. Here Fleming challenges the conventional view that the primary value of using drama in educational contexts (particularly in modern language teaching) is to replicate as closely as possible equivalent real experiences. Drama as an art form works more effectively by allowing the type of exploration of human situations which would not be possible in real life. Thus the exploration of culture can take place in the safety of the fictional world created in the drama, using non-realistic methods such as slowing down the action, voicing inner thoughts, replaying scenes with a different emphasis. In the example given in the chapter, drama was used to explore problems young people might encounter when visiting other countries. The dramatic context prompted a process of 'making strange', of seeing their own conventional behaviour through the eyes of a foreign visitor.

The chapter by Bolton and Heathcote describes a project which was undertaken with a group of year 9/10 pupils which was specifically designed to provide them with the conceptual tools to analyse cultural contexts. The theoretical background for this analysis was provided by the work of the anthropologist Hall, but it was made accessible to the participants through the use of fictional contexts created and managed to make increasing demands on them. In real life the analysis of complex situations might have been either too alien (in the case of the examination of other cultures) or too familiar (in cases where the demands are to reflect on what might otherwise be taken for granted). In the fictional context, however, situations can be artificially constructed with the express purpose of providing material for analysis and with the appropriate level of challenge, ranging from exploration of the underlying significance of a very specific act like picking up a piece of paper or a scene in a supermarket to the creation of a fictional culture. As the authors themselves argue, the signs in drama are all of significance, so selecting what is to count is not a problem; the analysis is thus rendered more manageable in the fictional context.

The chapter by Jensen and Hermer challenges traditional, cerebral approaches to language teaching which focus exclusively on the learning of vocabulary, analysing grammar and translating authors. They argue for the importance of engaging creatively and intuitively, using the whole body and all the senses to participate in the creation of language spontaneously. Their emphasis is very much on play and playfulness, experimenting with sound and movement where the initial emphasis is on unfettered expression rather than on meaning or accuracy. They describe a variety of exercises, some of which are of appealing simplicity, which arise from focus on a specific text. Their work is based on an approach which acknowledges that the 'word' isn't everything and the emphasis on the non-verbal finds echoes in the writing of Hall which underpinned the chapter by Bolton and Heathcote. Jensen and Hermer aim to foster the engagement in language more fully, to experience its texture and to help participants perceive their surroundings more sharply. Thus awareness of language in its cultural context underpins their general approach but they also incorporate exercises which are specifically designed to explore cultural differences.

Schmidt's paper describes a theatre project which has been running successfully for eleven years in which the participants produce a play in a foreign language. The primary aim is artistic, the creation of a piece of significant theatre, but the value in terms of increasing cultural understanding is evident. This operates at a very specific level, for example when the participants have to investigate another culture in order to transpose the action of the play into a foreign context. There is also, however, a more general raising of cultural awareness by virtue of the fact that the language is embedded in very real contexts for the participants. As with the previous chapter, the emphasis on language comes in the context of social relations developed in the course of exercises which use the whole body through movement and sound. Schmidt makes the interesting point that the use of foreign language, like drama itself, can provide a form of protection because the participants are more readily able to engage in situations which might otherwise be embarrassing. The exploration of other cultures can take place in the relative safety not just of the fiction but of the other language.

The final chapter by Schewe describes a drama project which was designed to introduce students of German as a foreign language to aspects of German culture through the study of a novel. The argument presented here is not only that the study of literature can provide the reader with a real feel for another culture but that the use of drama to facilitate the reading can deepen the extent to which that cultural understanding is based on an affective engagement with the text rather than mere surface acquisition of cultural knowledge. The activities are designed to open up the text for the reader and are based on a reader-response theoretical perspective which sees meaning as a function of the interaction between text and reader rather than residing exclusively in the objective text. The drama activities are designed to help the reader come to terms with the cultural content of the text. Schewe makes an interesting parallel between the model of reading literature which underpins this approach and the process of coming to know another culture.

Taken together, the chapters illustrate the wide variety of approaches possible when using drama in the classroom and the appropriateness of this particular art form for developing intercultural competence.

7 Cultural awareness and dramatic art forms

Michael Fleming

In recent years there has been considerable debate in this country about the appropriate form drama teaching should take in schools. The tradition of 'drama in education' which has been very influential in the last three decades has been criticised on the grounds that by concentrating on forms of dramatic play and improvisation, and, more recently, by promoting the notion of 'drama as learning' and 'drama across the curriculum' it has diminished the nature of dramatic art, relegating theatre craft, acting and study of plays to a minor or nonexistent role. Those criticisms have not gone unchallenged. The conception of drama underlying those views tends to be based on very fixed preconceptions drawn from traditional and narrow notions of theatre practice. Moreover, they fail to recognise that there has not been opposition to theatre and performance as such but more a recognition that particular approaches to drama are more appropriate for particular age groups and for the fulfilment of particular aims. More importantly, such criticisms take a very simplistic notion of what constitutes dramatic art, focusing on surface manifestations rather than deeper meanings and forms. It is not my intention, nor would it be appropriate here, to pursue the debate in any great detail, but I use this as my starting point because one particular aspect of the argument, the relationship between teaching method and educational objectives, is helpful in providing a focus for considering drama and its relationship to foreign language teaching and cultural awareness.

Critics of drama in education have opposed the use of drama across the curriculum to teach other subjects, the so-called use of drama 'as method'. That opposition stems in part from a belief that to use drama as a means to an end (as in the case when it is employed as a teaching methodology) is to distort the nature of the art form. The following comments illustrate the types of dichotomies which are identified.

> Those who believe in drama as an arts discipline would espouse ... a notion of learning *in* drama, not *through* it. And *that*

> difference is crucial for it exposes the difference between a general pedagogy and a distinctive discipline of the imagination. It is here in this distinction between drama as a device to facilitate learning and drama as an arts discipline centred on art that any critique of educational drama from an arts perspective must begin. (Abbs 1994:124)

To such critics the use of drama in the context of the teaching of foreign languages would constitute a betrayal of the art form. The simple reply to these concerns would be to argue that they are based on a false dichotomy, that pupils are always, whether they are engaged in dramatic activity in its own right or in the context of other subjects, simultaneously learning both *in* and *through* the drama. One could argue that pupils are always developing ability in drama skills as well as developing understanding of what the content of the drama is about. In the same way a simple pragmatic way of resolving the dilemma is to argue for the existence of drama on the school curriculum as both subject in its own right and as method. I think there is a great deal of sense in both those views but they do not take us further in examining whether the contrast between 'drama as a device to facilitate learning' and 'drama as an arts discipline' is valid, and that seems to be what is interesting about the debate.

I am aware that this discussion may appear to be primarily of concern to drama practitioners. It could be argued that to the teacher of foreign languages, history or geography it hardly matters that drama is being used as 'general pedagogy' rather than as an 'arts discipline'. In one sense drama can be seen as simply one choice amongst many possible pedagogical methods (use of video, audio-tapes, visits outside school) to bring variety and dynamism to the lesson. In that case the means chosen can be seen as contingent to the particular objectives being pursued. I want to suggest however that the distinction is of wider significance than merely an esoteric debate amongst drama practitioners because if instead of seeing drama as a contingent method, we see drama as offering forms of learning which are intrinsic to the nature of drama as art, there are important theoretical and practical consequences.

In my experience it is not uncommon for teachers who are new to drama to imagine that its primary value is as a substitute for real experience. The practical consequence of this view is to confine its expression to attempts at realism. It is easy to see why that view arises because the predominant form of drama which dominates our conception of the art form is derived from the realism of television and film. The purpose of participation in drama is seen therefore as a means of trying out situations which otherwise we might not get a chance to experience. As a foreign language teacher I may set up various role play activities (buying an article in a shop, seeking directions, asking the time) as a sort of second best to actually performing those activities in real life. I am not questioning the use of role play in that way but rather the implicit theory which accompanies it because it serves to limit the practical possibilities.

Alternative possibilities open up if we appreciate that drama like all art operates in the realm of the 'unreal'. A fruitful way of thinking about dramatic art is not to see it as merely replicating experience but to be aware of its potential to explore and examine experience in ways which would otherwise be denied to us in real life (Fleming 1997:4). Real communication, particularly in public contexts with strangers may be full of sub-texts, innuendo and self-consciousness which in drama can be subject to more conscious control and manipulation. It works paradoxically by revealing complexities through simplification; by editing out some of the features which are characteristic of encounters in real life, certain aspects of behaviour are thrown into relief and able to be subject to scrutiny. In practical terms that may mean freezing a moment in time, slowing the action down, replaying the action with different outcomes, juxtaposing thoughts with actual words spoken, repeating actions with different intonations, focusing on language without worrying about meaning, working towards fully-fledged performance and so on.

Such examples seem to me to have the possibility to exploit the potential of drama to the full, using it less as contingent method. Drama here is not serving merely as an arbitrary means to an end but is actually affecting the end or outcome. In this case the end 'learning a foreign language' changes to 'learning a foreign language in a way which focuses on the richness and complexity of human behaviour' or, to put it another way, it is to approach language in its cultural context.

The view that exploiting the full potential of dramatic art opens up possibilities rather than closes them down is contrary to the way in which the argument is sometimes presented. Advocates of drama as a distinctive discipline who criticise the use of drama across the curriculum imagine that drama as art only manifests itself in particular forms. The suggestion I am making however is that all manifestations including watching plays, rehearsing and performing, engaging in improvisations, depictions, various exercises, etc. represent possibilities of deepening understanding of human experience.

The first drama session I propose to describe was aimed not at teaching a foreign language but at exploring directly some of the problems encountered when young people visit other countries. All drama can be conceived as forms of cultural expression, but the intention of the session was to focus very specifically on attitudes to other cultures, aiming to help the pupils identify with the perspectives of others. I had been approached by a local teacher, a former student, with a request to visit the school with some of our present student teachers to work with her drama club (thirty or so pupils aged 12–14 years). She invited us to choose the context of the work and I decided we should aim to use drama to explore aspects of cultural awareness, particularly in the context of young people making visits abroad. Many pupils now engage in exchange visits to other countries and a number express the view that this is a stressful, even unhappy experience for them (Furnham 1994).

We planned to use some form of small group improvisation culminating in a sharing of work because this was a way of operating with which the pupils were familiar. However there are potential pitfalls in this approach given the chosen subject matter because representation of foreign cultures in improvisation can easily lead to stereotyped portrayals. There was every potential for humorous and entertaining 'skits' which would take us no further in fulfilling our aims.

We began by playing two games as ice-breakers in which the whole group (pupils and visiting teachers) participated. Having played one game of our choosing, the pupils were invited to teach us one of theirs – a form of cultural exchange! After a very simple introduction to the theme, the pupils were asked to produce in groups of four or five a tableau (still image) depicting a situation in which a foreign visitor has been made to feel uncomfortable. To help them they were given the following list of situations, although they did not have to confine their work to the examples represented here.

Making friends of your own age.
Shopping in a large supermarket.
Going on public transport (trains, buses, tubes).
Going to discotheques or dances.
Making British friends of your own age.
Making close friends from other countries of your own age.
Going to a small private party with English friends.
Going out with somebody who you are sexually attracted to.
Being with a group of people of your own age, but of the opposite sex.
Going into restaurants or cafés.
Going into a room full of people.
Being with older English people.
Meeting strangers and being introduced to new people.
Being with people that you don't know very well.
Approaching others – making the first move in starting up a friendship.

Making ordinary decisions (plans) affecting others (what to do in the evenings).
Getting to know people in depth (well, intimately).
Taking the initiative in keeping the conversation going.
People standing or sitting very close to you.
Talking about yourself or your feelings in a conversation.
Dealing with people staring at you.
Attending a formal dinner.
Complaining in public – dealing with unsatisfactory service in a shop where you think you have been cheated or misled.
Seeing a doctor.
Appearing in front of an audience (acting, giving a speech).
Being interviewed for something.
Being the leader (chairman) of a small group.
Dealing with people of higher status than you.
Reprimanding a subordinate – telling off someone below you for something that they have done wrong.
Going to a social occasion where there are many people of another national or cultural background to yourself.
Apologising to a superior if you have done wrong.
Understanding jokes, humour and sarcasm.
Dealing with somebody who is cross and aggressive (abusive).
Buying special goods (medicines, books, electrical goods, etc.).
Using public and private toilet facilities.
Waiting in a queue.
Getting very intimate with a person of the opposite sex.
Going into pubs.
Going to worship (church, temple, mosque).
Talking about serious matters (politics, religion) to people of your own age.

The list is based on research by Furnham and Bochner (1982) and represents typical everyday situations actually encountered by students as foreign travellers which they said caused problems. Its purpose was not simply to provide a source of ideas for the pupils but to get them thinking about the wide examples of fairly ordinary situations which could cause embarrassment or difficulties. Some chose examples from the list (mostly focusing on social encounters). One group, no doubt looking for more dramatic excitement and tension, chose to demonstrate the witnessing of a fight which offered an interesting dimension because it posed the question why should this be more stressful for a foreign visitor. This last example illustrates an interesting challenge for planning the drama on the chosen theme because very ordinary, everyday situations do not immediately have obvious potential for the tension which is an important ingredient of successful drama: the tension would need to derive not so much from inside the situations themselves but from the contrast between the situations as interpreted by some people and the reality of the intentions of the participants.

As an introductory activity this tableau exercise was relatively safe for the pupils, culminating in a concrete image which required no speech but asked them to concentrate on aspects of non-verbal behaviour. They were also free from the problem of deciding how to represent the speech and mannerisms of a foreign person in the drama, thus avoiding falling into immediate stereotypes. There was no need for detailed contextualisation – the pupils were required to show the expression of discomfort in a concrete situation but not the wider circumstances which led up to it. The exercise was intended to have them translate the generalised situations into concrete instances involving attitudes, stances, facial expressions, but without focusing on intention and motivation.

The next stage, after viewing and reading the tableaux, was to ask the pupils to repeat them but to be ready now to articulate the thoughts of the participants in the scene when invited. Here the focus was on the contrast between the way a scene might be construed by those involved (as observers) and the actual intentions of the participants. In some groups the participants revealed themselves to be oblivious to the discomfort of the foreign visitor, others were more conscious of the effects of their actions. This briefly then became the focus of discussion, the degree to which it is possible to know what the intentions are in human situations and the possibilities of misinterpretation.

The next stage of the project was to ask each group of pupils to interview one of the teachers in role as a foreign language traveller to England now being questioned back home by a group of people from their own country. The visitor had not been altogether happy during his/her stay abroad, the reasons for which would emerge in the interview.

The teacher role gave the opportunity to help the pupils distance themselves from their own culture and start to see themselves as 'other'. At first the task seemed a little strange, but soon the pupils took the cue from the teachers and began to enjoy talking about the British families and some of their idiosyncrasies and in some cases rather negative attitudes to foreign visitors: they had expectations of the visitors based on stereotypes; they had some strange social habits; they made few allowances in terms of their day to day behaviour and in some cases were actually rude.

The final stage of this first session was to build on the earlier work (which had been based on the way actions and motives can be misinterpreted) by asking the groups to demonstrate through improvisation what might actually have happened from the English family's point of view. Each improvisation began with the foreign visitor (now played by a pupil) articulating their version of what had happened in a brief monologue, followed by events as they had actually happened. Thus the account of the visitor who claimed to have been treated badly was followed by the family excitedly making plans for their visitor's arrival. The drama then showed the arrival of the visitor and the insensitivity of the family caused not by neglect or malice but by an excess of enthusiasm. Three levels emerged in the improvisation: the interpretation of events by the visitor, the intentions of the family, the actual encounter showing the explanation of the source of the difficulties. The actual content of the drama focused on everyday situations: meal-times, watching television, going out for the evening, with the pupils building into the work explanations of why the visitors were uncomfortable: assuming the French visitor would automatically know and care about the footballer Eric Cantona, making no concessions in their use of accent and dialect, providing fish and chips in newspaper with no explanation, assuming that their visitors would happily watch and understand 'Neighbours' (the soap opera). Whether the situations chosen were realistic or not as sources of discomfort seemed less important than the exploration of how people can unwittingly contribute to the culture shock experienced by visitors.

By now the question of how to represent the foreign visitor was not a problem because the pupils were more engaged with the task in hand. In one group the visitor started to use French and a French accent, although the absence of such attempts at realism in the other groups was not a problem. The session seemed to have been a helpful start towards fulfilling the aim of having the pupils appreciate other cultures by reflecting at a distance on their own. One pupil after the drama said she had found it very interesting because she was about to go on an exchange visit abroad herself. The project could be developed in a number of ways, placing the focus on visits from England to other countries, exploring what those visitors would need to know in order to make their visit more beneficial. By 'need to know' I do not just mean factual knowledge (although factual knowledge is part of it) but what they need to know about human behaviour in general. Perhaps with a foreign language teacher the project could be extended into brief scripted exchanges in the foreign language.

I have argued that if the potential for drama in educational contexts is circumscribed by a view which sees its use as a substitute for the equivalent real experience, then this represents a narrow view of its possibilities. It is, however, necessary to recognise that the power of drama resides precisely in that fact that it does *in some sense* mirror reality. That paradox is embodied in the way writers on aesthetics have discussed concepts such as 'mimesis', 'representation' and 'naturalism' which seek to describe the relationship between the art object and that which it is intended to depict. Aristotle's use of *mimesis* is at times equivalent to simple mimicry but he also extends the concept to, for example, the way music relates to the feelings, suggesting that to interpret *mimesis* as simple meaning 'imitation' is an oversimplification (Halliwell 1990). Representational views of art have been challenged because of the basic Kantian idea that what the artist sees depends on the subjective perspective (including cultural preconceptions) in which perception is necessarily rooted – pure imitation of things in the world is, in that sense, not possible (Gombrich 1960). Styan (1981) has pointed out that in the history of drama what was viewed as 'natural' in the theatre was always relative to the particular period, and changed as styles developed. As with all art, drama is grounded in reality, it has its 'field of reference in reality' (States 1994). Furthermore, although its origins derive from a human ability to imitate, its interest precisely derives from the fact that it is not real.

As suggested above, it is because much drama tends to be highly representative that its departure from the real is less frequently acknowledged. Photography is sometimes quoted as an extreme example of representation but one only has to consider the difference between looking at a scene and looking at an equivalent photograph to realise that representation entails transformation. The very fact that a human agent has intervened and has selected and isolated a particular moment carries the implicit message that at least says 'this was worth looking at'. There is a suspension of time; a moment which would have passed us by is held before us so that we can take in more of the detail than if we had been there. The isolation and selection allow us to penetrate the subject more deeply. The form isolates and displays. 'Transformation' rather than 'replication' is the key concept and the important practical point is that recognition of that fact can specifically determine a teacher's choice of strategies and approaches in drama.

The concept of 'transformation' can be taken further to involve a process of defamiliarisation. The emphasis is now not just on avoiding any notion that drama is simply trying to replicate reality but to go further so that the central aim is to destabilise and challenge normal ways in which the world is seen and experienced. This was one aspect of the drama project described above based on foreign visitors, because the pupils were asked to see their own taken-for-granted customs and behaviours in a different light.

The concept of defamiliarisation was central to another project which involved a year 10 group (fourteen year olds) working with student teachers. The drama which was structured around the notion of aliens visiting earth began with a piece of theatre performed by the teachers which the pupils had to read. The performance did not strive for realism but used simple signing to convey the necessary information, drawing on familiar images from television, film and science fiction literature.

The short scene established that a group of aliens were visiting earth to conduct anthropological research into the customs and practices of the inhabitants. The convention of a 'language device' (a small box worn on the belt) allowed the aliens to tune in to the host language so that their initial incomprehensible exchanges (which established their alien identity) gave way to them speaking in English. The convention of 'video' allowed the aliens to receive reports from their researchers on earth. Everyday earth scenes were shown (e.g. a dentist's waiting room and surgery, a modern office) and the aliens sought to comprehend what they saw, speculating for example whether what they were witnessing was some sort of punishment or torture inflicted on the young (the dentist's surgery) and whether the 'being' which seemed to need regular feeding was some sort of pet (the photocopier). The lack of realism in the drama operated at two levels: the whole scenario of aliens visiting earth and reporting back had to be accepted, as well as the unlikely idea that an intelligent race would be confounded by simple objects and customs. These were basic conventions on which the drama was built which were established and accepted not through discussion but in the initial performance. That is why the initial signing had to be simple – paradoxically, the more attempts at naturalism (elaborate costume for the aliens, providing contextual details such as name of planet, life-style, technical expertise) the less convincing the actual drama would have been. The purpose of the initial performance was to lay down the 'rules of the game' not to create verisimilitude.

Having established the basic convention in which the drama would operate, the task for the pupils was to create their own scenes which would similarly be read and interpreted by an alien race. The drama was now structured so that the pupils were to take on both roles of aliens and earthlings. This was crucial to the process of defamiliarisation. The 'play within a play' convention helped to establish the two required levels: the presentation of the 'video recorded' scene and the commentary which was also enacted in role. There were similarly two levels of engagement with the make-believe – the scenes from earth were more crafted and rehearsed, while the scenes in which the aliens analysed the recordings were more exploratory and open-ended.

An important ingredient which contributed to the quality of the work produced was a brief teacher-led discussion which followed the initial presentation. The short enacted scene which introduced the theme had established the basic convention; the setting of the drama task for the pupils needed more exploration. It was pointed out that the misunderstandings which were central to the drama could be a source of entertainment and humour but could also provide a deeper commentary on aspects of human life. The scenes chosen by the pupils aided by the student teachers provided precisely the vehicle for further thought which was required. They chose a funeral (which explored human reactions to death, mourning and conventions associated with death), winning the lottery (in which ironically the lottery was interpreted as a god), and a visit to a hairdresser's (which explored concepts of beauty and fashion). Each of the scenes was defamiliarised and looked at afresh through the conventions of the drama.

These examples of lessons embody some of the features which distinguish drama as art from drama as simulation or role play and which can also provide the teacher with a guide to practice. They can be described as the use of multi-levels, obliquity, distance and concealment (Fleming 1997). *Extra levels of meaning* can be injected into the drama by such devices as the use of subtext when one character speaks and another articulates the concealed or intended meanings. Alternatively, a still image or tableau can be accompanied by the diary of one of the participants which throws more light on the depicted scene. In the first drama example there was a contrast between the way the scene was constructed by those involved and the actual intentions of the participants which provided an extra layer of meaning. Drama works *obliquely* in as much as it is often not the central action which is the main source of interest but the implications. Detailed contextualisation is not always essential. In the first drama project, rather than enact their experiences abroad, it was appropriate to interview the pupils. In the second drama it was not so much the creation of an alien race or the interaction between one culture and another but the analysis or interpretation of everyday events which was of central importance. *Distancing* in drama is achieved by such conventions as the use of tableau, deliberate signing, play within a play. The objective of creating distance is contrary to the way drama in education was often conceived in the 1970s and 1980s when deep involvement, real feeling and belief in the make-belief were often seen to be the central objects. This distancing is essential to the notion of defamiliarisation and was realised in the structure of the second drama by the use of a play within a play. The notion of *concealment* refers to the process of holding in abeyance what one knows in order to advance the drama. This is contrary to the way improvised role play often works which uses what one knows in order to create and sustain the drama. In both examples of drama projects the participants at various stages were asked to assume ignorance of what was actually familiar to them. Such devices serve to provide the type of alternative perspectives essential to the objective of developing cultural awareness.

These brief descriptions of drama projects have served as examples of the way in which drama can work to subject to scrutiny human behaviour which we might normally take for granted; to examine things as they actually are as opposed to how they seem to be. At the start of this chapter I identified a contrast between drama as a methodology and drama as an arts discipline. It will be clear that I reject that distinction. It is the way drama operates as an art form which provides rich opportunities for learning.

Note:
Thanks are due to the pupils of St John's Comprehensive School, Bishop Auckland.

8 Teaching culture through drama

Dorothy Heathcote and Gavin Bolton

An introduction to a concept of drama education

The Puritan movement in England persisted through several centuries. One of its minor effects on education was the expulsion of the school play. The late 19th century saw a faint-hearted and somewhat oblique revival of this tradition in the form of play performances in a classical language. Greek and Latin apparently satisfied the most suspicious Puritan.

It was the beginning of the 20th century in England that saw the first examples of drama in the classroom as opposed to drama on stage. These instances are isolated, but nevertheless significant, for they introduced the notion of 'dramatisation', i.e. a method of *using* pretend behaviour in order to teach a school subject, such as arithmetic, history, nature study or literature and in a few, prestigious schools, the 'direct speaking' of Latin and Greek dialogue became part of the classics lesson.

By the 1920s interest in dramatisation seemed to fade in favour of drama as a branch of English language and literature, and it was felt by some authorities that its practice in the classroom could only be justified if it were linked with speech-training, so in many schools drama became exercises in correct articulation.

This particular bias was almost overtaken by a powerful input from the continent, first in the form of musical and dance education evolved by Emile Jacques-Rousseau and Rudolf Steiner and later 'movement education' as promoted by Rudolf Laban, who in the late 1930s became resident in England. It is interesting that the influence from the continent on British education was in respect of a form of expression that was *without* spoken language. Thus the 1920s, '30s and '40s saw drama translated either into speech-training or into a form of expression that dispensed with words and needed the space of a large hall.

Then there arrived a philosophy that required teachers to see drama as derived from child's play. If the movement work of Jacques-Rousseau can be described as 'drama without words', then Peter Slade's methodology can be thought of as 'drama without meaning', or rather, without significant content. At a time, in the 1950s, when formal education espoused the learning of facts, the introduction of drama into the curriculum as a subject that freed children from the burden of acquiring knowledge was widely welcomed. Children were free to be dramatically creative, improvising their own actions and words in playful harmony. The meaning of what they did was in the action, for 'drama is doing' was the catch-phrase of the time. If a child played the part of a waiter, he simulated cleaning the table-tops, laying a cloth, arranging the cutlery, writing down the customer's order – and if he was supposed to be a 'bad waiter', he would get the order mixed up and comedy would ensue – for drama also had to be 'fun'.

But 'dramatisation' or, 'role-play', as it was later called, never entirely disappeared. It often involved the reading aloud, with suitable actions, of short, prepared play scripts, specifically written to illuminate events of history in a history lesson, or excite interest in Bible stories in the religious education lesson, or, and this is more pertinent to this publication, to give practice in speaking a foreign language, such as French or German. The pupil can read his 'waiter' lines from a script.

The idea that drama can assist foreign language teaching has been around for some time. One of the authoritative publications on how to use improvised drama for language skills is by Schewe and Shaw (1993). The source of material on dramatic methodology is sparse, for there appears to be evidence of much talk but little practice. It is difficult to find teachers who use drama, scripted or improvised. One of the advantages of improvised drama, as described by Hawkins (1993) is 'exposure'. It is language 'exposure' rather than language 'study' that is going to promote skill and confidence. Our 'waiter' now needs to speak spontaneously in a concrete setting. The pupil playing that role may have learnt-off a series of 'waiter expressions' to fit the context, but having to repeat them *in situ* can make the language come more alive than normal classroom interaction.

But even in this contextual practice, the kind of language may belong to the textbook rather than to life, for improvisation may merely provide an 'image' of a context, resulting in an 'image' of language rather than a 'real' language exchange. One way of enlivening the process is to add an adjective to the waiter – he is 'tired' or 'forgetful' or 'deferential'. A further way is to turn the role-play into something that feels like 'real' drama: there are constraints on true thoughts or feelings being expressed: our waiter finds himself having to serve an ex-girlfriend and her new partner.

There is a deeper kind of context which may be worth considering, that of personal values. Supposing the waiter models himself on his deceased father who owned and ran the restaurant with such pride. On the other hand, supposing, now that his father has died he feels free at last from paternal scrutiny.

There is another kind of value – pertaining to this book – a *cultural* constraint. Supposing our waiter is learning the job in a foreign country. Or, more subtly, supposing a customer adopts a degree of familiarity, totally inappropriate to the waiter's upbringing. The subtlety of these latter exercises might only be achieved with teacher-in-role as the customer. Teacher-in-role is a device adopted during the last 30 years by the authors of this chapter as an integral part of drama teaching. One of its purposes is to bring a degree of authenticity beyond the expected ability of the students – and, as such, has potential in language methodology.

The cultural component of this last exercise, as we shall see in the second half of this chapter, becomes of central interest in respect of the application of drama to learning about cultural matters as opposed to the enhancement of language skills. Indeed, such an exercise takes us some way to understanding a development of drama education in this country over the last 20 years. If the 1950s approach to drama teaching was free of significant content, the methodology advocated by the authors of this chapter demands scrupulous attention to levels of meaning. For Dorothy Heathcote the main purpose of drama is to train pupils to look beyond the surface action, beyond our waiter's dining-room rituals to the personal and cultural values that sustain them.

There is a sense, therefore, in which we can claim that in our school drama we are always dealing with cultural values: we are always, to use Byram's expression, 'decentring from our own culture', that *that is what drama is*. It will not often occur that the cultural distinctions are national, but sub-culture boundaries are nearly always being explored – an older generation of waiters having to understand the new generation, for example. Improvised drama at its most superficial will engage the pupils' interest in a personality clash between two waiters; at its best their interest will extend to probing the embedded personal and cultural values.

So, to invite drama teachers to consider how they might use their methodology to teach about culture is no more than to ask them to ply their usual practice, but of course it is one thing to engage students in a fictional dramatic event with a view, ultimately, to drawing attention to underlying cultural implications; it is another matter to tackle directly the matter of training pupils to look for cultural implications.

Drama 'proper' tells lies; most drama is about characters for some reason withholding true facts, thoughts or feelings – our waiter, finding himself serving his ex-girlfriend is constrained to put on his waiter's smile. In the lesson which is described below which was taught as part of a research seminar held at the University of Durham, Dorothy Heathcote did not use drama of this kind, but rather, illustrative role-play, allowing the pupils to put behaviour under a microscope, to reflect upon what they had learnt and then articulate it for others.

Using drama to help students learning a foreign language study how culture(s) operate(s)

Introductory philosophy underlying the concept of 'theatre' and how some elements of theatre can be used in the classroom to teach about culture

Dramatic performance in the theatre intends that onlookers shall be affected by what they see and hear, so everything is biased towards the message to be understood and all the signs are there because they are *necessary* to the message. The watchers realise they are to watch and hear *everything* and regard it as truthful at the time.

Because they realise this they also know that the actors are in a 'no-penalty' zone. They need not fear that Othello after murdering Desdemona will be taken into custody or that they themselves will be arrested as accessories to the act. The actor may today play Othello and tomorrow the role of a modern spaceman. This especially applies in TV 'theatre' which may actually be occurring at the same time on different channels!

Our work for the grades 9 and 10 students and the delegates to the research conference on language and culture used *some* of these theatre elements, but more often used 'blurred genre' in the interests of the learning to be negotiated rather than entertainment. They varied their positions in relation to the dramatic elements. Sometimes they watched a short piece of theatre; sometimes made one themselves. At other times their tasks (drama demands a *doing* approach) were to read, comment, discuss, write, collaborate in planning, be in charge of the actions of others. But always at the heart of each task lay considerations of other people living out their culture: the focus in every task had elements of images of living people expressing their lives and attitudes.

All these tasks, tailored as precisely as possible to the social and intellectual levels of the class, placed the students and adults present in the position of observers of culture, but they recognised that in the main the cultures had to be *invented for the purpose*. It is this combination of people doing *real* tasks, behaving as themselves and thinking from out of their actual state of knowledge, and *invented* cultures, which is the unique contribution to learning of a drama approach. This is the 'no-penalty' zone borrowed from theatre.

A problem for this particular teaching occasion was that the people assembled had two different learning needs. In addition to the school students, there were representatives of a number of European countries and Japan. These delegates needed to be able to observe and evaluate at close quarters the students' responses to the different forms of work. With this objective in mind, the students were invited at the beginning of the session to break up into small groups and invite the 'visitors' to split themselves among the students, so that there were roughly one or two adults to a group of four to six students. These intimate groupings were sustained throughout the work, communicating more as they became more comfortable working together.

The main objective for the session, of course, was that the students were to be introduced to ways of observing elements of culture, so that they would have tools for more subtle and complex study as their own course in language learning progressed. A stated aim of the conference which guided our planning was given to us by Michael Byram: '... it is a question of developing attitudes, empathy, the ability to de-centre from one's own culture. *It is a process rather than a content*'.

John Mortimer (1994) quotes Chesterton's remark that '... Literature is a luxury but fiction is a necessity'. In the field of formal learning, drama fits the 'necessity' factor, because fictionalising situations creates distances and people *can* de-centre and becoming caring observers.

Theatre conventions

It is necessary for the *conventions* of theatre to be considered here, so that when we later discuss the range of tasks the delegates and students met, we can see how the outer forms of the exercises supported the inner meanings. Progression depends upon the coherence of the inner structure, because that inner coherence is the very *process of learning* to which Byram's statement refers.

Theatre art and life use the same communication systems. Both use a vast range of signs, but in life such usage is less selective and precise, so the participant or onlooker in the 'real' world must make sense of what is happening by discounting any signs they consider irrelevant. In theatre, of course, *all* the signs are relevant.

The communication system consists of the following elements:

What is heard (all sounds from noises to music, including talk – and at whatever volume or intensity);

What is significantly *not* heard (noticeable quietness; absence of the expected);
What is seen (arrangements of objects, people, surrounding backgrounds);
What is noticeably *not able* to be seen;
What moves and what is still.

These form the palette for a drama approach – teachers cannot 'learn' its rules – they can only absorb them into their imaginations and apply them in practice significantly to that waiting space that is theatre, 'waiting space' for a stage can never be empty: *it is filled with waiting*.

One of the theatre pieces we devised can be used here to clarify the palette available in drama so that when the 'blurred' tasks are considered, the inner coherent structure can more readily be seen. Notice, in the script below, the different forms of signing, blurring the conventions. Some objects were actually there – and indeed *must* be real – and carefully placed, signifying their relative places and distances (the chair for the cashier, the name labels on the actors and the coat-hanger, anorak, price tag, and the plastic 'named' shop carrier). Some objects existed because they were spatially represented by words – the words 'BIN', and 'CASH TILL' were placed accurately for use. Some objects were copied crudely (just a piece of card cut to appropriate size for a 'cash card' – thus avoiding the 'penalty zone' of a real one). And, of course, many objects were indicated by actions and gesture: the movement of the till, the key to activate the till drawer, the card processing device, the receipt and the pen for signing.

Scene A check-out counter in a clothing store

Setting The objects and names laid out as described in the above paragraph

Enter cashier (female) –pins label on herself.
Enter customer (male) – pins on name label – Muslim origin.
Cashier – puts imaginary key into cash machine. Waits. Watches customer.
Customer – examines anorak; checks size, stitching seams and price. Selects it and carries it to cashier.
Cashier – receives it, removes price tag and places it in view of both. Removes hanger and drops it into 'bin'.
Cashier: 'This style is very popular this year, sir.'
Customer: 'It is for my wife.'
Cashier (concerned) – lays down coat and looks at customer.
Customer – takes out 'cash card'.

> *Cashier* (deciding to speak): 'Excuse me, sir, but this anorak is meant to be worn by a man.'
> *Customer*: 'I like it. It will suit her very well. It is a good size for her.'
> *Cashier* – folds and bags anorak and sets it aside, taking up cash card and reading price tag.
> *Cashier*: 'That will be £43 pounds, sir.'
> *Customer*: '£35?'
> *Cashier* (showing price tag): 'It says £43, sir.'
> *Cashier* – indicates sliding 'card' into an imaginary machine and presents a 'receipt' with her 'pen' for his signature.
> *Customer* – 'signs' and returns 'pen'.
> *Cashier* – hands over bag enclosing the anorak.
> *Customer* – takes card and bag and turns to leave.
> *Cashier* (shrugs): 'Thank you, sir.'

In addition to the visual signals described above, the scene could be analysed in respect of its *elements of sound*: the words spoken, the clatter of the hanger dropping into the area of the 'bin', the feet of the customer moving around (in contrast to the cashier whose position is fixed, a movement/stillness element) and the rustle of the anorak as it goes in the bag. But the occasional silence may be significant too – the quiet scrutiny by the cashier of the customer's behaviour as he examines the anorak – neutral, benign, anticipatory – the concern when the purchase is for a woman and the judgemental gaze as he leaves the area.

The use of light and dark, here, as in most classroom work, is metaphorical only. For instance, the cashier 'lights up' the presence of her till by deliberate gesture. The customer 'keeps dark' his reasons for buying a man's anorak for his wife. However, there is a paradox operating here, for the actors, as opposed to the 'characters', 'shed light', for the sake of the audience, on the fact that innermost thoughts *are* being hidden.

It is this attention to detail in using all the above theatre elements which enables the teacher and students to employ dramatic forms in the interests of precision and planning for specific learning goals – and the self-spectator in each student must be actively aware that that is being done and how each is contributing.

Protection

But learning could only take place if the students were sufficiently comfortable with the unusual circumstances. They needed to be eased through demanding responsibilities – working in small groups with foreign adults, exposing their opinions and ideas to scrutiny by the rest of the class, pitching the voice publicly, even using their bodies to demonstrate 'how it *might* be', concentrating for a whole school day, etc. Protection was needed too by the conference delegates: they too had to gain the trust of their small group members. Both delegates and students needed to be given time to get used to the variety of language styles and accents.

Two main aspects of culture

We had decided that we would tackle two main aspects of culture and reinforce them by using as many forms of involvement as possible. The internal structure of every task had to be related directly with these two aspects, while the external appearance of the tasks should not feel repetitive to the students: many hammers were used to hit the same two nails!

The whole concept of the work was derived from the following assumptions:

(a) *Personal Values*: that individuals always *behave* in expressing their culture (indeed living persons cannot *not* behave!); that their behaviour carries their *personal* value systems which are deeply ingrained.

(b) *Cultural Values*: that all *cultures* develop a hierarchy of value systems: those which are mainly unperceived at a conscious level and are sustained tenaciously by all members who are formally bound to their inner laws; those rule-making values operating at a socio-political level, to which members are informally bound, often relying on professional interpreters, such as doctors, lawyers, engineers, etc. for guidance; those seemingly 'boundless' structures that permit individuals the freedom and responsibility to use their own judgement about behaving – 'seemingly' because, of course, 'their own judgement' is in turn dictated by the 'personal values' of (a) above.

The tasks

For the benefit of the reader, the tasks are listed as the final section of this chapter. It will be noted that the first and last of the 19 tasks gave an important sense of 'full circle'. Both delegates and students were invited (the teacher's tone was light, with some humour) at the very beginning of the session to scribble 'off the tops of their heads', using a long, communal roll of paper, what they knew about the other's culture.

These sheets were then returned to at the end – for considered alterations.

The first 'observation of role-play' tasks invited comments from the students, comments which became more technical and discriminating as the carefully graded role-play scenes became more sophisticated and as the students picked up the 'cultural' vocabulary with which to probe the illustrated behaviours. This 'vocabulary' reflected the 'Personal' and 'Cultural' values outlined above. The former, expressed on a blackboard as a hierarchical series of questions, and used at first by the teacher on the 'characters', was relatively easy for the students to ask, first of the actors and then of each other in their small groups and finally actually to 'teach' the delegates they were attached to; the latter, written up as concepts rather than questions were more difficult to absorb and needed the longer time (indeed longer than they were actually given), to apply them to the 'textual study' mode of private reading, mutual sharing and checking of understanding and the analytical task of scribbling classificatory labels on the text as they felt more confident in using the technical terms. For the 'culture values' the students' attention was continually moving between the printed texts and the 'live' scenes showing either an incident in the life of the two fictional tribes or a contemporary incident.

Below are details of the 'tasks', in order, laid out as if they were a lesson plan, giving some indication of the purpose behind each.

Detailed description of tasks

Task one

Cards are held by delegates indicating their country of origin.
Students, having read the cards write their impressions on large 'public' paper with thick pens.
Delegates, on a separate scroll, write their impressions of the British.

External form: Casual, permitting change of ideas, no pressure regarding standards.

Internal structure: to permit personal images to arise and not allow too much time for inventing 'safe to show teacher' phrases; freedom and 'power' to scrutinise delegates' written statements.

Content: What do we rely on when considering other nationalities?

Task two

'Actors' used to demonstrate an activity. The following questions are written large on a blackboard:

What are you doing?
What is your motive in doing that?
What makes it an important thing to be doing?
Where did you learn that such things must be done?
How should life be for you?

The teacher *formally* asks these questions of the actors. One set of answers went as follows:

I am telephoning my sister.
Because it's her birthday.
I always phone her on her birthday.
We've always remembered important dates in our family.
Celebrations keep a family together.

Three different actors showed different actions and then were pressed by the teacher to develop a mood or attitude to what they were doing. So, for instance, the 'birthday' one became:

I am telephoning my sister using a funny voice.
Because on my birthday she pretended to be the income tax office calling me.
We always play jokes like this.
Our parents were themselves always up to tricks.
You've got to seize every opportunity for a laugh.

External form: Watching people behave and feeling safe as audience.

Internal structure: Watching the five layers of personal values recur over and over again; familiarising themselves with the formal questions, without actually setting out to 'learn' them.

Content: That all individuals develop a deeply ingrained personal value system which they 'carry around'.

Task three

Exactly as for Task two, except groups are formed, behaviour selected and demonstrated by the students or delegates within their small group.

Content: In addition to reinforcing Task two, this is the first time students and foreign adults are to work together; first opportunity to get used to vocabulary and accents and show behaviour publicly.

Task four

The three 'actors' now, in turn, take on Shakespearean roles and demonstrate the relevant craft:

Snug the joiner (sawing wood)
Snout the tinker (mending a metal cooking pot)
Starvelling the tailor (sewing hem on cloak)

Less familiar people and crafts allow students to see familiar in strange – which becomes more like everybody else when 'attitudes' are injected into the answers. When Snug replies 'You have to work perfectly ...', and Snout says '... want to get home before dark ...' and Starvelling: '... must finish before dark ... my eyes aren't what they used to be', these people from Shakespeare come closer!

Content: All people of all times have developed personal value systems – it is not only our period or industrialised nations.

Task five

Students take up names of mechanicals (additionally, there were Bottom (weaver), Quince (carpenter), Flute (bellows-mender)) and in their small groups invent their own range of answers.

Content: It is possible to take on work we have never considered before and demonstrate it to other people by empathising with how their attitudes may be experienced. 'We can pretend' is the crudest level – but ability to empathise and show how it might be experienced by others is the level we aspire to!

Task six

Students listen to a short illustrated blackboard lecture introducing them to the second 'value' concept – the hierarchy of cultural values: *Formal*, *Informal* and *Technical*.

External form: Listening amongst peers to a teacher lecturing and explaining. This would most likely be the most familiar position for the students to find themselves in!

Internal structure: To keep developing (by style of talk and demonstration) the observer point of view. To introduce immediate examples from 'today's news broadcasts or local events'.

Contents: To label and show examples of the three cultural elements which define group behaviours.

Task seven

A demonstration (by 'actors') of an incident repeated twice to show three levels of culture.

Incident: A man enters the House of Women – by mistake.

1st level: Formal – Both must die.
2nd level: Informal – Both must rely on authorised experts to decide outcomes and abide by any decisions.
3rd level: Technical – The woman and the man must negotiate his exit according to her sense of outrage and his responses.

Content: To give opportunity for students to see culture in process and have precise examples to reveal stages of cultural shifts. (All cultures are continually reviewing, and revising these shifts. As soon as a formal value is questioned it can no longer remain mandatory – and becomes 'informal'.)

Task eight

Copies of 'The people of Ferradach Dhu' text are distributed to each student and delegate with the intention that they should note and mark all the cultural levels of social behaviour they could find. (See Appendix 1.)

Outer form: Reading and discussing, in their small groups, a given stimulus that requires their full attention.

Inner structure: A chance to put *their* interpretations on the text and thereby 'take power over it'.

Content: To recognise cultural patterns via a written account (looking like a typical 'school text').

Task nine

The students are to watch a role-taking situation representing a line of text from the account they have just read: '... they (the women) are skilled bargainers when outsiders come to trade.'

The scene, a foreigner coming to buy cloth, is played twice, first for its story-line and then to be interrupted as the students identify cultural patterns operating at any of the three levels. (They are invited to instruct the 'actors' to 'Freeze!', to make their comment, and then, 'Carry on!' to the actors to resume the text.) The text is as follows:

Situation: a primitive hut with two stools
a pottery dish
pieces of cloth

The 'seller' (a woman) arranges cloth.
The 'buyer' (a man in a cloak) puts aside 'curtain' of opening, stooping as he enters politely.
She indicates which stool he may sit on.
He gives her his hunting knife.
She places it a little way off in full view of both.
He waits; his coin bag is to be seen.
She brings cloth (one piece) for his inspection.
She indicates he may touch it.
He fingers the cloth, examining it closely.

Buyer: 'Is the dye heather root?'
She indicates that it is.
Buyer: 'How may I be certain?'
Seller: 'Because I have so said.'
Buyer: 'It is a man's cloth?'
She shakes her head.
Seller: (fetching another cloth) 'This is a cloth for men.'
He examines both and chooses one piece.
She folds it.
She indicates 'ten pieces' of coin by finger counting.
She places 5 pieces in the pottery dish and 5 in her bag purse.
She gives him the cloth and his knife.
He bows and leaves with the cloth.

Outer form: Watching a play.

Inner structure: Recognising behaviour patterns at speed; using their 'power' to interrupt actions. De-centring. Publicly explaining the evidence for their labelling.

Content: Empathising, without judging, with the motives, skills, assumptions of the culture they were observing.

Task ten

The check-out counter scene (purchase of anorak).

Content: Students to recognise that they can now de-centre, examine and empathise with any strangeness in a contemporary situation.

Task eleven

The students are now given copies of the text about the other culture, the people of Aest Bodrotria, to teasel out the cultural patterns. (See Appendix 2.)

Outer form: Looks exactly like the work of Task eight.

Inner structure: The task gives the same clear indicators of cultural patterns, but they have a more complex task. This time they are asked to keep in mind the convention used in peace-keeping between adjacent tribes whereby a son or daughter of the chief's family was reared as hostage in the neighbour's tribe. So a person with an individual value system, coming from a culture very different from that to which he will be sent is to be advised by the students as to how to observe, cope with, respect and survive such alien value systems – with a view, in adulthood, in the name of better understanding, to bring back enlightenment to his own people.

Content: Mediation between cultures must occur whenever they are in contact with each other. This is of immediate concern to the students who will shortly be visiting other countries on the continent.

Task twelve

The students watch two cultures in action in a role-play demonstrating that '... the horse is the main means of transport ...' of the people of Ferradach Dhu, and demonstrating that in the people of Aest Bodrotria an inherent inarticulacy has bred 'an inability to use words as their main basis for communication'.

Action: Two people of Ferradach Dhu, wearing cloaks, lead in three tall horses (conventionalised by 'holding rein' gesture and 'I am bringing my horse to ride and another to lend to our guest the son of the Chief of Aest Bodrotria' written on a card fixed to their backs). A third person, wearing an amber necklace and delicately patterned long gown, is the visiting son. On his back is the sign 'I am looking at the horses'.

Outer form: Watching a play – with empathy for both sides.

Inner structure: Identifying with value systems of both cultures.

Content: The observers are to perceive the dilemma of both cultures and discover (a) the individual value systems of each person by asking the five 'What are you doing?' questions used earlier in the day and (b) what cultural patterns of formal, informal and technical this event reflects for both tribes. By dealing with (a) first, they can more easily gain access to the tribal value systems through the statements offered in response to the five formal questions of act, motivation, investment, education and value system.

The Ferradach Dhu:

Act: I am bringing my horse.
Motive: So he can see all the valley in safety with us.
Investment: We want him to realise he'll be free to go where he wills once he knows the rules.
Education: When you're a foreigner it's important to know where you stand.
Value system: Life is for living. Use your opportunities.

The Son of Aest Bodrotria:

Act: I am looking at the horses.
Motive: Because I'm afraid of what they might do.
Investment: I should be polite and accept a horse.
Education: You should try to accommodate where and when you can.
Value system: Troubles between peoples should be avoided.

The students were now to take some responsibility in resolving the 'horse' problem.

Task thirteen

The group consider what the issues are and decide how they may mediate the situation, having reference to the two written texts, which are their main source of information.

Outer form: Teaching the guest about the cultural values of the host people and vice versa.

Inner structure: Explaining (by both demonstration and advice) two cultures to each other, so that they may interpret behaviour and rules of each other's responses. There is, of course, an ethical issue here – to what extent is it proper to assume that the foreign prince should *adopt* the ways of his host? This was not questioned by the students nor by the teacher, who was nevertheless aware of a problem being glossed over, but who saw it as a matter to be faced another time. In this two-session work, tackling such an issue in a way that gave it the attention it deserved, would have meant abandoning the sense of a 'complete circle' with which this final hour was to be rounded off. Thus the teacher had to keep to her planned priorities, for the sake of the delegates as well as for the students' immediate sense of having completed a piece of learning. In some circumstances of course, one would have to deal *straightaway* with some moral concern at whatever cost to the completion of a plan.

Content: We consider and empathise with two cultures at once and may realise where we would stand if *we* were in the position of either the host or the guest culture.

Task fourteen

They watch a modern example of the tribal situation.

Outer form: Watching a play which reveals contemporary sub-culture values.

Inner structure: Adjusting to a modern example and using modern mediation.

Content: Adjusting their reading of cultural values; recognising changes from passages of time.

Task fifteen

Students re-read the text of the two tribal cultures in their groups and select moments of action which could bring most danger of misunderstanding on either side having to educate a guest from another community.

Outer form: Sitting reading and talking quietly in groups.

Inner structure: The students' chance to see in their imagination, from the words on paper, moments when cultures reveal their values, and to identify the formal, informal and technical rules governing any such moment.

Content: We can take any short printed phrase, imagine it in action as it expresses the rule base operating at that moment PLUS the likely response of a stranger, differently reared.

Task sixteen

Students prepare and then show 'tricky' moments they have selected from the texts. They face questions from onlookers and explain their choices and perceptions.

Outer form: Performing short incidents.

Inner structure: Selecting the means and conventions of drama to reveal the problems.

Content: Thinking in drama forms; selecting message systems to communicate clearly their understanding and differentiation of operant culture value systems; sharing with peers as doers and watchers.

Task seventeen

Delegates hand out copies in their groups of their own texts, written before coming to the conference, about their own country and culture.

Outer form: Reading a previously unseen text in familiar groups.

Outer structure: *Registering* to delegates any areas of interest or difficulty students think might give rise to being misunderstood by foreign visitors. AND POINT OUT likely formal, informal and technical culture values which may be revealed or intimated by the accounts.

Content: These are the countries and cultures we may be encountering soon. This is of immediate concern. How will it affect me from England? How will I deal with it? feel about it? respond to it?

Task eighteen

Students select a situation from the delegates' texts and demonstrate an event where an English person is guest of another culture.

Outer form: Constructing a play to be shown.

Inner structure: Making sure the *problem* is revealed not just a peep-show story-line.

Content: We are pre-living, through role-play, situations we might meet soon in reality and trying out our tools for recognising roots of behaviour and cultural value systems in action in the immediate moment.

Task nineteen

Return to the original scrolls of large paper and browse around the statements.

Outer form: Wandering and pondering casually and writing or crossing out.

Inner structure: Considering to what extent the earlier notions and attitudes are now modified.

Content: What different or more developed considerations are available now? What alterations or additions, if any, will I make to reflect my thinking at this time?

It was when students were presented with the final, third text that their new cultural comprehension was tested. The delegates, before the conference, had been asked (with no explanation) to write down a description of the chief features of their own countries. These were not of course written, as were the 'fictional tribes' texts, with the content of the teaching in mind. It was the students themselves who brought a cultural hierarchy to bear on their interpretation of these texts from other countries. The 'distancing' of the 'Aest Bodrotria' and 'Ferradach Dhu' had enabled them to de-centre and *benignly* approach the cultural social basis of the mainly 'European neighbour's' accounts.

Appendix 1

The people of Ferradach Dhu

The chieftain and all his extended family of tribespeople live in a wide valley closed on three sides by high mountains and open to the sea on the fourth. A river flows from the mountains to the sea where there are high cliffs and dangerous currents.

Crops of rye, barley and flax are harvested as well as healing plants. Some deer abound for meat, and fish is plentiful. Two kinds of boats are skilfully built to withstand the seas and treacherous currents. One is used for time of high ceremony, such as celebrations of the seasons, deaths of chieftains and receiving of honoured guests – and strong light seagoing vessels are used in the daily labour of catching fish which they spear 'on the move'.

Wolves range the higher reaches of the mountains and are to some extent protected. Each male is permitted to hunt and slay (by the spear and dagger) one *male* wolf so that the skin can be fashioned into a warm hunting cloak. The wolf 'mask' is worn above the headbonnet as a sign that the spirit of the slain wolf has given itself to the one who slew it. Friends at the time of these wolf huntings may assist with their dogs to track the wolf, but the initiate must make the final kill alone.

The council hut where all public matters of concern are discussed contains a ship's carved figurehead made of wood. All fishermen take a sliver from this before taking their fishing boats to sea, to protect them from storm and current. This custom is currently under review.

The women are famous for their skills in dyeing and weaving – especially woollen and linen cloths. They are known to be skilled bargainers when outsiders come to trade for dried and salt fish, and dyes and fabrics. Because of the sea currents, the boats of these traders must be escorted into the valley.

A power balance is finely held between the priest-kind and the chieftain's family who keep the line by inheritance. All clansfolk may be consulted when events demand such discussion.

Celebrations are marked by a fast and furious game known as 'Cattle Raid' in which two teams participate on horseback carrying spears made with sharp points of wood. Each team protects a 'gateway' defined by two posts, and a calf's head, with its full pelt still attached, must be speared and carried through the 'gate' of the opposing team in spite of their best efforts to prevent it. The team which first hurls the calf's head seven times through the enemy gate is declared the winner.

All adults become skilled at 'scouting' – a system of keeping watch throughout the mountain ridges in order to protect their valley from incursions. It is deemed that Ferradach Dhu is a land of pure race people.

The horse is the main means of transport by land and the rough hill ponies are bred for stamina, surefootedness and agility. They are trained to stand as if tethered fast, when the rein is hung forward over the head and to keep silent at night even when the wolf smell arises or fire is kindled on the resin torches. All clan members in good health learn the ways of the horse.

All persons are expected to hold opinions and express them openly, and this enables the community life to be close and tolerant of a variety of attitudes and behaviours. Private space is not deemed important but tools and weapons are highly valued and protected by their owners.

Appendix 2

The people of Aest Bodrotria

The country of the Bodrotrian people is rich in minerals and unusual stones. Since time immemorial they have used these to fashion objects, jewellery and utensils of great beauty and embellished form. They have developed the skills of transformation of natural materials to a high degree. They have fine control of heat and flame, of moulding and carving and their artists and artisans are held in high esteem.

Those who can afford these luxuries see themselves as preservers and guardians and resist any movements which may bring about adverse changes to this condition. Wealth lies in acquiring and preserving and this includes giving the highest honours to the makers and formers.

Because of their skills, their reputation has caused many strangers to visit Bodrotria and they are always greeted with courtesy. However these strangers are never shown the highest and most skilful work. By common consent, makers and shapers have developed work dedicated only for trade and intended to depart the country. Thus there is an unspoken (and largely unrecognised) secretiveness.

Too much discussion, explanation, or questioning (in the young, for example) has led to a benign 'keeping of one's own counsel'. They have no poets, or tellers of myths, and ceremonies tend to be marked by processions, dancing – wearing elaborate garments and jewellery – and the bearing of processional objects.

They favour small plots for cultivation and dedicate much time to close observation. They have profound and intimate knowledge of the flora and fauna of their country and high skills in the different uses of plants – for healing and providing colour for dyes and paints – and they have detailed written records of weather charts, instructions for the learning of crafts and maps of all crop dispersal and cultivated areas of valued plants.

Physically they are of slight build, but are strong in endurance and on the rare occasions they have been made prisoner have shown great fortitude to endure, and extreme stubbornness in resisting pressure to teach strangers their skills.

It is believed that this is not due to unwillingness but rather to an inability to use words as their main basis of communication. Those they trade with have given them a reputation for sullenness and a suspicion of others.

They use no drums or cymbals for their dances or rituals, preferring pipes and reeds or shaking instruments, all of which are intricately built and tuned to work in harmony.

9 Learning by playing: learning foreign languages through the senses

Marianne Jensen and Arno Hermer

The daughter in Gregory Bateson's narrative about the gesticulating French asks quite innocently: 'Daddy, why do the French wave their arms about?' 'What do you mean?' 'I mean, when they speak. Why do they flail their arms about and everything?' After talking for a while with her father who never actually offers her any type of 'explanation' for this French peculiarity, but who takes seriously her own attempts at explanation, the daughter finally asks: 'Daddy, when they teach us French at school why don't they teach us how to use our hands too?' and her father replies: 'I don't know. Really I don't. It's probably one of the reasons why people find it so difficult to learn languages. Anyhow, it's absurd. I mean, the idea that language consists of words is completely ridiculous (. . .) because there is no such thing as "just" words. All that syntax and grammar, that's rubbish. Everything rests on the notion that there is such a thing as "just" words – but there isn't' (Bateson 1972).

Both of us, like many thousands of others, were taught various foreign languages traditionally: swotting up on vocabulary, analysing and learning grammar, translating authors. That led to the absurd situation of us being able to read newspapers, understand writers – but not be able to order a sandwich once abroad. We could not even properly understand the waiter who wanted to explain the menu to us. All the vocabulary and grammar was in our heads and not in our arms, mouths, eyes or feet. Such a disembodied language is regrettably quickly forgotten. The experience of being dumb-struck in a foreign country however is not one which is so easily forgotten.[1]

Our approach to teaching which seeks to go beyond disembodied language is intended to provide more lasting results than a purely

[1] In an examination of the efficacy of training methods of 200 people tested in the Instructional Methods Inventory (IMI) the following learning methods were rated as the most effective: '1: study trip, 2: visual presentation, 3: role-play in small groups, 4: practising in small groups.' In this some learning methods which we present here are still not even included. Cited from the Training and Development Journal, no place of publication given, June 1988.

cognitive method, but it is also a process of providing the learner with a richer engagement with the target language. It is in that general sense that our approach which seeks to promote a full sensory, physical and emotional appreciation of the language can be seen as a form of cultural education. In the practical examples which follow we also show how cultural awareness can be pursued as a more specific objective.

We are theatre performers. For more than a decade we have been travelling around schools, working with all age groups and with people of differing backgrounds. During this time it has been rewarding to see large numbers of pupils (and adults) engage in vigorous physical activity in lessons and serious seminars. They sing, perform pantomimes and nonsense poems, devise stories, create theatre – and in doing so they learn a great deal. Even suggestopaedia and 'superlearning' work exceptionally well with associated methods.

We have come to crystallise our approach more through a long process of practical trial and error rather than through systematic research or theorising. The theory which underpins our work however is not unique and the essential features of this practice are confirmed and reinforced by writing and research in the areas of play and learning.

In our work we approach texts, themes and ideas in exactly the same performance-based manner as we do in the examples which follow. What we describe is not intended to be prescriptive; there are many publications which simply list practical activities to be followed slavishly. What is offered is rather an invitation for teachers to develop their own activities and ideas and try out practically as many of these as possible. The approach is playful but has a serious intent; to adopt a performance-based stance towards teaching means that teaching must be taken very, very seriously.

Sometimes teachers whose classes are doing drama courses with us try to warn us off difficult pupils. To their amazement this warning proves superfluous in the vast majority of cases. The disruptive, the unwilling are transformed into leading lights who can carry along the entire class in workshops. Such experiences over the course of time have led us more and more to make use of these energies even in quite normal lessons. We hear pleasing results particularly from teachers of foreign languages (but not just from them): the objectives of the curriculum are learned more rapidly, with greater retention and with far more motivation.

A basic tenet of our approach is graphically illustrated by one of the practical warm-up exercises we use. Anyone who comes into contact with new material (or an unfamiliar teaching method) finds him/herself in the same position as a right-handed person who has to carry out familiar tasks with the left hand. We like to invite beginners to try this by carrying out some daily tasks (picking up a fork or drawing) with the wrong hand. They often find that after the initial fumbling, clumsy actions, they gradually become more skilled. Even the capabilities of the dominant hand are extended. Symmetrical activity is one of the basic exercises used for connecting the left and right halves of the brain which in turn is an indispensable aid to learning. In traditional teaching the left half of the brain responsible for linear, serial, logical thought is exercised. The right side of the brain which functions interconnectedly and chaotically, creatively and symbolically, intuitively and integrally remains unused. If learning is to endure, it is more likely to do so with the help of both halves of the brain – irrespective of which of the five senses a person favours for the organisation of his/her thoughts, whether he/she uses hearing or seeing, moving or a combination of several of these senses for this. Learning is for this reason about performance right from the very start:

> Scientific engagement with the child's aesthetic experience promoted the view that contact with the world occurs in ways which activate the imaginative capacity and the ability to visualise things. Contained in the child's aesthetic experience are symbolic and scenic, linguistic and gesticulatory messages and they show us something about the intrinsic side of learning, in which impressions are processed and previous experiences related. ... So whoever understands 'learning as cultural acquisition' knows that cultural acquisition can only occur in ways which themselves manage to re-release inner activity...
> (Duncker 1995:4)

Observation of children has taught us the most important basis for our teaching: they learn instinctively in a way which is best for them. They are highly specialised in processing what is new in the most appropriate way: they tirelessly imitate; they sing and dance; they paint; they think up and tell stories; they research matters without preconceptions and inhibitions. Such activities can be reclaimed for teaching – even (and perhaps especially) with adolescents and adults.

Every natural language uses the most elementary human reference system – it refers to the five senses in its figures of speech and metaphors: so one talks of 'bitter experience', envisages a 'dazzling future' and the 'dark ages', one takes care of 'pressing matters' or a 'hefty bill'. An approach we frequently use is to take the five senses and use them as a basis for teaching. One of the most exciting outcomes is providing opportunities for each pupil to find for him/herself a suitable in-road into the structure of language. Language then becomes:

sound	picture
movement	analytical sculpture
music	scene
body language	language through gesture

We have grown accustomed in preparing for a teaching unit to ask questions of a text related to the senses, such as:

- What special sound qualities do I find? What kind of music/what kind of rhythm does this text have?
- What activities/which verbs do I find in the text?
- Which of the five sensory areas are appealed to in this text?
- What scenes are contained in it? Which can I develop from the existing verbs, nouns, sentences, images?
- Which materials are being talked about? Which do I associate with the theme?

When we start preparing for a lesson there is no rejection of any suggestions. At this stage, every spontaneous thought is permitted and welcomed, however remote it may seem. Of course the same attitude is useful when you begin work with pupils. Only later do we select ideas which have turned out to be suitable in order to develop the work further through other activities:

- scenes;
- plays;
- team activities;
- creative writing;
- other forms of active presentation and teaching;
- pictures and sculptures;
- rhythms.

These ideas can best be illustrated with a specific example. For this we propose to use a German-language text which formed the basis of a cabaret theatre evening on which pupils from an 'East German' and a 'West German' school collaborated. The extract is reproduced here in translation. The ideas presented are not intended to be used exclusively with one particular age range or specific language level. We believe that at every level of learning some of the ideas can be used; this tends to be the case if one views text as material for performance and not just as content to be analysed. Readers who do not understand a word of German can imagine themselves hearing the text in German and will find themselves at the same starting point as those beginning a new foreign language in what follows. They can, so to speak, experiment on themselves with our ideas. The text is by Salli Sallmann:

Wissen Sie, daß mir Ausländer manchmal unheimlich vorkommen, nur so, vom Ansehen her?
Nein, bitte, vermuten Sie nun keinen versteckten Rassismus – es geht um einen Schinkentoast und noch unerforschte Kräfte. An einem meiner zahlreichen freien Nachmittage trat ich durch eine sich recht großzügig bewegende Schwingtür in ein Lokal und stellte fest, daß leider alle Tische besetzt waren. Da ich ein scheuer Mensch bin, setze ich mich ungern zu anderen. Zu irgendeiner Konversation ist man immer genötigt, zu einer negativen oder positiven, zu einer mit Worten oder einer ohne Worte, zu einer mit Blicken dieser oder jener Art.
Ich lief also auf und ab zwischen den Sitznischen und suchte nach einer Möglichkeit, alleine zu essen, und mit diesem Auf- and Ab-gelaufe stieg auch mein Appetit auf einen kleinen Happen. Da bekam ich von einem Inder mit weißem Turban, der solo in einer der Nischen an einem Vierertische saß, in Zeichensprache die unmißverständliche Aufforderung, bei ihm Platz zu nehmen. Innerlich zögerte ich, aus obengenannten Gründen, konnte aber schließlich das Angebot des Fremden nicht ablehnen, weil es einerseits so offensiv deutlich vorgetragen wurde und andererseits mein Appetit zu Hunger angeschwollen war. Ich lächelte also und setzte mich zu dem Herrn.[2]

(Do you know that foreigners often strike me as unnerving, only in their appearance that is?
No, before you start, please don't suspect that there's any veiled racism – it's about a ham and cheese toasty and as yet unresearched forces. On one of my countless free afternoons I walked into a restaurant through a set of liberally flapping swing doors and saw that unfortunately all the tables were already full. As I'm a retiring person, I dislike having to sit with other people. One is always compelled to hold some kind of conversation, negative or positive, verbal or non-verbal, one with glances of this or that kind.
So I walked up and down between the seating areas and looked for somewhere to eat alone, and with all this toing and froing my appetite grew to hunger. Then, from an Indian wearing a white turban who was sitting alone in one of the seating areas at a table for four, I got the unmistakable request in sign language to join him. I hesitated inwardly for the reasons given

[2] (Michael) Salli Sallmann: Nix Besonderes. Dirk Nishen Verlag, Berlin, 1983. Mit freundlicher Genehmigung des Autors.

> but could not in the end however reject the stranger's offer, as, on the one hand, it would clearly have come across as so offensive and, on the other, my hunger had turned to ravenousness. So, I smiled and joined the gentleman.)
> (Sallman, 1983 – with special permission of the author)

The first questions we pose are: 'Which sounds do I find? What music/what rhythm does the text have?' To establish the answers, we read the text aloud to the pupils several times over and ask each one to remember as precisely as possible at least three or four sounds/syllables/words – according to the sound – and then reproduce them in a small group. There, the group members teach each other the chosen sounds as precisely as possible and then perform this sound composition before the class – as a choir, as a concert with several vocalists with solo voices, etc.[3]

When we resume reading, we gather together first of all syllables and words (not all of them by any means) without applying any grammatical logic. At the beginning, no one has to observe the correct syllable division rules and so there is the opportunity to play around with the special features of German syllable division.

Prefixes	. . . ei . . .	. . . ie . . .	. . . er . . .	. . . ch . . .	Other
un	nein	sie	jener	ich	ung
vor	kein	nie	dieser	sich	län
an	mein	lief	der	lich	wiss
be	klein	schließ	her	nicht	bitt
ge	heim		gern	mich	manch
auf	reich		ner		rass
ab	leid		mer		heim
über	lein		ger		mut
aus			Herr		forsch

[3] Waldorf pedagogy after Rudolf Steiner has been working for decades on children learning by heart entire texts and stories in the foreign language, without them reading a line, without them understanding a word, without them understanding the language. So, the formation of the neuron networks is shaped through hearing. Later this is considerably reviewed by the learning of language meaning and the ability to speak.

Here the syllables are arranged simply according to their auditory value. (It will be noticed that an element of grammar has crept in – prefixes; they have such a clear sound value that it is tempting to include them as a category.) In this way, a really limitless variety of sound patterns can be constructed:

wiss – nur – nein	– sen – so – bitt – ei
– un – nei – groß	– zü – ner – der – ze
– lei – setz – nar – je	– ten – in – ner – sie

These are only a fraction of the possibilities. It is not the intention to include them all. This 'meaningless' conglomeration of sound-bites contains some meaning in that because it is spoken out loud, suddenly the quite special 'German' character, the sound – 'the music' of the German language – reveals itself. Now the pupils continue to develop other activities: they make up rhymes, rhythms; they combine together 'the unspeakable'; they sing the syllable sequences, etc.

This focus on sound is particularly appropriate for reading German. In her article 'Lesen und Lauschen', Margit Frenk (1991) shows the historical development of the exclusively auditory character of reading up to the dominance of the visual.[4] It is a strong encouragement to trust in hearing. As 'The Great Dictator' Hynkel, Charlie Chaplin does a brilliant pastiche on the sound of 'German' words in a demagogic speech in which the sounds are randomly arranged. In the middle section particularly of the speech, without knowing a word of German, he manages to make the sound 'authentic'. He uses lots of 'ü' and 'schtr' syllables.

For the second activity based on the second excerpt of text (from 'So, I walked up and down' to 'joined the gentleman') a basic knowledge of the German language is necessary because pupils have to differentiate between verbs and other types of words. They are asked to create a list of which activities/which verbs they recognise in the text. This list of words is then altered slightly to create an appropriate sequence. An object is chosen as an additional prop and already a 'story' begins to emerge. Of course, this is only one of the many possible stories – so each group of pupils can invent a completely self-made story perhaps using a different object. The players perform the relevant actions and when doing so they describe what they are doing. Thus, activity and the word sound/meaning are made to refer to each other and linked through the senses. Here is an example of a story invented in this way involving an apple:

[4] In Lettre Internation, German edition, volume 14, 111, quarterly 1991, p. 76ff.

Verb	Pupil's words	Pupil's actions
'to walk'	'I walk up and down.'	pupil moves round the room
'to look for'	'I'm looking for something to eat.'	pupil looks around
'to climb'	'I climb on a chair/table.'	
'to get'	'I get an apple.'	
'to refuse'	'I can't refuse it.'	
'to hesitate'	'I hesitate in eating it.'	
'to carry'	'I am carrying it around the room for a bit.'	
'to eat'	'I eat it.'	
'to grow'	'My stomach grows.'	
'to smile'	'I smile.'	
'to sit'	'I sit down.'	

With such performances in the class and in the groups who already know each other, we attach great importance to dispensing completely with corrections, judging whether what they have said is 'right' and 'wrong'. Every reference to a pronunciation or grammar error ('That's kilometer, not kilometer!') draws attention above all to the mistake, not the correct form. It is always only the teacher's example which acts as a guide to the correct grammar and pronunciation. In this way, knowledge and perception are extended. The experience of exemplary and non-corrective teaching has proved itself in practice in the widest variety of subjects, and is not restricted to foreign language teaching (Birkenbihl 1992).

Often the various groups hold little competitions to see whose story is the more original. The most important thing is that they play – and that they reinforce the words through the senses: they move and speak at the same time; they listen and watch simultaneously; they read and listen at the same time. In addition, of course, a 'commentator' can describe the action: 'Mr X walks up and down', or the spectators guess what he is doing. It then becomes a kind of charades.

A broader content-based approach to the text is illustrated by our third example based on a different extract.

> Und sofort trat jene Situation ein, die den Aufenthalt in Restaurants für mich so unangenehm macht: Immerzu muß man sich anblicken, obwohl man eigentlich nur speisen will.
> Ich sage es im voraus: Zwischen mir und dem Fremden fiel kein einziges Wort.
> Er beobachtete mich unter seinem Turban hervor, so daß ich nach Sekunden sturen Starrens meine Augen zu den benachbarten Tischen schweifen lassen mußte.
> Danach kam es zu einer kleinen Zwangspause. Er betrachtete mich intensiv, ohne auch nur einmal den Kopf in geringster Weise zu bewegen. Eigenartig.
> Mein Unbehagen wuchs.

> (And immediately that situation occurred which makes being in a restaurant so difficult for me: one has to constantly observe oneself, although one really only wants to eat.
> I'll say it now: not a single word passed between me and the stranger.
> He watched me from under his turban, so that after seconds of concerted staring I had to avert my eyes to the neighbouring table.
> Then it came to a short interval. He watched me intensely, without even moving his head in the slightest. Odd.
> My discomfort grew.)

What sense is being appealed to here? The visual, of course. The following terms concerned with the visual appear in the text: to observe oneself, to stare, to avert one's eyes, to watch intensely. The exercise for the participants then is to act with the eyes. What possibilities are there for doing this? Just a small extract acts as an initial inspiration for activities like the following:

- small scenes where a situation only changes through different looks – two people approach each other with lowered eyes/eye to eye/one has lowered his/her eyes, the other fixes his/her gaze; on meeting the looks alter. The spectators interpret what these looks tell in a story;
- small games using the eyes: in turn one of two players leads the other with his/her eyes;
- sayings which are connected with eyes/looking;
- enacting different ways of looking – or performing them and getting the audience to guess: 'gaping, goggling, blinking, rolling the eyes ...'.

There are other possibilities for working with the content of the passage, and the following example has the more specific objective of sharpening cultural awareness. It is widely accepted that it is not possible just to teach a foreign language – something of the foreign culture must always be mediated. This is true even in the cases of teachers who have not set foot in the country of origin of the language they are teaching. And the knowledge of the foreign culture – whether intended or not – makes one's own culture into just one model of living amongst many. So in the course of time, the confusion of culturally mediated norms dissolves into 'natural' behaviour. However, to do this also requires preconditions.[5]

[5] Ulrike Friedrichs (1995) describes how teachers at museums in Hamburg at the Museum for Ethnology practise the games of the American Navy Personnel Research and Development Center. See also Heathcote and Bolton in this volume with similar methods.

Perhaps it is a truism: cultural awareness presupposes awareness. By 'awareness' we understand the ability to perceive one's surroundings with all the senses, to arrange what is perceived into one's own construction of a sensorial context and thereby continually revise one's own assumptions and models of reality – and correct them when necessary. Associated with this idea, is the consideration of one's own culture as something foreign.

> What one discovers is not simply apprehended and perceived, but is examined and interpreted, ascertained and sounded out, compared and assessed. In this way a form of play with perspectives and viewpoints, a weighing up of what is important and what is inconsequential, a discovery of the original and the transferable emerges. (Duncker op. cit.)

We now attempt this with the situation which is described in the next excerpt of the chosen text:

> Die Kellnerin brachte die Karte.
> Eine willkommene Gelegenheit für mich, den bohrenden Blicken meines Gegenübers auszuweichen.
> Ich bestellte einen Schinkenkäsetoast und eine kleine Cola. Danach heftete ich meinen Blick auf eine verschnörkelte. Holzleiste an meinem Stuhl.
>
> (The waitress brought the menu.
> A welcome opportunity to evade the probing gazes of my companion. I ordered ham and cheese on toast and a small coke. Then I fixed my gaze on an ornate wooden strut on my chair.)

Not a pleasant situation in which the shy narrator has so far found himself – but for us it is a wonderful area. The pupils can now play around with this instruction: 'Sit down next to someone at a table ...' performing the activity in different ways:

- the way you do at home;
- in a way in which you would never do it;
- as you would do it in select company;
- as you do it in a completely foreign culture, etc.

The same 'alienation' technique lends itself to being enacted in the case of ordering a meal, handling the cutlery ... each everyday situation lends itself to being regarded as foreign, in order to discover the differences between one's own culture and the culture of the foreign country. Whether for example to an English person a German holds his fork the 'wrong way round', whether one counts change into someone's hand or onto the table, whether I use my hands a lot or not when talking – the acting and learning possibilities are infinite. The narrator of the text seems however to have fewer possibilities for learning:

> Die Blicke des Inders ruhten auf mir. Ich spürte es . . .
> Mein Selbstbewußtsein war gleich Null. Nach einigen Minuten wurde mein Genick völlig steif.
> Ich riß mich los von der Leiste und stürzte mich mit meinen Augen auf die auf dem Tisch liegenden Bierdeckel. Dann überprüfte ich den Sitz meiner Schürsenkel, anschließend widmete ich mich nochmals der Speisekarte.
> In der Spiegelung der Aluminiumzuckerdose lauerte der dunkle Blick. Dieser Fremde hatte eine starke Persönlichkeit!
> Des Inders überlegene Blicke trafen mich gnadenlos.
> Toast und Cola wurden serviert. Ich ergriff Messer und Gabel. Meine Nerven waren zum Zerreißen gespannt. Nur nicht auffallen jetzt, sagte ich mir, um Gottes willen nicht auffallen, Zähne zusammenbeißen und durch!
> Ich stach in den Schinkenkäsetoast. Nach dem dritten Bissen versuchte ich einen Kontrollblick, wurde aber abgeschmettert.
>
> (The Indian's glance came to rest on me. I felt it . . .
> My self-confidence was at rock-bottom. After a few minutes my neck was completely stiff. I tore my eyes away from the strut and my eyes fell upon the beer mat lying on the table. Then I checked my shoelaces and next I turned my attention to the menu again.
> The gaze settled in the reflection on the aluminium sugar container. This stranger had a powerful personality!
> The Indian's superior glances caught me mercilessly.
> Toasty and coke were served. I grabbed the knife and fork. My nerves were at their elastic limit. I mustn't be conspicuous I said to myself, for God's sake I mustn't be conspicuous, teeth clenched and pull through!
> I stabbed at the ham and cheese toasty. After the third bite I attempted to compose myself but was floored.)

'Classical' vocabulary exercises do not command a great deal of popularity amongst pupils. Teachers and above all pupils have introduced us to other alternatives. We do work with the content, but we do not use it simply to ask analytic questions of the extract ('What is the theme of the text?'), but we play with other meanings, for example, whether the objects which appear in the text allow themselves to be characterised by the pupils. Then they begin to speak as these objects – 'I am a menu. I know all the prices and dishes in this restaurant. I am immune to grease spots because I am wrapped in a plastic cover. Sometimes, when the restaurant is empty, I get bored to death. Then I wish I were a hymn book in church . . .' The actors try to move like the objects would. ('How on earth does a menu move?' – 'What qualities do you notice about it?' – 'Well, it's rigid.' – 'Try moving rigidly. What else do you notice about the menu?' – 'It's flat.' – 'What kind of movement do you get, when you make yourself flat? Move the menu around, throw it. How does it move in flight?' – 'In a zig-zag.' – 'How can you imitate this movement?' etc.). The objects encounter each other. We wept with laughter at a love scene involving a shoelace and a menu, which are constantly interrupted by the aluminium sugar container. Afterwards, the actors can write an object description in the foreign language without the slightest difficulty – this activity is traditionally one of the most despised in the language lesson.

Of course, charades and creative writing games are appropriate here as in the following example. Small groups are formed. Each player writes down five objects which appear in the text on five notelets (an object per notelet). All the notelets are piled up without revealing what is written on them. Then every player selects five notelets again. Each person is given five minutes to invent a completely free story in which each of the five objects appear – and in some way or other they should all be connected. One can invent many more on top of that.

But what does our xenophobic restaurant-goer discover?

> Mein Gott, mein Gott, sagte ich mir und spritzte etwas Worcestersauce über den Toast, hab Erbarmen! Nur nichts anmerken lassen, nur nicht auffallen! Meine Hände zitterten ganz leicht. Wieder spritzte ich etwas Worcestersauce auf einen Happen. Die Worcestersauce ergoß sich heftig und schäumte auf. Der Schinkenkäsetoast erhob sich bis zum Tellerrand und verharrte dort, leicht schaukelnd.
> Schweiß brach mir aus. Ich hatte die Worcestersaucenflasche mit der Colaflasche verwechselt! Was tun! Was sollte ich tun?!
>
> (Oh God, oh God I said to myself and sprinkled some Worcester sauce on the toasty, have mercy! Don't let anyone notice anything, mustn't be conspicuous! My hands shook slightly. Again I sprinkled some Worcester sauce on a piece. The Worcester sauce came out in a gush and foamed up. The cheese and ham toasty slid to the edge of the plate and remained there gently rocking.

> I broke out in a sweat. I had mistaken the coke bottle for the Worcester sauce bottle! What to do! What should I do?)

The number of variants in vocabulary and speech training is limitless. This time we play with the semantic field 'wechseln' and other verbs. We invent situations with the pupils in which something is changed (gewechselt), confused (verwechselt), exchanged (ausgewechselt), in which someone changes sides (die Seiten), something changes colour (etwas die das Farbe wechselt), etc.

Now it's high time to release the tortured restaurant-goer from his awful situation:

> Ich beobachtete, wie sich der Käse allmählich vom Schinken löste, während das Weißbrot auf den Grund des Tellers sank. Mit der Gabel tauchte ich den Toast unter, schnitt ab und steckte mir das schwammige Stück in den Mund. Die Kellnerin schüttelte den Kopf und sagte: „Der schöne Toast!"
> Um das Gesicht zu wahren, stammelte ich: „So schmeckt's auch."
> Der unheimliche Tischgenosse betrachtete mich weiter gnadenlos. Ein Grinsen war in seine Mundwinkel gestiegen. Hypnose! An den Nachbartischen war mein Mißgeschick nicht unbemerkt geblieben. Zwei Frauen kicherten.
> Aufgelöst grüßte ich zu ihnen hinüber, legte einen Zehnmarkschein neben Teller, rannte hinaus und flüchtete in die Volkshochschule, wo ich abendliche Kurse besuche.

> I watched the cheese gradually slide off the ham as the white bread sank into the base of the plate.
> I dived into the toast with my fork, cut some off and put the stodgy lump in my mouth. The waitress shook her head and said: 'The lovely toast!'
> To save face I said: 'It tastes great like this.'
> My strange companion carried on observing me without respite. A smile had begun to curl the corners of his mouth. Hypnosis! My mishap hadn't gone unnoticed on the neighbouring table. Two women giggled.
> Disconcerted, I nodded over to them, put a ten Mark note next to the plate, fled and sought refuge in the night school where I attended evening classes.

At last! He has escaped the restaurant without having to cross words with the Indian. But at what a cost! Nevertheless, the unfortunate man before his departure has presented us with a great opportunity to address the idea of 'lying through our teeth' with our pupils. 'Having to lie' could be the title of the theme which the last excerpt harbours. Or: 'What ways are there of getting out of a room?'

There are a few options which still remain to be added to what we can do with the text as a whole:

- retelling;
- the characters speak their thoughts out loud while they act;
- the players show different ways in which the scene could end; they develop different denouements through play;
- the characters speak using indirect speech;
- the scene is acted out with an altered cast: a man and a woman at a table or instead of the Indian a disabled person sits there – how does the situation change in both cases? And what do we learn in the process about our own culture/about the foreign culture/about the images we have in our own heads?
- the pupils create realistic/expressionistic set designs for this situation – and give the colours, the objects in them;
- they paint pictures and make sculptures which depict situations from the text – and then present their own work;
- they produce the music for the scene – and learn in the process the necessary terminology; they set the scene to opera;
- the class cooks a meal and casts the roles in the restaurant, etc.

In our experience the pupils are the best collaborators in a performance-based learning environment. They even find and devise exercises and games themselves, research situations and texts. Each pupil is an unbeatable specialist in his/her own way of learning, as Neuro-Linguistic Programming suggests (Bandler 1990). The role of the teacher is to facilitate the different levels of entry and be attentive to what pupils have to offer. Experience has shown that at the beginning this presents some difficulties because it is so different to anything we have ever done before in teaching. Later on however this additional work more than pays off.

Now – in contrast to our opening assertions something resembling a list of activities has been suggested. However, more important than the practical recommendation is recognition of the basic principle which understands teaching and learning as a reciprocal process of enrichment and astonishment; that is what we have hoped to achieve. Friedrich Hölderlin (1970:174) offers a very beautiful description for the passion which we encountered again and again in our work in the most different people:

> Each man to his own trade, you may say, and I too say so. Only he must toil with his very soul, he must not quell every force

within him which does not exactly befit his station, must not with this meagre fear be literally hypocritically that which it entitles him, he must be what he is in earnest, with love, so that there be spirit in his toil, and should he be pigeonholed so that even his spirit may not thrive, then he must refuse it with contempt and learn, may he learn to plough!

10 Intercultural theatre through a foreign language

Prisca Schmidt

Introduction

This chapter describes an experiment in intercultural theatre carried out for over a decade in a multiracial and disadvantaged suburb of Paris. It involves creating, writing and producing a play in English and other languages by a British theatre director, a French teacher of English and her students from many cultural origins who live in this underprivileged district. The ultimate challenge is to present the play to parents and the general public in a local theatre, and thereby to develop intercultural understanding. It may seem, on the surface, that theatre is not the obvious means to help people from different ethnic backgrounds understand one another, as it is the product of a particular culture and usually associated with a specific language and text. However, the value of theatre in establishing human relationships beyond the boundaries of languages becomes evident particularly in the research of Peter Brook (1968, 1988) and Patrice Pavis (1990), which emphasises the complexity of the factors that come into play in any cultural exchange and the difficulty of theorising about them, suggesting that intercultural theatre has a significant role to play. Intercultural theatre is always a challenge, but doing theatre in a foreign language is even more so in underprivileged areas, insofar as it seems to increase difficulties in communication. Furthermore, the research in intercultural theatre through a foreign language analysed in this study brings in a further complication by playing on and integrating into its artistic design the various languages and cultures of its participants. To the layman, it sounds like Babel and yet it attracts hundreds of young people and families to the theatre every season. In 1994, in three nights, over a thousand spectators attended a play performed in a foreign language (English) and various other languages, in the suburb of Saint-Denis, notorious for its roughness. The play was also performed in Glasgow where it was very well received. The project brings together a British professional theatre director, a French teacher of English and French students of different ethnic backgrounds.

Preliminary remarks

It is necessary to clarify initially a series of possible misunderstandings and ambiguities arising from the unusual character of this theatrical experiment in an attempt to define the work in a more precise way. It is often taken for granted that theatre should be practised in one's own language and it is therefore often assumed that the theatre workshop in English is a new method of teaching the language through theatre. Yet the aim is primarily artistic, and the English teacher does not, initially, correct either the grammatical or pronunciation mistakes made by students, unless they block the natural flow of communication with the theatre director, who is English. It is true that the students will improve their command of English but this is a by-product and not the primary aim. However, the fluency with which the students speak in the final production impresses the audiences so much that it is seen as an outstanding approach to the learning of a foreign language. The result is indeed remarkable, but it is the medium of theatre that puts students at ease with their body and their language since the latter is connected with the sensations and the emotions.

The point is not to promote a particular language. In this case, the English theatre director, when visiting the Saint-Denis high school and being asked by students to teach them the art of theatre, took up the challenge of running a theatre workshop in her own language with young people in a deprived area. It did not cross their minds that theatre had to be in any one particular language, maybe because they themselves came from different cultural backgrounds and also because their longing for a theatrical activity was stronger than any linguistic barrier. They had been doing drama in English language classes and this had given some of them enough confidence to learn theatre and perform in front of an audience, but they had experienced drama as a pedagogical tool as demonstrated in other chapters of this volume (Bolton, Heathcote, Fleming), whereas the aim of theatre is first and foremost artistic.

Although curing social problems in a 'concrete jungle' is not the goal of the experiment, the dire social circumstances in which the students live cannot be ignored. Therefore the social aspect is integrated into the artistic activity. What matters is the mediating role theatre can take between individuals, irrespective of whether they are poor or rich. It is where different people meet either through their personal artistic development and/or through the themes of the play. In a deprived district there is no denying that students have difficulties with the official language that is taught at school, because it is the language of study. It is almost a second language even for the underprivileged native speakers of French and constitutes a barrier because it is linked to the Establishment. Yet a number of pupils who fail not only in French but also in other subjects which rely on the standard national language, are able to enjoy success thanks to theatre in a foreign language. However, this is not the primary aim of the project and should be seen as a bonus not the main purpose.

The multicultural aspect included in the plays is another significant point. As one pupil from Chile once remarked, 'we are all equal before the English language in the theatre workshop'. Feeling equal allows the students to reveal their own languages and cultures, as a means of expressing themselves. It is an opportunity they never have in the French educational system, but then the experiment touches on a highly controversial subject. Many French people fear that if one lets the children of immigrants use the languages and cultures of their parents within the context of the school, it might weaken the official language and the homogeneity of the host country. However, the preoccupation in the workshop is theatre and the participants are encouraged to express their feelings and their imagination genuinely, otherwise artificiality creeps in. Furthermore, the fear of a threat to national unity is ill-founded as far as theatre is concerned, since it is a means both of integrating and of enriching the various cultures. The danger lies rather with immigrant students who, having been unable to connect with the French culture and language taught at school and having been rejected consequently by the French school system, fall back on their own cultures and hang about in the streets with immigrant friends. There is no fear of weakening the French language through intercultural theatre.

The previous remarks will help to explain how the complexity of research into intercultural theatre through a foreign language is a result of the interplay of three broad domains: psychology, sociology and anthropology. These different aspects are moulded through art, and it is the art form that gives them sense and value. As the basic aim of the workshop is theatre, the French Ministry of Culture has acknowledged the work since 1986 and has given its support to the experiment.

Approaching intercultural theatre through a foreign language

The first stage of the argument to be made here is to show first that there are universal elements in theatre training which can be understood by all regardless of nationality, and secondly how intercultural theatre draws on those elements. In a second stage it will become clear how a play in a foreign language can be developed from nonverbal theatre which simultaneously reflects a foreign country and yet is rooted in the students' lives.

Theatre can render abstract elements of a culture visual by using concrete means. Since Artaud, a certain type of theatre has looked to the four corners of the world for new theatrical influences not dependent on texts. Barthes has argued that 'le théâtre est une véritable polyphonie informationnelle' (1964:258). It was in this context that Peter Brook started his experimental theatre group in Paris in 1971, with actors of different cultural origins. These actors had to confront each other with the cultural stereotypes which emerged initially from their improvisations and which constitute the superficial layer of a culture before discovering a new cultural truth and new cultural links. Brook's (1988) quest for a universal theatrical language arising from what he calls 'the Culture of Links' has inspired Ruth Handlen's experimental youth theatre workshop based on a foreign language in a multiracial community.

In 1991 Brook addressed actors and teachers of a new examination in theatre studies, similar to A-level theatre studies in England, and told them that what blocked people most today was the word, that therefore one must not start with the word, with ideas, but that freeing the body was the first step. How even more valid this statement is when dealing with a multicultural workshop through a foreign language! One can imagine the inadequacy of starting with the text of a play by Shakespeare, for instance. It is obvious that one needs to work through improvisations in order to make the students establish relationships with one another and become aware of the body's resources. Initially, games and rhythm exercises are a prerequisite, not only because they are basic to group dynamics and to acting, but also because music and dance depend on rhythm and movement and are a universal means of communicating. Thus some students will teach a dance from their country or a song which will often be used later as a warming up exercise to bring the group together or to train their voices, as Brook does according to John Heilpern's account (1977:94). This is also a natural process of learning to value other cultures and of enriching one's own, through the joy given and shared in singing and dancing together. Westerners have been brought up on the written word whereas Africans rely on oracy, that is, story-telling and songs and dances which are ways of expressing the culture; because they are freer with their bodies and their voices, this spontaneous approach to literature can infuse some vitality into text-dominated European cultures. Therefore a physical approach unblocks those students who feel the weight of self-consciousness in French, the standard national language, and gives confidence to both native and immigrant students, especially as the common language spoken in the theatre workshop (English) is foreign to all.

The first step is to explore the signs of communication that are specific to theatre and to encourage nonverbal expression. Working in English makes it easier, precisely because the students are not very proficient in English. So body language becomes a means of surviving in the workshop along with a host of other practical ways of communicating that emerge through want of words in the improvisations. Movements, space, objects, images, etc. are used to convey meaning. The student experiences how a banal object (a bamboo cane) can become many things (an oar, a horsewhip, an arrow, a conductor's baton, a drumstick, a magic wand, etc.) according to the imaginative way he/she or the other participant handles it; and he/she realises he/she can create meaningful images from plain matter, such as a piece of material in *Conference of the Birds* (directed by Peter Brook at the Avignon Festival in July 1979) where it is made to move and look like a flying bird, or in *Mahabharata* (directed by Peter Brook at the Avignon Festival in July 1985) where the actress holds it against her breast like a suckling baby. There are visual ways of talking to one another which are exciting because they awaken our creative instincts, and that is where the magic of theatre beyond languages lies.

Since the very tune of the English tongue is alien to most participants in the project, conversing through sounds and improvising in nonsense language does not strike them as strange, but rather as a stimulating way of exploring the texture of languages. It also encourages those who possess another language to practise it unashamedly. Moreover, unfamiliar sounds like for example the English *th* or the French *r* are combined with similarly unfamiliar gestures, even more unusual when they reflect a non-European culture. Playing with partners from different countries makes students realise that there are different and very interesting ways of expressing oneself through a gesture and a sound. They are well aware that it cannot be just any movement or any noise, in as much as it has to carry a meaning for the building up of a scene together. This experience enlarges their range and acting skills. Furthermore, creating images together through nonverbal communication allows the participants to reach the essence of human relationships and understanding through a genuine act of theatre, leaving behind stereotypes and prejudices, hackneyed words and ham acting. There is no doubt that intercultural theatre widens the imagination and develops the creative powers of people; it is also a splendid process to establish true and joyful human relationships.

So the use of the English language might appear to be a technique to bring out the innate creative dramatic qualities of the students. It functions, as some professional actors who work with Ruth Handlen say, as a 'mask'. In other words, it seems that one dare express things one might not have dared to say in the official language. Whilst improvising on *As you like it*, I asked my group of young people to explore and then express feelings of both love and rejection, and it was clear that uttering such sensitive emotions through a foreign language helped them find a degree of sincerity that would probably have been impossible in their native language. It was a means of overcoming embarrassment. With a few simple words charged with emotion they were able to convey love and rejection. They feel it is not quite them, but at the same time it is them, just as the mask reveals some deep truth in the personality of the person wearing it, even though the actor may have the feeling of being concealed behind it. Acting in a foreign language is a journey into the unknown which precludes self-indulgence as one is deprived of one's landmarks, and yet it provides one with the freedom of daring to be oneself.

However, when the word eventually emerges, it is spoken out of necessity and it is absolutely right. The process is similar to giving birth. The word is rooted in the body and at the same time steeped in the situation. It sounds like a cry and will remain printed in the memory, as it is loaded with effort and feelings. Viewed in this light, it is easier to grasp what makes the utterances in a foreign language on stage so forceful and to understand how far from a standard exercise in translating into English this work is, and also how far from interpreting a standard English play the experiment is. Through the medium of theatre the process is a creative one. What Brook says on this subject is illuminating:

> A word does not start as a word – it is an end product which begins as an impulse, stimulated by attitude and behaviour which dictates the need for expression. (1968:15)

Creating an intercultural play

So the development of artistic expression in the intercultural workshop is based at the beginning mainly but not exclusively on nonverbal language, as it will lead to the creation of a play spoken mainly in English and also integrating other languages. The argument will be illus- trated by reference to a show entitled *Fragments of Clay*, from 1994.

What makes the project especially valuable is that the play is created from improvisations in English and other languages around themes that have been chosen and discussed by all. *Fragments of Clay* explored social issues such as unemployment, the homeless, the gap between the rich and the poor and 'the System' which destroys the individual, because these were the preoccupations of the students of that year. They bring the raw material which is full of energy and challenging matter to the making of the play, and this is where part of their French contribution lies. Theatre in a foreign language highlights the importance of letting young people express their anxieties and of giving their frustration a voice, since their impatience with society is channelled into creativity and they 'hold the mirror up to nature'.

The participants are then advised to read an English play where similar issues are dramatised in order to have a solid structure from which to create their own play. Very often the model is Shakespeare, but not always. In this case, it was Shaw's *Pygmalion*. The idea is to adapt those themes to the present so that they bear some relation to what the students want to say about their lives and the world. The play is thus steeped in their circumstances but at the same time connected with wider universal issues. By setting the action in a British context, it helps to distance the actors and the spectators from burning issues, whilst at the same time heightening awareness of the problems. There are echoes of Brecht's *alienation* and Diderot's *paradox of the actor*. It allows students to convey to and share their themes poignantly with the local population and, when played in Britain, with a Scottish audience. The English setting broadens the drama for a French audience and the native flavour of the French actor adds a wider dimension too for British people. It reflects the European scene and the intercultural play *Fragments of Clay* was as warmly applauded in the suburbs of Paris as in the suburbs of Glasgow.

However, transposing the action into a foreign context requires a careful investigation of the country's way of life. Theatre is illusion but not deception, and the eye of the foreign theatre director ensures the accuracy of the setting. For instance, an equivalent to the French '*J'ai faim*' written on a card held by someone begging in the street had to be found for the tableau on the homeless; the make and the actual packet of cigarettes that the housewife of the poor family smoked had to be correct; and the students discovered through theatre that a typical British working-class family is more likely to drink beer than wine. Thus the props provide another insight into the daily life of a foreign country and these cultural aspects must not be overlooked because they can otherwise cause offence. The same research was carried out on clothes.

It is not often so easy to transpose elements of one culture into another, because the history of a country and its traditions have moulded it so deeply that it becomes necessary to look for the essence of the set rather than for its direct translation. In another play, *Thank you, Charlie*, the director had to suggest a fish and chip bar to the students who wanted to convey the idea of a seedy French café. This was foreign to them, but they learnt in a concrete way what it was like through creating the decor and, whilst showing their play in Glasgow, they were excited to have a first hand experience. 'Living theatre' became living reality.

The work is monitored and structured by a British professional theatre director, Ruth Handlen, who is well versed in the literature of her country and who is infused with English culture. Indeed it is essential that the artistic mediator possesses those assets. Although what is described here is a privileged situation, one should nevertheless aim for the highest degree of quality in intercultural theatre. It is a marriage of two minds, as the British cultural heritage is conveyed to the students and infused into their play. The contribution to French theatre is a mixture of styles, with the introduction of comic scenes to lighten the atmosphere and also songs and dances in accordance with the British theatre tradition. The 'cocktail' is well received on both sides of the Channel, which proves how relevant variety of tones is to intercultural theatre. However, the handling of cultural links is a delicate process and one should bear in mind that the success of this intercultural research is partly due to the training of the theatre director at the international mime, movement and theatre school of Jacques Lecoq in Paris, and to her distancing herself from her own culture by living in France. These are vital elements contributing to the quality of intercultural theatre work.

With respect to the contribution from French culture, there are on the one hand, the students who speak French, even if some of them are not perfect, who are taught French culture at school, and who live in a French environment. On the other hand, there is the French mediator who, being a teacher of English, has some grasp of English culture and is well acquainted with French attitudes and backgrounds. However even within this ideal framework, there are limits to cultural understanding. Zarate (1986:27–32) asserts that it is impossible to master a whole culture in so far as we are bound to miss references and content because we cannot but filter experience through our own heritage. She argues that we need to distance ourselves from our own culture too, and that even so we still cannot perceive it objectively. Yet, acknowledging those limits, it can be argued that the British theatre director and the French teacher of English can rightly be called 'cultural mediators' and viewed as essential links between two cultures. The combination of three different elements – a 'displaced' British professional artist, a

French teacher of English trained in the mould of the official culture, and tough French students who are also 'displaced' – represents an exciting intercultural challenge.

Ensuring intercultural exchange

The research is founded on a genuine intercultural exchange which is quite unique. As Pavis points out (1990:196), in the *Mahabharata* Brook captures the spirit of the legend magnificently, yet the Indian culture is sifted through several filters: the different translations (French and English), the English culture of the theatre director, Brook himself, the French language, since the play was created in French, and the various cultures of the actors. On the other hand, in this theatre workshop both cultures permeate each other: the language is English, the theatre director is British and can check the authenticity of the setting, of the characters and of the dialogue as she writes the play from the recordings of the students' improvisations in English, but the themes come from the students and it is their story. The subtle balance between the different influences is best exemplified through the creation of the characters as there are no tailor-made roles and the artist cuts the cloth in accordance with what the students propose. Thus every actor is shown to advantage. As for the language, the theatre director works on the script in a similar manner, using the words of the students themselves, re-arranging, correcting, adapting them to the rhythm of the English language. The inter-penetration of cultural elements is a striking feature of this theatrical experiment.

The artistic design is however the most important part of research whose core is the creative process. One needs to refer to a good model to build a play from improvisations, otherwise one might produce a poor show. The starting point of *Fragments of Clay* was the Greek myth, and each student was asked to mould a piece of clay to create some shape in order not to begin with intellectual ideas about moulding a human being and to release their creative powers. It is often a fault of teaching to ignore the plastic approach to foreign languages in particular. Furthermore, exploring the theme physically and aesthetically is conducive to sensitive and imaginative improvisation. In this case the students fed their plastic discovery of their major theme, the moulding of the individual in today's society, into improvisations in which the individual was totally transformed, and this creative process gave rise to very powerful images. Thus ideas are explored from a physical basis and translated into visual theatre.

The moulding of the individual mentioned above became the drilling of a young girl by the business world which was made visual by a squad of people marching up and down the stage to the sound of the drum. Whenever the girl attempted to enter the faceless group and failed and fell, the blind squad marched on over her body till eventually she fell into rhythm with them. The image was made even more powerful through the use of sound effect: the beating of a bongo drum from the wings by a West Indian boy. Images often have a stronger emotional impact than speech since words often fail to evoke our deepest feelings. Referring to Brook again, a visual image can be much more expressive than a whole speech. Rhythm and music too affect our sensitivity and are powerful artistic means that must be taken into account in the making of an intercultural play.

However, one needs a supportive frame for the building of characters around a theme from improvisations and in this case dealing with the moulding of an individual, the obvious dramatic model that came to mind was, as mentioned earlier, *Pygmalion*. The story can then follow a solid dramatic pattern within which there is a large amount of freedom to devise a modern adaptation even to the extent of creating extra characters. Nevertheless the students express their own feelings and are themselves within the framework, and the theatre director ensures the aesthetic quality of the scenes.

In the same way the diverse cultural elements are integrated into the overall artistic pattern in an organic fashion. Intercultural theatre through a foreign language helps students from ethnic minorities to rise above the local community, connect with the world at large and find a fulfilment in creating an *alter ego*, like the West Indian boy from Guadeloupe, a street musician in the play, who decided that he would be a Jamaican in Great Britain. Many typical elements from those cultures can be woven into the play to enliven it, provided they are not used just as folklore. In fact, such aspects as dancing and singing must be an integral part of a character and contribute to the action. Consider, for example, a scene whose aim was to expose the shortcomings of European upbringing. A student from Madagascar who played the modern Mrs Pierce was able in her role to teach the son of the rich family where she was employed how to perform a dance from her own country in order to approach the girl he fancied. By contrast, the future heir, who was dominated by his mother and inhibited by his education, was lamely imitating her. Furthermore, the secure mask granted by theatre and the foreign language relieves such students from Western constraints so that they bring a spirit of joy on stage, and even give vent to humorous criticism of their own kind. Thus, the Malgache girl and the West Indian boy who both loved singing and dancing acknowledged each other immediately when they met as brother and sister from

Jamaica, establishing a wonderful complicity in an improvisation that was integrated into the show; and the scene developed into comedy as the 'so-called' sister relished debunking the flirtatiousness and fickleness of West Indian boys. When they are freed from the official language and feel they are appreciated, immigrant students can provide rich elements for a play, being heir to traditions that are still alive, when ours are dying from materialism.

Various languages are spoken when they epitomise a character and also in order to involve and sensitise an audience: when the Moroccan immigrant to Great Britain, a union leader, who has lost his job, addresses the public directly, he delivers his speech at first in French to the French audience and in English to the British audience in order to rouse the spectators of both countries to the plight of the unemployed, but later, on leaving the stage, the student being of Arab origin carries on railing in Arabic against the injustice of today's society to the surprise of both audiences and the particular delight of the Arab community.

The foreign theatre director together with both French and immigrant students invent a language in which the dreams of the young people are realised through theatre in a foreign language.

Conclusion

Doing theatre in a foreign language in an underprivileged area is a rich theatrical experience. It makes people take into account the culture of other countries and become conscious of their own. It makes them aware that language is not a simple tool and, having rediscovered its value, they live and actively experience it. Above all, it develops a common imaginative language which establishes an artistic understanding of the world between people of different cultures. Such an experiment could be achieved in a different country in a different language provided it were carried out by 'mediators' of both countries and by professionals. The theatre director must be 'displaced' and ideally, as is the case with Ruth Handlen's international company, there should be actors from various origins, or at least from a country where the target language is spoken. These conditions are essential for the creation of genuine intercultural theatre. Experimenting through a foreign language in this manner might even help revive an ailing theatre that is suffering at present from the ruthlessness of a system dominated by economic competition, exclusion and wars, as it seems to be attempting to re-find its humanity through 'cultural links' within and across borders, thus to reflect a changing society.

11 Culture through literature through drama

Manfred Schewe

Knowing about bare facts
involves only a small part
of one's self. (Arnaud Reid)

Artists treat facts
as stimuli for imagination,
whereas scientists
use imagination
to coordinate facts. (Koestler)

Introduction

This chapter is based on a project in German as a Foreign Language that arose out of a teacher training seminar at the University of Oldenburg/North Germany. For the purposes of this seminar my colleague (and also highly regarded teacher!) Heinz Wilms and I set out to develop a drama approach to literature that would pave the way to cultural learning. We decided to work on a novel that in our view was 'culturally rich' and thus suitable for introducing foreign students to central aspects of German culture. We did not embark on this project, however, in the naive assumption that literature can be taken as a purely factual document of a specific society at a specific time, but certainly in the belief that literature has rich potential for learning processes geared to cultural understanding – which for example Collie and Slater (1992:4) characterise as follows:

> It is true of course that the 'world' of a novel, play, or short story is a created one, yet it offers a full and vivid context in which characters from many social backgrounds can be depicted. A reader can discover their thoughts, feelings, customs, possessions; what they buy, believe in, fear, enjoy; how they speak and behave behind closed doors. This vivid imagined

> world can quickly give the foreign reader a feel for the codes and preoccupations that structure a real society. Reading the literature of a historical period is, after all, one of the ways we have to help us imagine what life was like in that other foreign territory: our own country's past.

To 'give the foreign reader a feel for ... a real society' summarises well what we tried to achieve with our project which was greatly influenced by the active participation of 10 student teachers and resulted in the production of teaching materials for the foreign language classroom (Schewe and Wilms 1995).

In this complementary chapter I will focus on some of the theoretical assumptions underlying this project, and in doing so will also raise questions of a more general nature with regard to cultural learning. In what follows I will give five selected examples of our drama approach to literature and look at the implications of our way of working. I would like to ask you, the reader, to remain patient, if I withhold information (title of novel, author, plot, etc.) for didactic reasons which I hope become obvious as we go along.

Example I

> Soon there won't be places anymore
> where people can meet.

If you know that this phrase is spoken by a character in a novel which is set in a German context and by a German author: Which concrete situation do you associate with this phrase? Could you allow yourself a few minutes – before reading on – and answer the following questions?

- Who is the speaker? To whom does s/he speak?
- Where (inside or outside? public or private place?) is this phrase spoken?
- When (year/month/day/time of day?) does s/he say these words?

Reader activity 1

Which situation sprang to your mind: A council meeting somewhere in Hamburg in 1995 in which a member of the Green Party is addressing the members of the council and warning against the increasing urbanisation of the environment? Or did possibly the time of the Weimar Republic come into your mind – Rosa Luxemburg talking to Karl

Liebknecht in some Kudamm-café in Berlin about the dangers of the rise of the National Socialists?

Probably neither of the two, for this 'decontextualised phrase' releases mental images that will vary from reader to reader. But, guided by the accompanying questions, the reader's/learner's imagination is stimulated and channelled so that s/he conjures up images which are related to her/his cultural knowledge about Germany. Admittedly this phrase 'Soon there won't be places anymore where people can meet' is a very open phrase, open in fact to the totality of German culture, past and present.

Why did we decide on such a lead-in to our novel? The answer is characteristic of our overall approach: Instead of showering the student with our teacher knowledge we initially want the student to become aware of her/his own links with the foreign culture. In what appears to be a simple lead-in exercise, the students (working in small groups) are motivated to produce images of the foreign culture which seem to be stored in some sort of 'personal image archive'. An interesting discussion can follow this exercise revolving around questions like: Did I have images to choose from in my image archive? Why is it that I opted for this image and no other? What 'cultural truth' is there in my image(s)?

These are important questions to ask in a teaching/learning context, bearing in mind the immediate connection between the acts of imagining and understanding:

> Our ability to understand depends on our ability to imagine – that is, it depends upon our ability to create or 'apply' images through which we 'grasp' meaning. (Eisner 1991:7)

If what we are trying to do in our foreign language classrooms is to further an understanding of foreign culture and give students an insight into it, we need to develop techniques, exercises and materials that involve them in imaginative reflection and make them 'see'. 'Grasping' the meaning of the phrase 'Soon there won't be places anymore where people can meet' becomes possible, if we ask and answer questions like those above and thus do what any playwright does who is writing a play and creating dramatic meaning: We build characters and let them act within certain constraints of time and space.

What I find important to note about this lead-in exercise:

- By applying the dramatic principle of withholding information and just offering a (carefully selected) phrase taken from the novel in hand, the teacher surprises the students and arouses their curiosity and interest.
- Each student produces a 'personal image' of the foreign culture.

- By sharing these personal images in class (e.g. in small groups) an interesting 'imagic variety' is on display. The student's images instead of (often banal) images from textbooks, etc. can be compared and discussed with regard to their situational/cultural appropriateness.

In our drama approach we would in fact make the students show their images to each other by using appropriate drama conventions (e.g. tableaux), thus increasing the power of the images.

What the students have presented can then be used further by the teacher. S/he can focus on the presentations that came nearest to the content of the novel and build a bridge to its socio-historical background, telling the students at this stage that they are going to read the novel *Sansibar oder der letzte Grund* which is set in Nazi Germany around the year 1936 and was written by the German author Alfred Andersch in 1957 (published by Diogenes Verlag/Zurich). Before the teacher however supplies more information in the form of a list with selected events/dates relevant to the historical background of the novel s/he asks them to answer the following questions in small groups:

Example II

What do you know about:

- Adolf Hitler?
- the National Socialists/Nazis?
- The Third Reich in Germany?
- The Second World War?

After the students have thus collected their historio-cultural knowledge, they are encouraged to compare the foreign country and their own by working similarly on the question: What happened in your country from 1933–1945? In doing this exercise the students become aware of the limitations of their own cultural knowledge, but at the same time begin to realise how much knowledge they can gather between them. Working on those questions will certainly help the student who faces the challenge of reading a literary text in the foreign language to understand better the historical and cultural context of the novel. In our project we in fact supply the students at various points with cultural background information (maps, pictures, tables of events/dates, socio-historical, biographical information) in a much more extensive form than we would envisage for students who read a literary text in their mother tongue. The more information is available to them, the easier they can see connections. If for example the students know that in 1937 an exhibition of 'Degenerate Art' took place in Germany and if they know why it took place, this will help them to deduce why this nameless shadowy character in the novel intends to confiscate a piece of art; or if they know that according to regulations issued by the Nazi government from 1938 onwards the passports of Jews were stamped with a 'J', this will help them to realise the symbolical significance of this letter when the teacher sets up and participates in a scene modelled on an extract from the novel. I will give a more detailed description of this drama exercise further below (see Example V), but first I would like you, the reader, to try out a different exercise.

Example III

You are given four short (translated) text extracts, each of which is devoted to one of the central characters in the novel *Sansibar oder der letzte Grund* by Alfred Andersch.

Read them through carefully and each time ask yourself:

- Who is this person?
- What is s/he doing?
- What is s/he thinking?

> 1.
> Knudsen, said the priest. You'll not go out until it is dark. He added: please, I'm asking you. Knudsen questioningly looked up to the priest who stood a little above him on the quay wall, a tall slim man with a severe, reddened face, with a small beard over the mouth, a black beard with grey threads woven into it. Rimless glasses were flashing in front of his eyes, flashing like crystal in the passionate face which revealed a leaning towards violent temper and formed the top of a body in black clothes which bent a little over the stick. I have to ask you to sail to Skillinge for me and take something on board with you, Helander said.
>
> 2.
> Shit, Knudsen thought, the whole thing is shit. And all of a sudden he had an idea: Once I'm out, he considered, I'll throw the thing overboard, that's the simplest, and then I'll go for the cod, and tomorrow I will return with a load of fish. Nobody will be asking me questions and I will live in peace.
>
> 3.
> She was sitting on the bed of a guest room in the 'Wappen von Wismar' and rummaging in her handbag. The suitcase stood

> beside the door and Judith had not taken off her raincoat as she wanted to go out right away. Then she looked out of the window: a tiled roof under a bright, northern, completely empty autumn sky. Judith trembled. I should have got myself a room with a front view, she thought, so I would have at least seen the harbour, could have seen whether foreign boats are there that can take me with them. If I only knew a bit more about ships, she thought, I'm afraid I can't tell a Danish or Swedish steamer from a German one.
>
> 4.
> Gregor was afraid. The comrade from Rerik still hasn't come, he thought. Either I can't rely on him or something has happened. Gregor was always afraid when he was at a meeting place. On his way from one meeting place to the next he was also afraid, but not as much as at the meeting place itself. At the meeting place itself there was always a moment at which he would have preferred to run away. I'll give him another five minutes, he thought, then I'll leave. He caught himself thinking that it would be best if he did not turn up at all. Then I'd already have carried out my last order. Finish, he thought, it must finish. I won't play along anymore.

Now, before you go on reading this chapter, speculate on whether the characters presented in the above extract belong together and what they can possibly have got to do with each other.

Reader activity 2

In class this exercise would be set up differently in that there would be one group of students for each extract. After reading their extract and answering the above questions each group of students would – on the basis of their answers to those questions – describe their character to the rest of the class. Again, this withholding of information arouses more curiosity and interest and very likely leads to a lively interaction between the groups who are keen to find out what the other characters are like and if there is any connection between them.

The basic idea of this exercise is to introduce the students to the central characters of the novel. By having them anticipate the character relationships and the dramatic action in the novel they are put in the role of authors. On other occasions in our drama-based approach to foreign language teaching the students take on the role of director, actor or audience (cf. Schewe and Shaw 1993:14–16).

Whatever character relationships and dramatic action you, the reader, may have anticipated, very probably you will have been wondering about the 'thing' which Knudsen is annoyed about and wants to throw overboard. Having worked with this exercise in various groups of learners I know that at this point all kinds of different suggestions can be expected for what the 'thing' stands for: money, a gun, a microfilm, a corpse.

This is an ideal moment for the teacher to lift the secret and show the students a picture of – a part of – 'the thing' and tell them that it is a wooden sculpture.

The students are now asked to do the following which you, the reader, could try out as well:

Example IV

Study the head on the photocopy carefully. Touch it, following its lines and parts. What strikes you? Which of these lines and parts are important? Try to draw the face/head.

Reader activity 3

It is only after this creative exercise that the students are given a first short extract from the novel and are asked to read it. In this extract Alfred Andersch describes the sculpture in minute detail, i.e. through the eyes of one of the main characters. While Gregor, a communist functionary, is waiting for his party comrade Knudsen in a church where their secret meeting is to take place, he just cannot take his eyes off the reading monk ...

Why such an exercise? And what has it got to do with cultural learning?

In the novel the author does not explicitly mention (but obviously refers to) a sculpture by well-known German artist Ernst Barlach (1870–1938) and lets the novel's dramatic action revolve around it: all of the four main characters that have been introduced earlier on (cf. Example III) participate, willingly or not, in the rescue of this sculpture from the Nazis.

Given the pivotal role of this German piece of art in the novel, we decided to focus the students' attention on it immediately. And again, before we as teachers give them any information about this German artefact or the sculptor who made it, we encourage the students to touch and draw it and – via this tactile or perceptual experience – familiarise themselves with it. And only after they have formed their own impression of it, do they read about Gregor's first encounter with the sculpture.

Our principle of activating the students' imagination before confronting them with foreign (literary) language and culture is also applied in the next example which I will not describe in full but in which the teacher basically asks the students to do the following:

- Once again have a look at the sculpture (next page) and study it carefully.
- Sit down exactly as the sculpted figure sits and while doing so concentrate on the upper part of your body, on your shoulders, arms, hands and feet.
- Remain seated and have a look at the book that is lying on your knees.
- Close your eyes and imagine you have become this figure, and as this figure answer the following questions:
  - Where do you sit? Outside or inside?
  - What do you sit on?
  - Are you sitting comfortably?
  - Are you relaxed or do you feel any tension in your body?

- Have you been sitting like this for a long time?
- The book you are reading: Have you chosen it carefully or was it rather an accidental choice?
- Are you reading slowly and in a concentrated way or fast and superficially?
- What is the book's title?
- Which part are you reading just now? What are you thinking of while you are reading these lines? How do you feel?
- Will you go on reading for longer or will you stop reading soon?

- What will you do when you have finished reading?
- Look at the part again which you are just reading – and write these lines on a piece of paper!
- Read the lines out aloud to us ...

It may be a bit difficult for you, the reader, to do this exercise on your own, but it would be a good idea to try it before going on.

Reader activity 4

The images that form in the students' minds will differ of course, but in my experience also will have a great deal in common. Have a look, e.g. at a few of the book titles and phrases that students in the first year German course 94/95 at University College Cork came up with at the end of this exercise:

1. The Bible: An account of the march to Calvary with the cross: 'And Jesus fell for the third time.'
2. The Bible: 'From the 6th to the 9th hour darkness came over the land.'
3. The Bible: 'Let there be light!'
4. The Bible: 'Fear no evil!'
5. The Eclipse: 'The occurrence of an eclipse is a very rare thing. It occurs when the moon totally covers the sun and as a result the world is left in total darkness for a number of hours.'
6. World Disasters: 'Millions of lives were lost and the place was left in total confusion.'
7. Journey into the Unknown: 'What was this loud, waif-like wailing? Who or even what awaited us as we anchored the ship? Oh God, would we even be finished with this terrifying voyage ...'

Many of the students evoked a biblical theme, and dominant in their associations (even implicit in examples 1 and 2) was an atmosphere of gloom, a sense of imminent catastrophe. When the students read the phrases out aloud in class, this had a big surprise effect for the other students (and the teacher!) and created powerful resonances. It was not difficult for the teacher to establish a connection between the students' associations and the content of the novel which is set against the bleak reality of the Third Reich. Thus this exercise in imaginative empathy works on an affective level that so often is ignored or is at best peripheral in the foreign language classroom. It is especially this level, however, that drama operates on, achieving learning processes that in my view should complement those on a cognitive level whenever possible. Had I given the students 'cultural facts' only – e.g. that Ernst

Barlach called his sculpture 'Der Lesende Klosterschüler' ('The Reading Monk'), that he made the sculpture in 1931, etc. – I would rather have prevented the students from 'entering into the inside of the sculpture', i.e. into the mind of the reading monk. In order to understand this piece of German art however, they need to – bear in mind the quotation from Eisner above – form images they can connect with it and further reflect on, in the ensuing evaluation of the experience.

Using drama as a tool in the classroom can in fact lead to 'deeper understanding' because drama does not remain at the surface of abstraction as is so typical of academic teaching and learning (e.g.: Millions of Jews were persecuted and killed during the Third Reich). It rather studies the concrete case and tests our individual reactions to it. This will be further illustrated in the following example.

Example V

Let us focus on another of the main characters in the novel: Judith, a Jewish girl who tries to escape abroad from Rerik. The following two extracts from the novel will give you a taste of Andersch's writing and introduce you to the dilemma Judith finds herself in:

> 1.
> She was sitting on the bed of a guest room in the 'Wappen von Wismar' and rummaging in her handbag. The suitcase stood beside the door and Judith had not taken off her raincoat as she wanted to go out right away. Then she looked out of the window: a tiled roof under a bright, northern, completely empty autumn sky. Judith trembled. I should have got myself a room with a front view, she thought, so I would have at least seen the harbour, could have seen whether foreign boats are there that can take me with them. If I only knew a bit more about ships, she thought, I'm afraid I can't tell a Danish or Swedish steamer from a German one.
>
> Moreover, after she had arrived by the midday train from Lübeck, she had not seen a single steamer before she had entered the 'Wappen von Wismar'. Only a few trawlers and an old rusty schooner that had apparently been out of use for years.
>
> For the first time she was having second thoughts whether Mama's advice to try from Rerik had been good. Travemünde, Kiel, Flensburg, Rostock – all of them are kept under surveillance, Mama had said, you have to try in Rerik, this is a small and lifeless place, nobody thinks of it. Only the small Swedish

wood steamers unload there. You simply have to offer them money, a lot of money, then they take you with them without further ado. Mama had always kept up a sentimental liking for Rerik since she had seen the town with Papa twenty years previously, on their way back from a happy summer in Rügen, but a happy day in Rerik was certainly quite different from a day on the run in Rerik under an empty late autumn sky.

In between this and the following extract Judith remembers her paralysed mother who had committed suicide the day before. By doing so, she attempted to facilitate her daughter's timely escape. After that Judith had packed her suitcase and had gone to Rerik, following her mother's advice.

2.
She had imagined Rerik totally differently. As small and lively and friendly. But it was small and empty, empty and dead under its giant red towers. Only when Judith walked out of the station and spotted the towers did she remember how Mama had been delighted with those towers. They are not towers, she had always said, they are monsters, wonderful red monsters you can stroke. Under the cold sky, however, they seemed to Judith to be bad monsters. In any case, Judith felt, they were towers that did not care about Mama's fatal poisoning. Nor about her escape. There was nothing to be expected from these towers. She had quickly passed by them crossing the town to the harbour. There she was able to catch a glimpse of the open sea. The sea was icy and ultramarine. And no steamer, no matter how small, stood in the harbour.

Then she had gone to the 'Wappen of Wismar' because it was tidy and painted in light oil-paint. The landlord, a solid-looking type with a white and greasy face, appeared to be glad to see the unexpected guest. Well, Miss, what are you doing in Rerik so late in the year? Judith had mumbled something about the churches; she wanted to see the churches. He nodded and slipped her the visitor's book. She entered her name: Judith Leffing. This sounded quite typically northern German. The landlord had not demanded to see her passport. Rerik really seemed to be a dead place.

Judith stopped rummaging in her handbag and thought of her name: Judith Levin. It was a proud name, a name with disastrous implications, a name that had to be hidden. It was terrible to be Judith Levin in a dead town that was inhabited by red monsters under a cold sky.

Before I describe how I worked on these literary extracts in class I would like to make a more general point on the use of drama in the (foreign language) classroom. Using drama in the (foreign language) classroom in my view requires of the teacher two things:

1. S/he needs to have developed an 'artistic feeling', i.e. a feeling for the potential of drama as an art form.
2. S/he needs to have an 'artistic grammar', i.e. be familiar with strategies/techniques that help to structure 'scenarios' in which students actively participate as actors, directors, playwrights and audience.

In all art, including drama (as a form of 'teaching art'), the aspect of form is of crucial importance. 'Artistic feeling' implies a special feeling for the form or the power of the form. When I read the novel from a dramaturgical point of view and came across the above extracts I could not help but focus on the passport of the Jewish girl, on her fate being inextricably bound up with (the form of) her passport.

I structured a drama sequence which I tried out for the first time in a multicultural group of students of German as a Foreign Language. This involved the actual making of a passport – out of cardboard, nothing elaborate, but looking fairly authentic with the imperial eagle and swastika on the front and: 'Judith Levin' and a large 'J' written into a yellow background, suggesting the star of David. This passport I used in an improvisation that – corresponding to the plot of the novel – was to follow the above extracts: Judith comes down from her room, takes a seat in the breakfast room, orders something to eat and drink. The greasy-looking landlord comes back with sandwich and tea ... The scene evolves from here.

My 'artistic grammar' came into play, for example, when I asked the student who volunteered to play 'Judith' to go to a designated part of the classroom and, according to my instructions, immerse herself into the role of Judith sitting in her upstairs room, all kinds of thoughts buzzing through her head while rummaging in her handbag and finally preparing herself for going downstairs into the breakfast room. While she was doing this, the other students (as audience) sat in a half circle. I explained to them quietly, so that 'Judith' could not listen, that I would pass something round the circle which each student should briefly look at without saying anything: Judith Levin's passport. I could read in the students' faces that, physically holding and seeing the inside of this passport affected them and created an air of expectancy which was increased even further when I went to the student in role as 'Judith' and handed her the passport saying: 'Decide what you will do with this, before you go down into the breakfast room.'

What I achieved with this preparatory work preceding the enactment was:

a) catching the audience's attention, making them active 'percipients' and
b) increasing the agitation of 'Judith', thus fuelling emotional energy into the ensuing improvisation.

I will not go into any further detail regarding the careful structuring of this scene (cf. Schewe and Wilms 1995), but instead I will give two examples of students' responses to the improvised scene in which 'Judith' (student in role) tries hard not to give in to the landlord's (teacher in role) insistent questions and keep her identity hidden.

Their texts, written shortly after the experience, highlight the intensity of learning processes that can be achieved through drama. The first was actually written from the student-actress's point of view, the second from the perspective of a member of the audience who happened to be a Palestinian student of German as a Foreign Language.

> 1.
> I got my first fright when a passport with a large letter 'J' was handed to me. Suddenly I felt a big lump in my throat and this thought flashed through my head: 'How must Judith or any other Jewish person have felt in those times?' I was so shocked and emotionally moved that I lost track of the sequence of the scene I was going to play.
>
> Then the actual improvisation began. Like it had been explained to me I went down the stairs in order to get outside, past the landlord. He now talked at me so vehemently and came so near to me that I felt as if ice was running down my back. Frantically I tried to recall the scene from the book in order to be able to answer to the landlord's phrases like: 'You look so foreign!' – I just couldn't. I felt very uncomfortable and I found it hard to think clearly. I wanted to say something, wanted to explain: 'My grandparents are from Italy' or something like that, but already after the first syllable he cut me short. I felt so helpless, not up to the situation, because he looked at me more and more insistently and talked at me with growing pungency. My mouth was dry, my heart pounded. Alternately I thought: How should I behave? How do I appear to those in the audience? How had she behaved in the book?
>
> The helplessness was the worst. I felt at mercy and had a completely irrational fear. Even if this sounds stupid: I felt a great closeness to Judith, in kindred spirits with her. To an extent I identified with her. (Conny Lausch-Jäger)

> 2.
> This symbol (the Star of David) causes many discrepancies for me as a Palestinian. As a symbol it plays an important role for the Arabs (especially the Palestinians) as well as for the Jews, because it's got to do with the political survival, the homogenous cohesion of each of the two sides: the oppressed and the oppressors. Those who at present act as oppressors were persecuted and killed in the country I live in today, in Germany.
>
> I see the Star of David in two colours: pale yellow in Germany; deep blue in Israel. In Germany the yellow star recalls the sufferings and destruction of the Jews, while the blue one in Israel frightens the Palestinians.
>
> I personally experienced an awful fear and angst when the symbol in the short improvisation all of a sudden took on the meaning of: she will be found out, she is trapped, this is her death sentence!
>
> This fear – I felt my blood pump, incessantly pounding – took deep root in me when the landlord talked at Judith with growing pungency and finally grabbed her arm. Exactly at this point of the scene my thoughts circled around Kafka's 'Kleine Fabel', and I saw myself as the mouse which – in slow motion – happens to get into the trap.
>
> These thoughts I have written down flashed through my head during the improvisation: from the showing of the passport with the Star of David inside, until the grabbing of Judith's arm.
>
> I found it very good that through the showing of the passport the audience was drawn into the improvisation and became part of it. (Khalled Khatib)

Note that the word 'feel' or an equivalent is repeatedly used by the students which bears out a point made earlier: drama primarily operates on an affective level and can evoke strong emotional responses that can 'show' physically ('I felt a big lump in my throat', 'I felt my blood pump, incessantly pounding'). I would claim that the students – through working on this experiential feeling level – come to a 'deeper (cultural) understanding' than would be possible through reading only or in a discussion about the text. In this case it is an 'empathic understanding' of Judith's dilemma which stands for the fate of thousands of Jewish emigrants during the Third Reich in Germany. Note in this context Knights' article 'Literature and the Education of Feeling' in which he states, for example:

> Literature certainly has to do with feelings ... What it does is ... to arouse them in relation to other existences, other experi-

> ences than our own, and thereby to realize them, make them more real to us. This realization is a complicated process. It is enough to say here that the feelings in question are not mere reactions, something that we undergo, as with passions: they are active, exploratory, and (to anticipate) they are inseparable from intelligence and perception, which are certainly active and creative powers. (Knights 1989:63)

Having tested their individual reactions to Judith's dilemma, the students usually will raise further questions in the 'reflection phase' after the improvisation and will be open to any further information on the mental side of German culture during the Third Reich, i.e. the ideas and values inherent in the Nazi ideology which justified and prepared the ground for the pogrom of the Jews. What the student in role (Conny) writes at the end of her text could, I feel, be used to establish a connection to cultural learning in general and raise the questions: Should we as teachers of a foreign language not give up the idea, expressed explicitly or implicitly in many cultural studies programmes, of a 'full understanding of/identification with' a foreign or even our own culture? How could one ever, be it German or Non-German national, 'fully understand' the pogrom of the Jews?[1] Bearing in mind Conny's words, isn't achieving 'a great closeness' to our own or another culture more than challenge enough?

At least since the discussions revolving around reception aesthetics (e.g. Iser 1994; Eagleton 1985) we know that there is no such thing as the understanding of a literary text (and its cultural implications!). Hans Magnus Enzensberger, a well-known contemporary writer illustrates this nicely:

> If ten people read a literary text, this results in ten different readings. Everybody knows that. Many factors influence the act of reading which in no way can be controlled, e.g. the social and psychic history of the reader, her/his expectations and interests, the inner state the reader is in at the moment of reading, the situation in which s/he reads – all of these being factors which are not only legitimate and to be taken seriously, but are the precondition really for a reading process to happen. The result is not determined and cannot be determined.
> (Enzensberger 1985: 16–17, my translation)

[1] Note that Posner (1991), in the face of divergent definitions of culture, suggests a concentration on three aspects of culture: social, material and mental. The mental side would include ideas and values and the conventions used to apply and present these ideas and values.

When using literary texts in the foreign classroom as a means of teaching culture, the reading and analysing of text cannot be completely arbitrary though. We are facing a double challenge. A text ought to be understood in the context of its world, its times, its conditions; on the other hand the reader cannot but refer to her/his experience and individual understanding of the world. In any case – and I have tried to show this in my examples – we as teachers should enable the students to refer to their experiences and understandings before we supply our (factual) teacher knowledge. It is important that the students 'produce their own (cultural) film' before they see ours:

> Fictional texts produce a film in our head. During this production fragments of our own world are projected into the other imagined reality. The fictional text written in a foreign language creates an in-between-world, a world between our own world and that of the culturally specific text. (Krusche 1993: 120, my translation)

For Krusche, whose area is literary theory and its application in language teaching, it is clear that the learner becomes an active part in the reading process, because s/he uses her or his 'imaginative consciousness' as a sort of inner stage for the production of textual events.

But – in the context of teaching culture through literature through drama – I would even go a step further. We must not stop at 'inner activities' in our classrooms. The films in our head need to be made and shown. And this is obviously where drama can play an important part. Which medium would be a better or more immediate 'showing-medium' than drama? In drama we use our hands and our feet, we make gestures and faces, we move through the room and project our voice: we wholeheartedly become involved in 'outer activities'.

What we should strive for in our foreign language classrooms – and drama is one of the most effective learning media here – is a productive interplay between inner and outer activities. The students need to be given opportunities to turn what they carry inside to the outside. They need to show their 'in-between-worlds', i.e. imagined reality between one's own and the reality of a different culture. It is by looking at and comparing these in-between-worlds and by checking them against the constructions of others (teacher, author, media, etc.), that they are likely to achieve 'a great closeness' to the foreign culture.

Andersch's novel in parts reads like a documentary report. In recent years, since the fall of the Berlin Wall, many a friend of (German) literature has taken advantage of the new freedom of travel in order to visit Rerik in East Germany, the place of action in Andersch's novel. But, according to Jan Schulz-Ojala's observations (1992:7, translation) these people 'stand estranged in a place which seems to turn away from its (fictitious) history'. For most of them it is disappointing to find out that the station where Judith and also Gregor arrive does not exist, that there is no river 'Treene' under whose bridges the boy who works on Knudsen's boat dreams of 'Sansibar' – which in his imagination is the opposite of the boring Rerik he hates. Furthermore they realise that Rerik is not a harbour town really as suggested in the novel, and even have to accept that 'The Reading Monk' has never left Rerik. Barlach's sculpture has always remained in his home town, Güstrow. The author Alfred Andersch obviously decided to do what any good artist naturally does: he treated facts as stimuli for the imagination, in the (tacit) knowledge that culture is not only facts but also what is beneath, in-between and beyond the facts.

In this context I would like to raise a few questions that are forming in my mind while writing these concluding lines: Isn't the understanding of culture similar to an understanding of a piece of art? Doesn't each new stroke that we see in a painting alter the pattern and each new nuance in colour we discover affect our perception of the whole? Don't we have to go back to a painting and look at it again and again to be able to create new meaning for ourselves? If (foreign) culture was like a painting with many different surfaces, shapes and deep layers, wouldn't we have to become more aware of its resonances?

Note:
The extracts from *Sansibar oder der letzte Grund* were translated by 3rd year students of German at University College Cork, in Harald Schmidl's translation class (no English edition of this popular novel is available).

Part 3 Approaches through ethnography: teacher and researcher perspectives

Introduction

Much of this volume so far has been concerned with learners and their needs. In the first section we focused on defining and describing what learners have to acquire and do to become interculturally competent and able to communicate across cultural frontiers. The second section illustrated how different methods drawing from drama might facilitate the acquisition of intercultural communicative competence. These include a strong emphasis on experiential learning, and issues of identity and reflexivity. The demands made on teachers, as we have become more aware of the complexity of intercultural communication, are therefore not only a matter of developing an improved intellectual grasp of the complexities. They also introduce new dimensions into methodology. Experiential learning, reflexivity, and the questioning of identities require teachers themselves to take risks and new roles.

This section of the book is, therefore, concerned with teachers and researchers as learners in intercultural realities. For teachers remain learners. Those who are themselves foreign speakers of the language they teach are constantly faced with new learning, in their role as mediators between the foreign language and culture on the one side and their learners on the other. They are obliged constantly to review their own understanding of the foreign and of their own language and culture. A second group, those teachers who are native speakers of the language in question, are no longer in the privileged position of the past, as Kramsch argued earlier, but are equally obliged to mediate, to review, to re-learn what they had taken for granted in their own cultural environment, and to relate to the language and culture of their learners.

It is the teacher and researcher's experience of discovering new perspectives which Morgan describes in her account of intercultural interaction as part of an international curriculum development project. In the first section of this volume, Byram and Cain described this project in the more conventional way, explaining its purpose and outcomes for learners. Morgan gives an unusual insight into the process from the perspective of the teachers and researchers involved, demonstrating how they too undergo demanding, experiential learning, not usually part of the training and education of language teachers. For, as the earlier chapters by Coleman and by Barro, Jordan and Roberts indicate, mere exposure even for a substantial period of residence in another country does not lead necessarily to positive learning; it needs careful preparation and the development of an ethnographic awareness. Morgan demonstrates that it is not only learners with little experience of another country who may feel threatened in their identity and need to become reflexive in their response. Language teachers' identities as individuals, and as professionals involved in intercultural communication are also at issue.

It is the question of the professional identity and self definition of language teachers which is addressed in Risager's chapter. She describes research, by survey and interview in Denmark and England, which analyses how language teachers see their role in a changing Europe. A fundamental question is how teachers see the purposes of language teaching as Europe changes, becomes in some senses more integrated, and might require language teachers to re-think their task inside and beyond the classroom. The chapter concentrates on how the relationship between language and culture within language teaching has changed, and how teachers in the survey describe their own view on the change. Perhaps not surprisingly, she demonstrates that there is a wide range of responses. However, these include a 'transcultural' approach which takes a radically different view of the responsibilities of the language teacher, and implies a significant change in professional identity and skills.

In the final chapter, Sercu demonstrates in concrete and detailed ways how teachers might be helped to develop these skills and identity. The volume opened with Kramsch's reflections on the nature of the intercultural speaker inspired in part by work from an in-service teacher education course, and it is fitting that it closes with a detailed description of a similar course, whose principal aims are not just to impart new methods, but also to incite teachers to reflect on the nature of their task.

Sercu emphasises in her course what must also be one of the main purposes of this volume: to give teachers and other readers 'a sense of having acquired a number of insights and tools that will allow them to take an active part in the search for the modern language contribution to international understanding and peacemaking at home and abroad'.

12 Cross-cultural encounters

Carol Morgan

The project context

One of the goals of culture and language teaching is fostering the ability to cope with intercultural encounter (Kramsch 1993; Byram, Morgan *et al.* 1994). The account below looks at a particular level of intercultural encounter within the context of a joint cross-cultural project with teams of researchers and teachers during the period 1990–93 in educational establishments in Durham (England) and Paris. This project is described in more detail in an earlier chapter by Byram and Cain. While the content of the project focused on introducing cultural awareness teaching into the curriculum at upper secondary level in England and at lower and upper secondary level in France, the process of the research involved cross-cultural contact between the research and teaching teams from England and France.

Two factors became evident during the period of this cross-cultural collaboration: firstly that linguistic proficiency did not automatically equal cultural proficiency. All team members were able to communicate fluently in the language of the other team and yet this did not prevent cross-cultural misunderstanding. Secondly, despite some difficulties and misunderstanding, the collaboration was successful. This success can be gauged from the positive and complimentary comments from members of both teams, from the changes the teams made in their modus operandi to accommodate ideas from their partner team, and from the fact that collaboration has continued between different team members on further joint research projects since that time.

One of my own interests as a researcher in the Durham team was to try to identify the particular parameters within the project which had brought about these successful outcomes.

The account below looks at different variables identified in studies of cross-cultural encounter in an attempt to locate those particular factors which militate for and against success and to place the Durham-Paris collaboration within this framework.

To some extent the dynamics of the Durham-Paris collaboration reflect the dynamics of any collaboration: namely the recognition of difference between partners, the need for compromise, respect, etc. These factors are, however, given a sharper focus in a cross-cultural collaboration. There is no common first language; behavioural, proxemic and politeness codes are not shared; and stereotypes exist which may damagingly be invoked as suspected reasons for misinterpreted cultural infringements.

The Durham-Paris project offered a unique opportunity for considering cross-cultural encounter from several different perspectives: contact was established between the two teams both at a group level and a personal, individual level; each team experienced the 'shock' of being in a different country with seminars and meetings held alternately in Paris and Durham; team visits abroad included not only meetings but also visits to the schools where the teachers in the team worked and where the pilot materials were trialled, thus affording an opportunity to understand the context of the project in each country; colleagues from each team were able to provide teaching material for each other on a reciprocal basis; several meetings and seminars were held over the two and a half years (ten in all) allowing for different kinds of encounter and time in which to reflect; and perhaps most importantly, the project not only afforded opportunity for cross-cultural encounter, but was in its very essence focused on that very kind of encounter, be it cross-cultural encounter with text, video, native speaker or the target country itself. Clarke and Grünzweig comment on the richness of this 'doubling up' in their description of a cultural analysis of the US undertaken by Austrian students in Ohio:

> The mix of academic and experiential learning ... where the field of study is ... identical with the place of study, can be said to facilitate 'learning' in a much broader sense. (1988:64)

The account below considers the experiences of the teams, at various stages in the project, to contextualise the circumstances of our own particular experiences, the cultural differences discovered during our encounters, the positive and negative factors identified in analyses of cross-cultural encounters, and the outcomes of our cross-cultural contact.

Contact between the two teams was of two types: week-long seminars with most members of both teams present (two were held in Paris and one in Durham) and three- or four-day meetings between the researchers (three were held in Durham and four in Paris). From the first meeting between the researchers it became clear that radical differences existed between the two teams on several levels: the demands of the institutions who were funding the research, profound differences in attitude and expectations with regard to research methods, the role of the teacher and various facets of the education system. (Broadfoot and Osborn comment on similar intercultural differences in their study of primary teachers' self-image in the Aix and Bristol areas, 1993.)

A working paper was written by the Durham team for discussion by both teams. This outlined our interpretation of the French view of teaching 'civilisation', our own reactions to this, our interpretation of our own view of teaching culture studies, and our interpretation of how we imagined the French team might react to our comments. The main differences outlined were between (as we perceived it) a French model based on the transmission of a body of knowledge, rational argument and accuracy, with the teacher's authority paramount in presenting the truth, and an English model based on learner-centred, experiential activities, incorporating cognitive *and* affective domains, where the teacher operates as a facilitator. These two models bear some resemblance to those given by Zarate in her description of models that currently pertain or should pertain in classrooms in France:

> Modèle 1 ... la compétence culturelle conçue comme une addition de savoirs ... le bon professeur, le bon manuel, le bon élève, la bonne réponse disent le vrai ... l'institution scolaire invite son élève à faire acte de foi dans l'autorité de ses sources d'information ... Modèle 2 ... fournir à l'élève des outils de l'interprétation d'une culture étrangère et lui apprendre à les mettre en oeuvre. (1988:24–25)

> Model 1 ... cultural competence conceived as a sum of knowledge with the good teacher, the good textbook, the good pupil and the right answer speaking the truth ... the educational institution asks the pupil to perform an act of faith in accepting the authority of its sources of information ... Model 2 ... provides the pupil with the tools to interpret a foreign culture and teaches him or her to put them into action. (My translation)

Zarate also stresses the need for relativisation and for learning by comparing the target culture with one's own culture in the second model (1988: 25–26); both of these needs were seen as key features by the two teams. The different approaches to the purpose and style of teaching cultural studies however were not shared, as had been seen from the outset, and this difference in approach informed the whole of our joint contact as teams. It could in addition be seen as representing the two different traditions of education in France and England (Maclean 1990).

Two extreme options were open to the two teams: to support a single agenda for both teams, with the necessary adjustments on both sides or to run two quite separate but parallel programmes. The composition of the Paris team to include both lower and upper secondary, added a further potentially complicating factor. A variety of options exist between these two extremes, and, in the end, our joint programmes, while starting out at the 'separate but parallel' end of the scale, moved gradually towards the 'amalgamated' end of the scale, over the two years, with different perspectives adopted in the two teams and some sharing in the choice of topics.

The shifts experienced by both teams were accompanied by both difficulties and bonuses. It is useful here to look at those features identified in the literature on cross-cultural contact as potentially damaging or beneficial, in order to identify more closely the pattern of our own cross-cultural growth. In reporting this, my own subjective bias, of course, needs to be taken into account. Visible differences in the two teams in changes in teaching style or approach can be reported relatively neutrally, as can opinions voiced by members of both teams, but the account that follows is inevitably coloured by my own experiences, coming from a background of little prolonged contact with French native speakers and no long-term residence in France. For most of the team members cross-cultural contact and residence in the target country had been significantly longer.

My own perspectives too in describing and evaluating the project are also likely in themselves to be culture-bound (Kramsch 1991), with the pragmatic, the experiential and the synchronic perhaps likely to receive undue favourable weighting.

Key parameters

Cross-cultural encounters of various kinds have been the object of scrutiny in several works written in the 1980s, particularly those appearing in the United States (for example, Brislin 1981; Bochner 1982a and b; Furnham and Bochner 1986; Robinson 1988). Encounters may take place for a variety of reasons: tourism, business, study, migration, etc. and be of varying duration. Brislin gives fourteen different categories of sojourner (1981:8–10), naming also research which has focused on these different kinds of stay. Although motives and conditions will vary, many of the experiences of sojourners abroad are similar and it is these that a variety of cross-cultural training programmes have sought to address (Adelman and Levine 1982; Seelye 1988; Brislin *et al.* 1986, for example).

Furnham and Bochner (1986) in their review of literature on cross-cultural encounter cite seven key parameters for interpretation, mainly focusing on affective factors and the individual: grief, fatalism, selective migration, expectations, negative life-events, social support and value differences, offering finally their own solution, social skills training. Brislin (1981) gives a further eight influential factors, mainly concentrating on situational variables, which overlap with these: the historical context, the individual, the group, the situation, the task, the organisations, the groups in situations, and cross-cultural adjustment. Robinson (1988) adds further suggestions in the cognitive and affective domains: the importance of the senses, the importance of time, anxiety resulting from forewarning, distortion for consistency, and the salience of negative information. Other writers mention further factors: fatigue (Seelye 1988), equal status and superordinate goals (Klineberg 1982), person attribution and situation contribution (Jaspers and Hewstone 1982) and social distance (Furnham and Bochner 1982 and 1986).

From this wealth of identified variables it is clear that cross-cultural contact is construed as a complex operation. In the analysis below I suggest that these variables fall into two major categories: those linked to the 'situation' and those identified as cognitive or affective factors. The Durham-Paris project has been adjudged in terms of these variables (as far as this is possible) and possible reasons for its success suggested.

Situational factors

It is clear from numerous experiments that the mere bringing together of people from different cultures does not guarantee success (Bochner 1982b:159). The example of the increased hostility between Turkish and German adolescents brought together described by Apitzsch and Dittmar bears witness to this possible outcome (1987:51–72). What then were the particular circumstances which signalled possible failure in our project? And what were those that militated for success?

Firstly, the particular situation within which we were located was significant. As we saw from the initial contacts between the teams, the outlook of each team was embedded in the differing educational traditions of their own country. In addition very differing circumstances prevailed in the educational establishment in the two countries. In France, upper secondary students study the same range of subjects, including English, with a centralised curriculum and often up to 30 or 40 students in a class. In England, students study a range of different subjects in addition to French, with a choice of curricula and with numbers varying from 1 to 20 (see Brislin's 'situation' and 'organisation'

1981). The existence of an additional team preparing lower secondary materials in France also created a different context. These unavoidable circumstances inevitably dictated some of the possibilities open to teachers, thus creating potential divisions. On the other hand, certain other organisational or institutional factors were beneficial: finance was available to fund visits to the other country and to obtain time free from school, and teachers and researchers had the benefits of being able to draw on the resources of the larger organisations hosting the project (Durham University and the Institut National de Recherche Pédagogique).

Other factors pertaining to the logistics of the project also tended to be favourable. Furnham and Bochner cite selective migration as a possible key factor: the notion that those suitable for migration self-select themselves or are selected by others in a Darwinian fashion (1986:172–73: cf. also Brislin's 'individual' and 'group' 1981). In much the same way it could be argued that the freedom to select team members likely to be in tune with the aims of the project, as was the case in both teams, augured well for the likelihood of successful outcomes. Klineberg suggests that equal status and superordinate goals also promote successful encounters (1982:53–54; cf. also Robinson 1988:64). These two factors were certainly strongly to the fore in the inter-team contact. Each team was given equal opportunity to present their own teaching materials and ideas to the other and these were debated and discussed at length. Meetings between the researchers allowed for the frank exchange of views on differences in approach to assessment and evaluation. The overriding aim or superordinate goal for both teams was to produce teaching material to aid students in understanding their own and the target cultures and in so doing to further the teams' own understanding on both counts as well.

Some projects of course suffer from internal 'cultural' clashes among participants, perhaps where the needs of a variety of stakeholders have to be satisfied, where there are a large number of participants who are not in contact with each other or where there is a perceived rift between university research priorities and those of participating schools. Shipman *et al.* describe problems of this sort in the Keele Integrated Studies Project 1968–71 (1974). Luckily, in our team circumstances again were auspicious for us: the Durham part of the project was funded by a charitable trust (Leverhulme) with no stipulated policy or resources outcomes expected, beyond a report of activity; only a small number of participants were involved; the teachers were fully integrated into the research, taking responsibility for writing curriculum materials and evaluating materials from other colleagues; and perhaps most importantly a preparatory orientation phase was built into the first year of the project to allow the team (both researchers and teacher-researchers) to become acquainted with the theoretical social-anthropological/ethnographic background.

Robinson in her exploration of cross-cultural understanding suggests that time is also a crucial factor in turning cross-cultural encounter to good effect:

> understanding is a gradual process ... time is a critical condition in modifying negative perceptions of other people ... some psychological studies suggest that mere exposure and continued proximity to another person increase liking. (1988:3, 81)

As mentioned above, the structure of the project with both short and extended periods of contact spread over the two years allowed for experiences to be repeated and reflected upon and for the teams to come to know each other.

In this personal orientation process another kind of disorientation was also present, linked to the unexpected and often mystifying differences which became evident. Even for team members long acquainted with the other country, such close co-operation revealed a deeper layer of difference. Differences in outlook and behaviour are discussed in further detail below. The end-result of frequent cross-cultural encounters and involvement can also lead to a kind of disorientation with oneself. As one of our team members put it: 'I spend so much time in France that I don't know whether I'm English or French any more.' This kind of marginality may be an inevitable outcome of cross-cultural understanding but it may also be a useful pre-condition. Zarate, in her work on teaching culture, comments on the productiveness of the initial marginal state of disorientation where differences may be perceived freshly:

> l'étranger, nouveau venu dans un pays, peut ... 'voir' des pratiques invisibles aux yeux des natifs ... ce point de vue est privilégié dans le mesure où il induit la contingence, la relativité de tout système de valeurs en place ... L'étranger en étant celui qui ne participe pas à la connivence générale, devient un observateur particulier. Il est dans cette position limite qui lui fait appréhendre le réel dans les conditions rendant possible une objectivité maximale. (1986: 32)

> The foreigner ... newly arrived in a country can ... 'see' those customs which are invisible to the natives of that country ... this point of view is privileged in that it implies the contingency and the relativity of the whole value system which is in place ... The foreigner, by being the person who does not subscribe to

> the general consensus, becomes a special kind of observer. He or she occupies a liminal position which allows him or her to be aware of what is real in any situation affording maximum objectivity (my translation).

Bochner gives marginality as one of four possible responses in a cross-cultural encounter:

> [1] reject culture of origins ... 'passing' ... [2] reject second culture ... chauvinistic ... [3] vacillate between the two cultures ... marginal ... [and 4] synthesize both cultures ... mediating. (1982a:27)

Marginality is thus an ambiguous state with both inherent anxieties and beneficial potentialities. One could also postulate a 'halo effect' for both teams in that our very identity as representatives of the target culture meant that we were 'special', of interest to each other.

Brislin's categories of 'group' and 'individual' (1981:109–37) are also relevant here. In situations of contact between two groups, the individual may experience difficulty in reconciling loyalty to self with loyalty to the group.

In our project meetings, opportunities for breaking the potential deadlock of 'this group against that group' were afforded by the splintering of each team, matching partners from the two teams: some of the team members were entertained and accommodated where possible in each other's houses; school visits were arranged on an individual or group basis and workshops during the seminars allowed for work with small mixed groups from both teams. From these personal contacts flourished a pattern of further visits, exchanges of teaching materials and possibilities of future school exchanges.

A monocultural group is however not always a problem. To some extent the group can cushion or neutralise some of the negative or extreme effects of cross-cultural encounter. These effects are described at some length in the literature on cross-cultural contact. Seelye predicts an inevitability of disorientation:

> An American abroad suffers from the inevitable malaise of cross-cultural fatigue ... Everyone experiences difficulties as s/he attempts to function effectively in another culture. (1984:98–99)

Furnham and Bochner also comment on the interpretation of reaction to an unfamiliar environment as negative, a kind of grief or bereavement at the loss of one's own country (1986:163–66) or in terms of a negative life-event associated with change:

> because migration involves a great number of potentially stressful changes, the development of psychological or physical illnesses may be attributable directly to them. (1986:180)

Short visits may be seen as of a different order to migration but the frequency of illness when on holiday may serve as an indicator of change inducing stress, even with holidaymaking being a relatively 'shielded' activity (Argyle 1982:61). Fatigue, stress, illness, even 'grief' can all be buffered by the support of a group (Brislin 1981:113; Furnham and Bochner 1986:186; Clarke and Grünzweig 1988:68). Membership of a group can thus be both divisive and supportive.

One further dimension for understanding identity can be found in comments by Pearce (1982). Zarate in her 'modèle 2' of culture teaching emphasised the importance of relativisation, of working from the mother culture to the target culture:

> l'approche d'une culture étrangère se fait prioritairement à travers la relation entre la culture maternelle de l'élève et la (les) culture(s) enseignée(s). (1988:25)

> the approach to a foreign culture is primarily achieved through relating the home culture of the pupil to the culture(s) being taught. (My translation)

Contact with a foreign country can lead specifically to a re-evaluation of one's own country. Thus in Pearce's survey of tourists on package tours to Greece and Morocco, the holidaymakers showed evidence of a change in beliefs about Britain even after a short and relatively shielded encounter:

> The tourists to Morocco ... changed some of their perceptions of the British after travelling. Their fellow countrymen were now seen as less tense and more affluent than prior to the travel experience. (1982:212)

Although such reactions may be seen as a rejection of the foreign culture and a hardening of ethnocentric attitudes (Bochner's 'chauvinistic' category in one of four categories of sojourner 1982a:27), there is nevertheless evidence here of re-evaluation and of a shift in attitudes.

A more positive scenario, afforded to the sojourner with closer and longer contact with the target culture, is that of the 'mediator' for whom the 'norms of both cultures [are] salient and perceived as capable of being integrated' (Bochner 1982a:27). Two German writers have interesting comments to offer here. Winter, in reviewing his students' experiences on reciprocal German-American university exchanges, identifies three different kinds of interaction: two negative variants of cultural adjustment with, first, an egocentric, deductive dominant distortion of the target culture, 'the self-concept is insulated against potential corrective information or experience', or, second, an inductive over-responsive total acceptance of the target culture resulting in a 'façade of smooth and worldly cosmopolitanism' (1986:326–7). Winter's third and positive variant is one of:

> stable self images ... [where] relationship with ... [one's] own national origin remains fully intact without becoming exaggerated (in either inflated or deflated terms). (1986:327)

Meyer in his description of differing levels of cultural competence similarly located the highest level as:

> *transcultural* ... [where] the learner is able to evaluate intercultural differences and solve intercultural problems by appeal to principles of international co-operation and communication which give each culture its proper right and which allow the learner to develop his own identity *in the light* of cross-cultural understanding. (1991:143)

These three levels also equate with those strategies identified by Schumann in his study of integration and acculturation processes: assimilation/total adoption and acculturation/maintaining balance (1978; see also Grünzweig's comments on dialogue 1988:76). Such stability of self-image and balancing of the equal values of different cultures were fostered in our own project by the particular structuring of the contact between teams. Public presentation of team reports and teaching material accorded a seriousness which demanded attention. Theoretical readings and investigations also provided a validation of different viewpoints and an opportunity to broaden out from the personal to the general.

Affective factors

Many of the points made above concerning disorientation, its effects and the dissipation of them, centre on an affective response. A true understanding of a culture involves a response with all the senses. Robinson confirms this appreciation of the range of response involved in her overview of cross-cultural interactions:

> Understanding kept increasing as more of the senses were involved ... physiological, emotional, kinaesthetic, tactile and other sensory modes of perception and response influence

> understanding as much as cognitive modes which focus on knowledge about others. (1988:4)

Such a range of response is probably only made possible by being in the target country itself. Clarke's description of the bewildering number of required responses that may be encountered in a taxi ride on first arriving anywhere abroad portrays the enormity of 'cultural shock' in a first encounter with a foreign culture with its accompanying confusions:

> Getting a taxi driver to understand where you want to go; attempting to discover if he has indeed understood you, given that he says he has, but continues to drive in the wrong direction; and searching frantically all the while for the proper phrases to express yourself so that you don't appear stupid or patronizing: all of this combines to give a simple ride across town Kafkaesque proportions which cannot easily be put in perspective by the person who has suffered through them. (1976:380)

Although familiarity lessens this shock on one level it may also reveal further unexpected areas of difference, as more is revealed and encountered. Visits to the target country in our project allowed the teams first-hand experience of culture shock of various kinds and learning through all the senses.

Cognitive factors

Robinson also mentions the cognitive processes which are invoked in cross-cultural understanding, and indeed most of the manuals for intercultural training focus on the provision of information about the target culture to cater for these processes. In the United States there is a tradition of 'situation training' with students presented with typical situations in the foreign country ('culture assimilators'), given multiple choice answers (replicating their own possible responses), with explanations provided for the rightness or wrongness of these answers. There are several examples in Seelye's work on teaching culture (1988), and Brislin *et al.* give 100 examples of situations of intercultural misunderstanding. Brislin's argument, supporting his cultural assimilators from many different continents and countries, is that 'reading 100 incidents best mimics the actual cross-cultural long-term experience' (1986:19).

Adelman and Levine (1982) go beyond guesses and explanations for behaviour in their ESL textbook for migrants accommodating to an

American way of life. They provide information on American behaviour and value systems and then ask students to consider their own and other cultures in an attempt to understand the limits of their own subjective perceptions and the relativity of different systems. For example, in the chapter on intercultural differences in perception of time and space, they provide five different seating arrangements possible in a classroom and ask students to comment on the formality or informality of these and whether these pertain in their own country (1982:169–70).

Grünzweig set up an interesting simulation exercise with a group of 15 American and 15 Austrian students in different situations asking them to role-play both their own and the other nationality (1988:75–85). This allowed students 'an understanding of the foreign culture ... [and a] rethinking [of] one's own cultural contexts and traditions' (1988:84). Retrospectively for teachers of both teams in our own project, the encounters and experiences of the two-year programme could form the basis of just such intercultural teaching material for their own students. The fact that concurrent with our own experience of cross-cultural encounter, the teams were also reading about cross-cultural contact in the widest sense and preparing their students for it, provided particularly fertile ground for understanding.

Other cognitive processes involved in cross-cultural encounter, apart from the application of learnt knowledge, could also be assessed retrospectively. Robinson neatly sums up three coping strategies for facing difficult situations ('fight ... flight ... [or] benign reappraisal' (1988:88). The essentially successful outcomes of the project allowed for benign reappraisal of our experiences both privately and in discussions with members of our own and our partner team.

Three particular cognitive factors are mentioned in the literature on cross-cultural encounter which in my own retrospective 'benign reappraisal' most closely replicated my own shifts in thinking: salience, consistency and attribution. All three factors are mentioned by Robinson. In her description of 'cue salience' Robinson points to the fact that factors which are different and negative are remembered more:

> Negative evaluations which are related to distinctive features tend to be more available in memory: therefore these impressions are more lasting and harder to change than positive ones. (1988:66)

Thus in initial encounters it is differences, in behaviour, in attitude, in values, and in taste, smell and appearance, which are most noticeable and potentially alienating, particularly those which are perceived as negative.

To turn this on its head, we may invoke Heider's notion of balance or consistency (Robinson 1988:62; Morgan 1993). Heider (1957) demonstrates that people who like each other expect to have similar likes and dislikes and will adopt a variety of strategies to achieve a semblance of consistency. Byrne's investigation into attitudes and attraction also establishes a strong link between attitude similarity and pairs of friends (1969). The most interesting of these strategies in the context of our project and in line with Robinson's benign reappraisal, is that of cognitive differentiation, suggested by Sampson (1971) in his review of Heider. This differentiation relies on recognising that different reactions may mean reference to different aspects of a single complex focus, in other words that individual differences are the result of focusing on different aspects of a single subject (1971:104). Thus benign reappraisal can accommodate difference. Certainly in our own team encounters, the fact that we liked each other motivated us to understand in greater detail how apparent differences might be subsumed by a coherent whole, and to see that our differences could be seen as complementary rather than confrontational.

The third cognitive factor, that of attribution, is an altogether more subtle and unconscious process which may often only be understood retrospectively. Attribution theory suggests that understanding the reasons for a person's actions or statements will vary according to whether one is the 'actor' (the person actually involved) or the 'observer'. The observer is more likely to attribute actions to the personal characteristics of the actor; the actor is more likely to attribute them to situational factors (see Bochner 1982a:19–21). Thus in a situation where a parent strikes a child, the child might see the parent as vicious or cruel (personality/person attribution) and the parent might attribute his or her action to tiredness or stress (situation attribution). The 'person' attribution of the observer is also heightened in an intercultural situation by a potential ingroup/outgroup differentiation. Jaspars and Hewstone include Heider's explanation in their own:

> If the choice in causal attribution is between a person and a situation attribution, 'person' and 'situation' are constituted, in the case of inter-group relations, by members of in- and out-group or (one of) its members and blaming them as scapegoats then 'exonerates the members of the in-group from any blame for their conditions and prevents a lowering of the self-esteem of the in-group members' (Heider 1944:369). (1982:135)

Jaspars and Hewstone point out earlier that attributing behaviour or action to the personality of the actor by the observer, also absolves the observer from further involvement or presumably from thoughts of his own possible culpability.

> The fact that a person is seen as first or 'local' cause beyond which we do not retrace the chain of causal inferences implies that (the effects of) the behaviour can much more easily and justifiably be annulled by 'destroying' the absolute origin of the effects. (1982:134–35)

Given time, observers are likely to accord situational attributions to the 'actors' they encounter:

> the better we get to know other people the more do we come to regard them as we regard ourselves, i.e. in situational terms. (Bochner 1982a:20)

In our case the length of the two years of the project allowed time to reassess any judgements which might earlier have hinged on personal attribution and to reorientate to situational attribution.

From the descriptions above it can be seen that the cross-cultural encounters between the French and English teams were not immune from potential and actual difficulties. A variety of circumstances were however propitious and allowed for the resolution of differences.

Behaviour and language

In the closing section of this analysis I wish to consider the nature of these differences further and also the outcomes that I believe resulted from the cross-cultural contact, although here my analysis is perhaps likely to be even more subjective.

In his analysis of cross-cultural adjustment stress Weaver provides a useful diagrammatic scheme for the factors involved (1986:135).

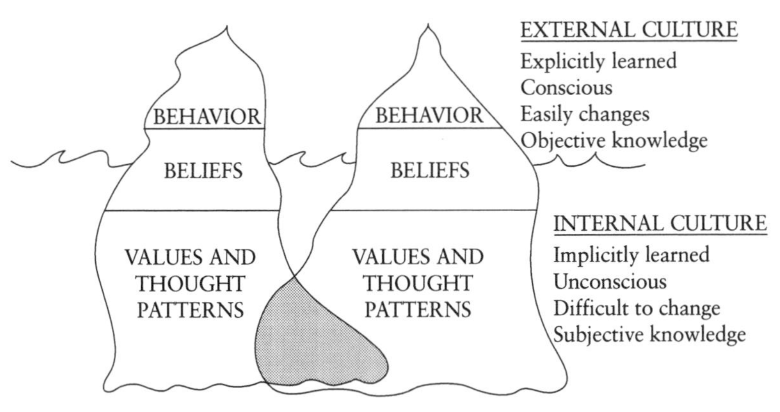

The 'Iceberg analogy' of culture

To his 'iceberg' models I would add the further factor of 'language' at the tip of the icebergs. In other words, we first encounter the behaviour and the language of another culture behind which lie the differing beliefs, values and thought patterns. Because of the nature of our project, the submerged sections of the iceberg, the more abstract schemata linked with cognition, seem also to be those most to the fore in discussion and easier to apprehend as being different. Differences in behaviour and language were less immediately available for debate, although being immediately apprehended as different. There is perhaps a more personal identification with one's own behaviour and language than with one's ideas. The latter exist often as a more recognised range of options (Billig 1987; Morgan 1993) and can often be attributed to influence from others. Thus, in the descriptions above, it is differences in situations, beliefs, value systems and thought patterns that I have commented on since these were also our first focus for discussion in the contact between the two teams. It was only later in the project with increased mutual trust and understanding that differences in behaviour and language were foregrounded and discussed.

Behavioural differences are seen as a key factor in cross-cultural misunderstanding in the training programmes mentioned above. The 'cultural assimilators' (Brislin *et al.* 1986; Seelye 1988), 'culture clusters' and 'mini-dramas' (Seelye 1988) contained in these programmes focus on decoding these differences. Here matters such as punctuality, intimacy, politeness, etc. are all-important. Discourse analysis of cross-cultural encounters reveals differences in 'frames' between speakers from different countries, differences in turn-taking and patterns of presentation (Roberts and Sayer 1987:111–35). Differences in verbal and non-verbal communication (eye-contact, tolerance of silence, gestures, volume of sound) are the subject of several exercises in Adelman and Levine (1982:39, 56–64). One example from our own experience may serve to illustrate behavioural difference.

Mole in his handbook on international business *Mind Your Manners* identifies many useful areas of difference in etiquette and behaviour (1990). Most striking amongst these for me were the descriptions of expected behaviour at business meetings since these replicated my own experiences. Mole outlines, amongst other parameters, overall distinctions of expected consensus in English meetings and accepted levels of dissent at French meetings. (See also Carolle's analysis of differences in American and French public levels of demonstrated dissent 1987: 106–09.) A further point which is not raised by Mole but mentioned by Archer (1986) is the question of tolerance of numbers of people talking. In her analyses of cross-cultural clashes, Archer identifies the difference between the polychronic speaking style of Latin American students set against the monochronic conventions of speaking expected by the American teacher (1986:171–3). Both these differences (consensus versus debate, polychronic versus monochronic) were experienced by myself in the joint meetings between the teams. For me there was a clash of expectations and reality. It seems likely that for members of both teams there were thus similar differences in what was expected in terms of contributions and in how this was articulated and what was experienced with the other team: a disorientation which however dissipated itself as the differing styles became understood.

More subtle differences exist in the area of language. The identification of the fusion of culture and language has been well established by critics (Byram and Esarte-Sarries 1991:7–8; Kramsch 1991:218; Brislin *et al.* 1986:276). Widdowson, while rejecting a symbolic relationship between the two, concedes their indexical relationship (1988:18). Two aspects of this indexical relationship surfaced in our team encounters: the use of expressions which have no direct translatable equivalent and the location of lexical items in differing semantic categories. Three of the key criteria in the French team's objectives for teaching *civilisation* were: 'le fil conducteur', 'l'écart de contenu' and 'les repères coordonnés'. These items are not easily translatable; they represent the desire to have a single co-ordinating point of focus running through the teaching material, texts which represent different and contrasting points of view, and themes which would link in an interdisciplinary way to other subjects in the curriculum. The importance of control, order and the sharpening of critical faculties through differentiation are all evident here and as such are embedded in the traditions of educational excellence in France. The interdisciplinary aspect is, for example, one that is required by the centralised French curriculum regulations.

Another area of linguistic confusion was in the understanding of evaluation/assessment. In England the process of retrospective consideration may contain both evaluation and assessment: a consideration of effectiveness of the programme and a measurement of learners' success. We use two different words in English. In French only one category exists, 'l'évaluation', which subsumes both notions. To turn the tables, the term 'comparative' in English usually suggests both contrasts and comparison, whereas in French 'comparatif' refers only to comparison. The matrix of different types of differentiation is much more clearly defined in the French language than in English. In these two examples the understanding of the language and thought behind it is further complicated by the lexical items being so similar in both languages. One could easily assume direct translatable equivalents.

The notion of the boundary

Behaviour and language then in our cross-cultural encounter were less easy to decode than the broader issues of value-systems and beliefs. In order to understand why behaviour and language are experienced as more personal, it is useful to analyse the notion of 'boundary'. Bozon in his ethnographic study of the small town of Villefranche describes how social groups establish their identity by their different patterns of sociability (and, one would suspect also, language), by establishing boundaries between themselves and other groups:

> Le dynamisme de la vie associative ... multiplie les possibilités de rencontres face à face entre individus et entre groupes sociaux. Dans ces occasions, les caractéristiques propres de chaque groupe s'exacerbent plus qu'elles ne s'atténuent. (1984:266)
>
> The dynamic of the life of clubs and societies ... multiplies the possibilities of face-to-face encounters between individuals and social groups. On these occasions the individual characteristics of each group become more rather than less pronounced. (My translation)

The establishing of these boundaries often entails rejection of the other group:

> La vie associative paraît être un lieu où s'affirme avec force des identités sociales distinctives et où se mettent en scène de véritables rivalités symboliques. (1984:266)
>
> The life of clubs and societies seems to be a place where distinctive social identities are asserted with force and where truly symbolic rivalries come to the fore. (My translation)

Thus it could be said that on relinquishing the boundaries of our own identity in recognising the validity of others, we threaten our own sense of identity. It is in the public area of behaviour and language that identity is proclaimed. These are thus more difficult to relinquish.

Outcomes

If identity is potentially threatened in cross-cultural encounter it could also be said that innumerable benefits may accrue. On a first basis, as already mentioned, team members were able directly to help each other with practical matters such as the acquisition of materials and information. Brislin suggests four beneficial effects of a sojourn, each contributing to a broadening of outlook and increasing self-confidence: '[1] Worldmindedness ... [2] decline in authoritarianism ... [3] internal control ... [4] achievement values ... people can influence their destinies through their own efforts' (1981:293–5). He also speculates that cross-cultural contact may foster 'creativity ... multiculturality ... [and the ability to act as] creative mediators' (1981:296–9). Whether such effects take place immediately or are long-term is difficult to assess. Certainly for myself, and I believe the other team members, the two years provided a richness of experience not encountered elsewhere.

The continuing collaboration between team members bears witness to the potential fruitfulness of such encounters and to the value gained from the visible cross-fertilisation in the materials produced (the welcoming of a more 'French' historical perspective and emphasis on the transmission of knowledge by the English team and the interest of the French team in the 'English' affective perspective with focus on empathy and ethnography).

To some extent any collaboration depends on mutual liking between team members. However, there do also seem to be variables that can be gauged in advance which will help to promote success. Of those identified above, time and accorded equality of status emerge as two of the most influential. These are perhaps factors not always given sufficient attention by researchers when joint projects are planned and organised.

13 Language teaching and the process of European integration

Karen Risager

Language teaching facing European integration

General foreign language education includes among its goals the development of learners' understanding of culture, and this is often expressed by the phrase that language teaching should 'offer insights into the culture and the civilisation of the countries where the language is spoken' (among others, the official guidelines for language teaching in England/Wales and Denmark, see below).

Such a phrase presupposes the existence of countries whose culture and civilisation can be clearly delimited. However, the process of European (and global) integration, seen as an increasing cross-national entanglement at the economic, political, cultural and linguistic level, tends to blur national borders. This development actually undermines a teaching which is still decidedly influenced by the idea of the national language and the national culture. How does language teaching in Europe respond to this development?

Language teachers' understanding of culture and descriptions of their own practice as teachers of culture

This general question can be seen as the guiding question for an international project on the cultural dimension of language teaching. The project, which focuses on how language teachers view the situation, is entitled: 'Language Teachers' Identity and the Process of European Integration', and its purpose is to investigate how language teachers in England and Denmark view their own role as mediators of culture in the process of European integration. Empirically the project concerns language teachers in English secondary schools, where learners study languages from age 11 to 18, and teachers of English, German and French in Danish comprehensive schools (*folkeskole*), where learners study languages from age 10 to 16 (then proceeding to upper secondary school). The data of the project have been collected in both countries by means of a questionnaire and an interview. The present article reflects results from the Danish part of the project, based on 653 responses to questionnaires and 43 in-depth interviews. It should be noted that most *folkeskole* teachers teach many subjects, and if they teach foreign languages, they very often teach two or three.

Four approaches to foreign language teaching

Results from the project suggest that foreign language teaching is facing a profound change in content and methods, chiefly brought about by the development of pupil exchanges and the use of information technology on a broad European basis. In what follows, I will describe four different approaches to foreign language teaching, and use data from the project to illustrate especially approaches 3 and 4:

1. The foreign-cultural approach, which has been losing ground since the 1980s;
2. The intercultural approach, which has replaced the foreign-cultural approach, and is the dominant one today;
3. The multicultural approach, which has made its appearance since the 1980s, but is still in a marginal position;
4. The transcultural approach, which is just beginning to appear as a result of internationalisation.

It should be noted that these approaches are to be understood as ideal-typical. In the actual course of teaching they may coexist, thus reflecting a widespread eclecticism within language teaching. The four analytical concepts are inspired by Welsch (1995), who discusses four corresponding concepts of culture from a philosophical point of view.

The foreign-cultural approach

The foreign-cultural approach is, largely implicitly, based on the concept of the single culture, associated with a specific people, a specific language, and normally with a specific territory. This approach focuses on the culture of the country or countries where the language is spoken (target countries) (cf. the approach that Murphy (1988) calls the monocultural), and does not deal with the learners' own country, nor with relations between the target countries and the learners' own, or other countries. The conception of the target country in question may include geographic, social or subcultural variation, but it is still said to be variation within one culture: French culture, German culture, etc.

Attitudes may be characterised by admiration for the foreign culture: the teaching may be francophile, anglophile, germanophile, allowing and enhancing positive stereotypes (cf. Risager (1988), where I call this phenomenon secondary ethnocentrism: ethnocentrism transferred to the target country).

In this approach the target language is taught only as if it were the first language for the population. The teaching aim is to develop in learners a native speaker communicative and cultural competence, i.e. a competence that approaches as much as possible the competence of 'the native speaker', without any awareness of the difficulties involved in this concept as described by Kramsch in this volume.

The current situation of the foreign-cultural approach

This approach is well-known, as it has been the dominant paradigm within foreign language teaching in Western countries from the last century until the 1980s. Today it is being strongly called into question in the pedagogical debate, mainly because it rests upon a concept of culture that does not include relationships between cultures – as the next approach does.

The intercultural approach

The intercultural approach is based on a concept of culture that takes its point of departure in the fact that different cultures are structurally related to each other. Accordingly this concept encompasses the encounter or interplay of cultures, including attempts to deal with, understand and recognise each other. As in the foreign-cultural approach, the primary focus of the intercultural approach is on the target country or countries, but the intercultural approach also deals with the learners' own country, and with relations between the target countries and the pupil's own, and possibly with other countries – including relations of dominance, and intercultural attitudes.

The teaching typically stresses the importance of factors of national identity. It may include comparisons between the target countries and the learners' country, thereby inviting learners to develop a reflective attitude to the culture and civilisation of their own country. The teaching may be characterised by attitudes of cultural relativism, the wish for a non-ethnocentric view of the countries involved.

Here too, the target language is taught as if it were a first language for the population in question, but the aim is to develop an intercultural and communicative competence, a competence that enables the learner to function as a mediator between the two cultures, and to use the target language as contact language with people who use this language as a first language (this use of the language is called by Ammon (1991) asymmetrically dominant: one individual uses the language as a first language, the other as a foreign language).

The current situation of the intercultural approach

Since the 1980s, language teaching has become increasingly influenced by the intercultural perspective. Among other things, there is an interest in looking at learners' opportunities for reflecting upon and gaining an understanding of their own country. That is what is expressed in the current descriptions of the aims of foreign language teaching in England and in Denmark.

The National Curriculum for England and Wales (DES 1990:3) contains the following aims concerning the cultural dimension:

- to offer insights into *the culture and the civilisation of the countries where the language is spoken*;
- to encourage positive attitudes to foreign language learning and to speakers of foreign languages and a sympathetic approach to other cultures and civilisations;
- to develop *pupils' understanding of themselves and their own culture*. (My emphasis)

The Danish aims for foreign language teaching in the *folkeskole* (Undervisningsministeriet 1994:15, 74, 78) state the following, concerning the cultural dimension:

- The teaching should offer insights *into the cultural and societal conditions of English-speaking/German-speaking/French-speaking countries*, thereby enhancing pupils' international understanding and *understanding of their own culture*. (My emphasis and translation)

In the aims of both countries there is first a statement related to the foreign-cultural approach (focused on the countries where the language is spoken), and a later statement related to the intercultural approach (focused on learners' own culture). So the aims reflect the general history of language teaching.

In language teaching today, there is a keen interest both in the cultural encounter and in similarities and dissimilarities between the target countries and the learners' country – and no doubt a lesser interest in relations of dominance. Attitudes may be characterised by cultural relativism, but intentions to foster positive attitudes can also be found, cf. the English statement 'to encourage positive attitudes' and 'a sympathetic approach'. In the Danish guidelines there is a more neutral expression: 'international understanding'.

The following response from one of the interviews in the project on the identity of language teachers is typical, because teachers are generally convinced about the relevance of the intercultural perspective, especially regarding personal contacts:

> I am quite sure that when you meet people from other countries and talk with them, you have to look at yourself, you will think about who you are, what you want, and what you stand for. I have experienced that very much, when I was abroad, because you are regarded as a representative of your country. They look at you, and they ask you all kinds of things, and what you tell them that's a bit about Denmark, and they stick to that. They really listen to that. (no. 281, a woman in her 20s, who teaches French) (my translation of all Danish interviews)

The pure intercultural approach rests upon a concept of culture that presupposes an understanding of each of the cultures as a homogeneous entity – though perhaps geographically and socially varied – interacting with the others. In my view, this approach is inadequate as an influential paradigm in language teaching, because it is blind to the actual multicultural (and multilingual) character of almost all existing countries or states. The next approach takes account of this.

The multicultural approach

The multicultural approach rests upon a concept of culture that reflects the fact that several cultures may coexist within the boundaries of one and the same society or state. For some groups in the society in question the 'national' or standard/official language is their first language, for others it is their second language, for still others it is a foreign language.

Thus the multicultural approach includes a specific focus on the ethnic and linguistic diversity of the target country or countries, e.g. Bretons and Moroccans and indigenous French in France. It also deals with the ethnic and linguistic diversity of the learners' own country, and with the relations between the target countries and the learners' own, and other countries, including migratory relations (where do immigrants and refugees come from, and why?). The teaching may be focused on national and ethnic identities. It may include comparisons between the target countries and the learners' own, thereby inviting learners to develop a reflective attitude to the cultures of their own country. The teaching may reflect wishes for a balanced and anti-racist view of the cultures involved.

The teaching deals with the target language both as a first language for parts of the population, and as a second language for other parts. Typically the teaching will include work with cultures that are currently or originally expressed in another language than the target language, e.g. Arabic, Berber or Basque.

As in the intercultural approach, the ideal is the mediator's competence: intercultural and communicative competence, but this time at a partly different level. It is a competence enabling learners to use the target language as a *lingua franca*, speaking with people who on the one hand belong to the society where the target language is also spoken as a first language, e.g. France, but on the other hand belong to another culture, e.g. Moroccan culture, and who may speak another language as their first language, e.g. Moroccan Arabic.

The current situation of the multicultural approach

The multicultural approach was anticipated in the foreign-cultural and the intercultural approaches in the sense that regionalism and immigrant workers have been included in the range of sociopolitical topics, along with women, young people, black people, etc. But it was not until the 1980s that the teaching began to focus on different ethnic identities in their own right, and to consider it relevant to teach specifically about these cultures.

Several factors are contributing to the further development of this approach. Firstly, there is the growing importance of the post-colonial countries as subject matter for the teaching. In this case the teaching typically deals with the target language as second language (official language) for the majority of the population – which may be ethnically very diverse.

Secondly, the multicultural perspective may become more pronounced with the increase in the number of multicultural classes, where one can build to a greater extent on the cultural experiences of bi- or multilingual learners, e.g. in working with topics related to these experiences, for instance Islam in France and in Denmark.

Thirdly, an important factor in the development of the multicultural approach is the increase in pupil exchanges (see also Lasnel 1994). In the interviews carried out in connection with the project on language teachers, some statements illustrate how exchanges may create an environment furthering the awareness of the culture of ethnic minorities:

> The district we visit, the school we have contact with, is situated in a suburban area outside Strasbourg, where there are many

> blocks of flats. I mean, we have contact with a school that has many foreign workers or many people of foreign origin, as they say, and it's a very good thing for us to experience. And I must say that our school doesn't have as many. And that means that we experience something that widens our horizon, I think. Also some negative things, they widen the horizon in another direction as well (...) And there are some social differences, because we can see that pupils live with different types of families. And some live with Moslems, where you eat in a special way. We have been there during the period called Ramadan, where we experienced that they are not allowed to eat during the daytime, and in spite of that they offered the Danish guest lots of things. And we have experienced that sometimes they move out of the bedroom, and they don't have room enough, you see, their living conditions are different. Maybe that's something you might experience just by exchanging with a class in Tåstrup [a Danish town, KR]. But now it's France by chance, and that's why it comes up like this. (no. 639, a woman in her 40s, who teaches French, Danish, needlework, drama, music and art)

However, the concept of multiculturality resembles the concept of interculturality, as it presupposes that the cultures existing within one and the same society are each a homogeneous entity interacting with the others. So the multicultural approach misses the awareness that internationalisation implies a blurring of both national and ethnic borders, leading to an increased cultural complexity at all levels.

The transcultural approach

The transcultural approach takes as its point of departure the interwoven character of cultures as a common condition for the whole world: cultures penetrate each other in changing combinations by virtue of extensive migration and tourism, world wide communication systems for mass and private communication, economic interdependence, and the globalisation of the production of goods (Hannerz 1992; Barth 1989). The widespread use of a number of languages as *lingua franca*s (i.e. used in situations where none of the speakers has the language in question as his or her first language) is one of the expressions of the internationalised world.

The transcultural approach focuses on the life of individuals and groups in contexts characterised by more or less cultural and linguistic complexity: television channels, the city street, the multicultural classroom, the supermarket – situations where the target language is used, but in such a way that learners also become aware of other languages being used (English in Germany, French in Britain, etc.) (Risager 1993). The teaching deals not only with the traditional target countries, but also with other countries, areas or cultural contexts, if this may contribute to language learning, e.g. communication in English, German, French with Dutch or Polish learners/pen friends, etc. The teaching may stress complex identities, possibly third culture identities: a kind of complex identity resulting from having lived for long periods in several countries.

Consequently, the teaching deals with the target language both as first language, second language and international language. The ideal is still the mediator's competence: intercultural and communicative competence, but with new tasks: the competence to use the language as contact language in all kinds of situations characterised by cultural and linguistic complexity, among others as a *lingua franca* in international and interethnic communication. (This type of competence resembles, but should not be confused with what Meyer (1991) calls intercultural performance at the transcultural level.)

The current situation of the transcultural approach

A driving force as regards this approach is the growing importance of cross-cultural personal contacts between learners (and teachers and families, etc.), especially in situations where the target language is used as a *lingua franca*. This establishes a culturally complex situation encompassing at least three different cultures, including the cultural background of the target language. A number of teachers in the research project speak very enthusiastically about the value of learners' personal contacts with young people in countries other than traditional target countries. Generally speaking, teachers do not have reservations as to the value of these personal contacts as regards the development of tolerance (cf. Christ, 1993):

> I think it's very important that pupils have or get contacts to especially young people of their own age from other language communities. It's not so important whether it is a community where the language is taught, or whether it is the same language community that we teach about. Our school has had exchange trips to Prague for some years. Here pupils can make acquaintance with a language community they don't know otherwise, and with a cultural background that may be valuable for them to get into contact with, which is an opportunity they seldom think about. In that case we chiefly use English and German as

> communication languages, of course ... (no. 261, a man in his 40s, who teaches English, German, and French)

> We have got a lot out of our exchanges with England, with Sweden, with Norway, with different places in Germany, and recently in Potsdam, in the former East Germany. We can also foresee that some Poles will visit us, and maybe some from the Baltic countries. (no. 624, a man in his 50s, who teaches German and geography)

> I did an exchange to Spain with the class I had as a form teacher, and in that situation I would of course have read some Hemingway, 'The Sun Also Rises', of course. And then a long time before I had bought 'The European', because every week there is something about every country, and I cut some things out, so you see I would have given them some teaching on Spain in English. But normally I would not begin telling them a lot about France, for example, or about Germany. I would concentrate on America and England. (no. 350, a woman in her 30s, who teaches English, Danish, history and religion)

Some teachers talk about learners' contacts via letters, electronic mail and similar forms of communication:

> For the moment my German class participates, via contacts to England, in a computer program with an English class that is studying German at beginner's level. They are supposed to send messages – by way of diskette or modem – of what information they want on Denmark in German. Correspondingly, we send them messages about what we would like to know about them and their area. As you see, this is a data-base relationship. And it is clear that this kind of communication offers more than the old-fashioned geography lessons. It is an experiment we have, and of course it is to be extended to other countries. (no. 520, a man in his 50s, who teaches English, German, French, Danish and geography)

> As a teacher of English I have always taken care that my classes have got pupils to correspond with in other countries. And I have had a class corresponding with Holland, and they took part in an air pollution project, where they corresponded with Hungary and with Latvia. And as a matter of fact, the class I have today, that's an 8th form [ages 14/15, KR], they got a letter correspondence started already in the 5th form (...) if it's an English girl or boy they are going to correspond with in the

> 5th form, then they (the English) would know the language, and then they (my pupils) would immediately feel inferior. But the fact that they receive letters that are written in a language just as helpless as their own, makes them less anxious about writing. (no. 8, a woman in her 40s, who teaches English, Danish and history)

Some are very internationally orientated, and wish to prepare learners to become cosmopolitan:

> One of the places I like to visit, precisely because it is so incredibly central internationally, is Luxembourg. A wonderful place. And they have a language mix-up that's enchanting (. . .) I would like to make these people (the pupils) cosmopolitan, so that they can live everywhere. The journey home to mum and dad is no further than a train or flight ticket. (no. 520, a man in his 50s, who teaches English, German, French, Danish and geography – cited above)

It should be added that concurrently with the use of the language as *lingua franca* in another country, one often finds phrases about nationalities, phrases that can be related to the intercultural approach. In this example, the class has been in Greece:

> ... you talk about what other peoples are like. And among other things the prejudices we have, that Italians steal, and Finns carry knives, and people from Southern Europe are generally scruffy. And then they say 'Except the Greeks'. Then I say 'Why not the Greeks?' 'No, no, for we know them, they are not scruffy.' And then I say 'Then Italians need not be like that either.' 'No, that's right, but Greeks are certainly not like that, and Greeks are not lazy either, even if they don't work between 12 and 16, that's because it's so hot ...' (no. 8, a woman in her 40s, who teaches English, Danish and history – cited above)

These few statements illustrate that some language teachers in the Danish *folkeskole* are engaged in an approach that is revolutionising language teaching at that level, not least the cultural dimension. Pupil exchanges to various European countries beyond target countries in the strict sense make new demands on the teachers. In addition to the current requirement that they should have some insight into the culture and the civilisation of the target countries, as well as an insight into pedagogical methods for mediating between the cultures concerned, they also – with short notice – have to be able to provide themselves with a basic insight into the culture and civilisation of other countries or areas, and teach learners to function as mediators between the country/area concerned, and their own. The same thing applies, of course, when learners communicate through traditional or electronic mail at the class level.

Language teachers' definitions of culture

As already mentioned, the project on the identity of language teachers includes a questionnaire study and an interview study which elucidate a series of questions concerning the cultural dimension of language teaching. One of the open questions in the questionnaire was: 'What do you understand by the word *culture*?' Respondents were given a space of 7 to 8 lines for the answer. The question on culture was placed relatively early in the questionnaire as a kind of prelude to the following sections where teachers were directed by our structuring of the topic area. The Danish material consists of 630 answers from all over the country (Risager 1995). In the interview study, teachers were invited to comment further on the definition they had given in the questionnaire.

About half the teachers give a definition of culture that associates culture with a country or people or society, that is, a nationally oriented definition, for example: 'Culture is what people do – the way of life of people. To understand other people's way of life you have to ask: What is it like to be a Dane, a German and so on?' (no. 1), and : 'The geography of the country – ways of life and customs, tourist attractions' (127). Very few teachers make explicit an understanding of culture that associates it with more than one society, for example: 'Everything related to life and ways of living in the country concerned, and to its relationship with the rest of the world' (129), and: 'Communicating and being together. From German Sauerkraut to the European history of religion, and all that is in between' (382). And very few mention cultural diversity within one country, for example: 'A group's work, art, customs, values, and language' (78). About half the respondents express themselves in a more general way in relation to these categories, but no awareness of cultural diversity or complexity is explicitly expressed, for example: 'Daily life – how people live together – social conditions – religious conditions – holidays and festivities' (25).

These results concern only *folkeskole* teachers teaching foreign languages. A minor control study was accomplished in 1994 by Karen-Margrethe Frederiksen (Roskilde University) and me among teachers of Danish as a second language for adult immigrants/refugees, encompassing 87 teachers. In that investigation the picture was partly different. Proportionally there were far fewer definitions that were nationally orientated, and there were more teachers who thought that culture should be described as something specific to groups. Answers that were more general were proportionately of the same number as for *folkeskole* teachers, i.e. about half the respondents.

These two investigations suggest that it is specifically foreign language (*folkeskole*) teachers, and not second language teachers, who in their immediate answers exhibit definitions of culture that are influenced by the nationally oriented conception. The difference may have something to do with the fact that foreign language teaching has a long tradition of conceiving culture in terms of nationality and national history, connecting nation, people and language closely with one another. Second language teaching is in a different situation. The difference may also be partly explained by the different connections between the two groups of teachers and their respective subject matter. Foreign language teachers' distance to the target countries may enhance the tendency to take a bird's eye view of the countries in question. Second language teachers are placed in the midst of the society that they teach about, and that may be one of the reasons why they are more aware of the cultures of different groups.

Of course, these definitions do not give a fair picture of the overall cultural awareness of teachers. They tell us something about their first associations with the concept of culture, associations which are supplemented and differentiated by some of the statements in the interviews, among others those concerning experiences of pupil exchanges.

Conclusion

As regards foreign language teaching in Denmark, the European integration process primarily comes out in the increase in the number of personal contacts across borders, where the languages are used in situations where they are asymmetrically dominant, or function as *lingua franca*s, connected with thematic contents that can in principle relate to any country or area, including Denmark. To the extent that exchanges and other visits are accomplished on a class (i.e. not individual or private) basis, they chiefly concern European countries, not countries outside of Europe.

The teachers' understanding of culture can be described at different levels, and I have touched upon two: how they describe the word 'culture', and how they describe their pedagogical practice in relation to personal cultural encounters. At the former level the understanding of culture points in a certain sense backwards towards the traditional concept of the national (or the single) culture. At the latter level the understanding of culture points partly to the future, by describing practices that can be related to the multicultural and the transcultural perspective. At the same time, the nationally oriented conception exists in the form of numerous references to 'the other peoples', in an attempt to cope with national stereotypes.

Note:
I wish to thank Tove Skutnabb-Kangas, Robert Phillipson, Michael Byram and Gerd Gabrielsen for valuable comments on the earlier version of this chapter.
The members of the project group are, in Denmark: Karen Risager, Roskilde University, Gerd Gabrielsen and John Gulløv Christensen, The Royal Danish School of Educational Studies, and Pia List, Odense University; and in England: Michael Byram, Kate Lloyd and Régine Schneider, University of Durham.

14 In-service teacher training and the acquisition of intercultural competence

Lies Sercu

Introduction

When telling foreign language teachers in Belgium that there is need for a change you are sure to face the difficult task of conquering immediately arising scepticism with regard to 'this intercultural wave'. Telling them, further, that the theory behind the change and the necessary concepts are already there (Müller 1986; Bredella and Legutke 1985; Byram, Morgan *et al.* 1994) will not help as teachers have, to say the least, mixed feelings about theory and theoretical concepts.

The problem with theory is twofold. Teachers may either regard a theory as *per se* proven and requiring no further substantiation or else, as a result of professional pride, they may reject theory altogether. The teacher has then become a practitioner, a term with which s/he wishes to say that school and teaching cannot be loaded down with an unnecessary ballast of grey theory. Consequently, if in-service teacher training (INSET) wants to contribute to bringing about changes it cannot simply *pass on* the results of 'the latest research' and 'the newest theories' to the teachers as a form of transmission of knowledge, without considering the relationship between theory and practice, between externally-based theoretical demands and the actual school and classroom situation (Edelhoff 1992). Its task is rather to attract the teacher and to supply him/her with the skills, abilities and reflective attitudes which are necessary if s/he is to participate actively in the process of change. In concrete terms this means that the teacher should be enabled to apply and test theories him/herself instead of simply training to be able to use ready-made recipes. Thus teacher education should provide 'for situations which cannot be unquestioningly accommodated into preconceived patterns of response but which require a modification of hitherto held views on one's teaching' (Widdowson 1987). Seen in this way, in-service teacher education and training is in every respect a critical process.

When developing in-service course concepts on the acquisition of intercultural competence, it is crucial to make teachers experience that the innovation at hand requires changes in their self-concept, in their professional qualifications, in their attitudes and skills. Thus INSET becomes a highly personal and individual matter where teachers need to start seeing themselves not only as trainers, but also as trainees.

Edelhoff (1987:76ff) summarised the main points of teacher qualifications for intercultural foreign language teaching as follows:

*(i) **Attitudes***

- Teachers who are meant to educate learners towards international and intercultural learning must be international and intercultural learners themselves.
- Teachers should be prepared to consider how others see them and be curious about themselves and others.
- Teachers should be prepared to experiment and negotiate in order to achieve understanding on both sides.
- Teachers should be prepared to share meanings, experience and affects with both people from other countries and their own learners in the classroom.
- Teachers should be prepared to take an active part in the search for the modern language contribution to international understanding and peacemaking at home and abroad.
- Teachers should aim to adopt the role and function of a social and intercultural interpreter, not an ambassador.

*(ii) **Knowledge***

- Teachers should have and seek knowledge about the socio-cultural environment and background of the target language community(ies) or country(ies).
- Teachers should have and seek knowledge about their own country and community and how others see them.
- Teachers' knowledge should be active knowledge ready to apply and interpret and to make accessible to the learning situation and styles of their learners.
- Teachers should know how language works in communication and how it is used successfully for understanding. They should know about the shortcomings of language and foreign language users and how misunderstandings can be avoided.

*(iii) **Skills***

- Teachers should have and develop further appropriate communication skills in the foreign language suitable for negotiation both in the classroom and in international communication situations at home and abroad.

- Teachers should have and develop further text skills, i.e. the ability to deal with authentic data in all media (print, audio, audio-visual) and in face-to-face interaction.
- Teachers should have and develop further the necessary skills to connect the student experience with ideas, things and objects outside their direct reach and to create learning environments which lend themselves to experiential learning, negotiation and experiment.

The teacher training course on the acquisition of intercultural competence presented here tries to take into account the teacher qualifications advocated by Edelhoff. The course was designed for Flemish foreign language teachers and tries to reflect and address the changes required for that particular group to become mediators of cultural knowledge and skills in the foreign language classroom. It takes into consideration the twofold learning process that is likely to occur: the teachers will be equally involved in a personal as well as in a professional learning process.

The Belgian context

Belgian teaching is largely dominated by the knowledge dimension of learning, and teachers feel uneasy having to deal with affective or behavioural aspects of the learning process. Also, they have a hard time reflecting on their own teaching practices, partly because they have not acquired the necessary professional terminology to discuss and reflect upon theories and proposals for practical applications. The professional identity of language teachers, too, is a very traditional one. Most language teachers think of themselves as 'language people'. Their courses, traditionally, consist of language work and are sometimes complemented with literature or 'kennis van land en volk' (knowledge of the country and its people), which is said to bring a welcome change from teaching but which is not felt to be an important objective of foreign language teaching. As it appears in schoolbooks, 'kennis van land en volk' is eclectic in content and method. It does not support reflective learning nor does it aim at enhancing the learners' intercultural competence. The teachers themselves are often well-informed about the foreign country(ies) of which they teach the foreign language(s) but do not perceive themselves as 'cultural mediators' (Buttjes and Byram 1991).

Nevertheless, with the growing impact of the Vlaams Blok, the Flemish extreme right-wing political party, and the resulting feelings of unease accompanying the party's members' intolerance towards foreigners and foreign cultures, teachers feel responsible for turning that tide. Language teachers especially feel they are in a good position to open up learners to other cultures but are at a loss how to do it. In 1993 all Flemish educational networks signed a non-discrimination agreement, which stipulates on the one hand that all teaching should be interculturally oriented and on the other hand that schools can no longer refuse to admit immigrant children. A number of experimental intercultural projects have been set up in literature, history and language classes. Although a lot of attention is devoted to the acquisition of Dutch as a second language, the cultural aspects involved are largely disregarded. The pioneer spirit that for the moment enthuses a number of teachers does not meet with sufficient support on the part of teacher training institutions.

A further element in the picture is that language teaching is largely confined to the classroom. Owing to fixed schedules and lack of self-access centres there are very few opportunities for independent and experiential learning. The use of computers or other tools which can assist language learning and bring the outside world into the language classroom, such as multimedia, e-mail or www, is very limited. As a consequence, learners perceive themselves as more or less passive participants in the teaching-and-learning process, which seems, to put it sharply, guided by the teacher and the textbook only. The images of other countries they gain from family visits or from the media – every pupil has access to French, German, British, Italian, Spanish, Turkish, Dutch, Luxembourg and even American television stations – remain largely unquestioned in the language classroom. As pointed out by Kramsch (1991:233), however, 'television can be the greatest obstacle to appreciate and understand cultural differences, if it is not critically "deconstructed" and placed in its own discourse framework'. Moreover, as part of the hidden curriculum learners learn that their feelings and their daily life experiences lose in interest in the course of growing up and moving on to more abstract levels of thinking and reasoning.

Designing the course

Presenting a brief sketch of the Flemish language teacher's identity and work situation seemed a necessary prerequisite for justifying the fundamentals that underlie the course outline. The course was designed for a two-day in-service teacher training seminar, intended for teachers of languages in the upper years of secondary education. As will be clear from the introduction, the course aims at presenting a comprehensive and coherent picture of 'teaching-and-learning language-and-culture', a term coined by Byram, Morgan *et al.* (1994), through combining reflection on a number of methodological culture-general key concepts and theoretical insights on the one hand and the presentation of a practice-oriented exercise typology on the other. Intelligent and informed reflection on the classroom situation was considered essential to achieving 'principled decision making in practice' (Duff 1988:vi).

For the sake of clarity of presentation, theory precedes practice. However, from the very start theoretical insights are related to teaching practice and vice versa; the exercise typology that is presented is examined in the light of the newly acquired theoretical insights.

The first part of the course has a culture-general character, which constitutes the second principle underlying the course design. The question of culture-general versus culture-specific training has been an ongoing controversy (Gudykunst and Hammer 1983). We, for our part, did not want to pass on culture-specific knowledge, thereby committing ourselves to the objectives of traditional *Landeskunde* teaching. Our primary goal was to give the participants an intellectual understanding of the concept of culture, of culture theory and of culture learning theory and to create a solid framework for the teachers', and ultimately their learners', personal development. Nevertheless, while completing seminar tasks, teachers from the different language sections (French, English, German, Dutch as a second language) were invited a number of times to sit together and discuss the issue at hand with their particular common language-and-culture teaching background in mind. While confirming the importance of a sound culture-specific knowledge basis it is shown at the same time how unreflected and simplified descriptions of certain aspects of the foreign culture may increase the participants' use of stereotypes and give them the false impression that they 'know' the culture.

A third principle guiding the course design was our concern to involve the participants in as active a way as possible. Culture-general courses traditionally include lectures in fields such as anthropology, intercultural communication or intercultural psychology or on the participants' own culture, reducing the audience to more or less passive receivers of, no doubt, interesting information. This format did not seem adequate to our purposes. We opted for an activity and task oriented experiential learning format.

A fourth principle guiding the format of the seminar should have been to supplement classroom teaching with field work outside the classroom, thus offering further opportunities for truly experiential learning, for example in the format of a field study conducted in the way described by Roberts (1995) and Barro *et al.* in this volume. Even if this physical going-into-the-field dimension was absent, discussing the methodological principles and objectives of field research as an activity to be carried out by learners was a welcome starting point for considering the problems connected with confining language-and-culture teaching-and-learning to the classroom. First, classroom teaching, arranging for common activities at a common speed, does not offer sufficient opportunities for autonomous learning. Second, the acquisition of intercultural competence requires contact with members of other cultures in as active and direct a way as possible. In ordinary classroom teaching, attempts have been made with role playing, where some have played themselves and others have played members of other cultures, possibly supplemented by actual cultural artefacts from the foreign country. Such a 'contact' with members of a foreign culture remains, however, an inadequate alternative.

Course outline

It will now be shown how the above-mentioned principles have been translated into a concrete teacher training seminar. Some of the materials used are in German, others are in English or in French. The

1 *Intercultural competence*

1.1 **Key concepts**
- 1.1.1 My own culture?
- 1.1.2 Observation and interpretation: the foreign perspective – empathy
- 1.1.3 Concept investigation
- 1.1.4 Geography, Landeskunde, intercultural language teaching

1.2 **Defining intercultural competence**

2 *A curriculum for intercultural language teaching*

2.1 **Intercultural competence and language production**

2.2 **Linguistic awareness of cultures: an exercise typology**
- 2.2.1 Conjunctions, adverbs, particles and negations (Grammar)
- 2.2.2 Concepts and their culture-specific meaning (Vocabulary)
- 2.2.3 Non-verbal communicative behaviour
- 2.2.4 Communicative styles

2.3 **Prejudices and stereotypes**

programme consists of three main parts. First, a number of key concepts related to the acquisition of intercultural competence are introduced. The core objectives for intercultural language teaching are discussed and a working definition of intercultural competence is examined. In the second part an exercise typology is presented and discussed in various stages. A final part consists of the evaluation of existing teaching materials with respect to the acquisition of intercultural competence.

The actual course outline is presented on p. 260. Only a limited number of the exercises and tasks that make up the course will be presented. All materials serve a threefold purpose: for one thing they aim at the teacher's professional development, for another at the teacher's personal learning and thirdly they aim at guiding the pupil's language-and-culture learning processes.

1 Intercultural competence

1.1 Key concepts

The aim of this part is to introduce the participants to the notion of *Fremdverstehen* (critical understanding of otherness) and its related concepts, to arrive at a working definition of intercultural competence, and to point out their pertinence to foreign language-and-culture teaching.

According to Müller (1986) the attainment target of intercultural language teaching is 'critical understanding of otherness'. A first condition for acquiring this ability is that one gains some insight into one's own culture and into the conditions of observation. As pointed out by Kræmer (1973) it is important to realise that true self-awareness is not the same as increased 'knowledge of one's own culture' as such. It is the recognition that one's own culture influences one's observations, interpretations and behaviour, and the awareness of when and how this happens. Secondly, in order to reach a high degree of empathy one should learn to compare interculturally. Accurately defined objects from different cultures need to be evaluated with regard to similar criteria, which are, it should not be forgotten, never objective but always culturally determined. One should try to find reasons for differences and similarities from within the foreign culture, always keeping a certain emotional distance. Thirdly, although the only adequate attitude is an all-questioning one, also with regard to the sources of one's knowledge, one should be able to live with a certain amount of ambiguity, with temporarily incomplete pictures of the phenomena under consideration, ensuring of course that this tolerance does not evolve into indifference, thus making a stereotype live on. Finally, *Fremdverstehen* requires the ability to mediate between cultures through metacommunication and negotiation of meaning: one should learn to verbalise uncertainties, ambiguities, similarities, differences, one's emotions and reactions towards aspects of the other culture.

In what follows, a number of tasks and activities are presented that make the course participants aware of the many facets of learning-and-teaching involved in the acquisition of intercultural competence. They will show ways to help develop the habits of reflection on and analysis of intercultural communicative situations.

1.1.1 My own culture?

Activity 1: Cartoon/picture

The participants are each presented with one half of a picture or cartoon (see Appendix 1 for an example) making a statement about the Flemings or the Belgians. The pictures comment on Flemish mentality, values or taboo subjects (e.g. the royal family, living in a small country and community, sensitivity to language issues). The participants first have to find their partner and then discuss what aspects of Flemish culture are being revealed and how they would explain these to a member of a foreign country of their choice.

This challenging activity incites people to investigate their own culture and introduces the concept of 'shared cultural knowledge', which moves on from the traditional *Landeskunde* concept of knowledge as information.

1.1.2 Observation and interpretation: the foreign perspective – empathy

Activity 2: Atlas

The participants are given blind maps of Belgium (image of one's own culture), Holland, Germany or Great Britain (images of other cultures) and are asked to fill them out with whatever cultural elements they can think of. They are encouraged to draw as well as write. (See Appendix 2 for an example.)

The activity points out that 'images' differ between individuals. Foreigners, then, will also hold very differentiated views on Flemish culture. As a consequence, in the foreign language classroom too, one cannot pass on 'the' picture of another culture. As most participants make reference to such things as objects, buildings, companies, products, landscape only, omitting aspects of mentality, ways of thinking or behaving, which are, of course, essential if one wants to really understand a culture, the concept 'culture' itself is briefly touched upon.

Activity 3: Policeman
The participants work in groups. Each group gets one of the two different versions of the same picture. In the example in Appendix 3 the face of a German, Spanish, British, etc. policeman is 'separated' from his uniform. Some groups are given a picture of the face only, other groups one of the person in uniform. The groups are to describe what they observe.

Pictures are ideally suited to trigger off immediate unreflected and therefore revealing reactions. The so-called objective descriptions that are given are all very different, making it clear that people, when they observe, immediately also interpret what they see. Nothing can be derived from the pictures with regard to family life, for example, but participants come up with complete stories.

Activity 4: Mücke, Henne und Löwe
The participants read the poem (see Appendix 4), which serves as a starting point for a discussion of empathy and intercultural comparison.

Accurately defined objects from different cultures need to be evaluated with regard to similar criteria, which are, it should not be forgotten, never objective but always culturally determined. One should try to put oneself in someone else's shoes and find reasons for differences and similarities from within the foreign culture before judging something as 'komisch', i.e. weird, abnormal or comical.

Activity 5: Critical incidents
The participants receive photocopies of pages 84–87 from Tomalin and Stempleski's *Cultural Awareness* (1993). They work on the tasks suggested on those pages and further illustrate the notion of 'critical incident' with personal experiences, trying to explicate what underlying reasons caused the misunderstanding.

Discovering the underlying principles that are central in the assignment of meaning in a given culture is a difficult task. Anthropologists managed to point out what culture-general and culture-specific principles guide a great number of cultures. They depart from the superficial visual level of cultures and dig deeper for invisible links and structures. The next activity consists of the critical reading of some anthropological texts, notably a number of extracts from the work of E. T. Hall, an anthropologist who focuses on the communicative process and on nonverbal communication in part of his work and who points out underlying cultural differences guiding the behaviour of, for example, Germans, Americans and French, all people of interest to foreign language teachers in upper secondary education in Belgium.

Activity 6: Anthropology
The participants read the chapter *Proxémie comparée des cultures allemande, anglaise, française* from Hall's *The Hidden Dimension* (1966). A number of questions guide their reading. They include: (1) Why is it that Germans get irritated at Americans talking to each other in such a way as if they were the only ones in the room? (2) Why do Germans get irritated at Americans leaving their doors open at work? What do open and closed doors mean for both groups? (3) Why is it that a Briton talking to an American gets the impression that s/he is not being listened to?

The participants are invited first to formulate their own hypothetical answers to those questions before looking for the answers suggested in the text. The hypotheses and answers are then discussed, as are the table of contents from *The Hidden Dimension* and a schematic representation of the chapter on monochronic and polychronic time from Hall's *The Dance of Life. The Other Dimension of Time* (1983). Teachers are invited to draw up questions for their learners on this last chapter.

1.1.3 Concept investigation

It has, by now, become clear that one can never be certain of having a valid perception of what is foreign. Really understanding otherness implies trying to understand from within. One should, therefore, take on the role of a cultural investigator, of an ethnographer and 'put oneself through the mysterious process of doing fieldwork' (Roberts 1995:89; and Barro *et al.* in this volume). The programme developed at Thames Valley University and described in an earlier chapter, aims at preparing university language learners for an ethnographic study they are to carry out during their obligatory year abroad. Of course, given the conditions in which language-and-culture teaching is taking place in secondary language classrooms, the proposals have to be narrowed down to what I would call a 'concept investigation', which can for instance be carried out during a school visit to a foreign country.

In the seminar a concept investigation of the notion 'café' is presented. Carrying out such an investigation implies that one first learns the basic skill of asking the right kind of questions. A random foreign concept and its counterpart in one's own culture may seem identical at first sight. However, after more thorough examination they seem to differ in a number of respects. The grid of questions guiding the investigation of the concept 'café' as it features in a foreign culture is presented in Appendix 5. From the grid it is clear that an investigator will not limit him/herself to examining the concept in its present state, but also consider it from a developmental, notably a historical, sociological, social, economic, intercultural, etc. point of view. The different steps learners need to take in order to carry out an investigation are discussed too, using the grid in Appendix 6. Careful preparation of the investigation activity in the classroom is essential to its success. Teachers have to help learners decide on what concept to investigate, carefully thinking about what linguistic or practical difficulties are involved in investigating that particular concept. Also, the issues of how to formulate hypotheses accurately and how to present one's findings, need to be addressed. In the seminar some examples of ways of summarising the findings of the investigation are presented: A number of papers written by learners at Bayreuth university (Jung 1994) and some drawings illustrate how learners can account for the different steps they took to carry out the investigation, on the insights they gained from it, and how findings can be presented in less linguistically demanding ways. (See Appendix 7 for examples.)

1.1.4 Geography, Landeskunde, intercultural language teaching

Activity 7: Terminology

Different groups receive different slips of paper containing either the word 'geography', 'Landeskunde' or 'intercultural foreign language teaching'. The participants prepare in groups what they understand by these concepts and what contents and methodologies they associate with them. The results of the group work are discussed in a plenary session.

This task promotes the participants' understanding of how intercultural foreign language teaching differs from traditional *Landeskunde* teaching, whilst at the same time promoting their use of professional metalanguage relevant to the field of teaching-and-learning language-and-culture.

1.2 Defining intercultural competence

Activity 8: Core objectives for intercultural language teaching

The participants are presented with part of a questionnaire (see Appendix 8) designed for an international research project on language teachers' identity, described by Risager in this volume. The questionnaire includes questions on the role attributed to the cultural dimension in language teaching and on the objectives and contents of foreign language-and-culture teaching courses. Having completed it, the participants exchange information in small groups. They then listen to a taped version of the answers of a British teacher participating in the above-mentioned research project. The interview transcript then allows the participants to discuss how far their professional views differ from those expressed by their British colleague. A presentation of four *savoirs*

(Byram and Zarate 1994 – see Appendix 9) further enhances the participants' understanding of the attainment targets of an intercultural language course and of how its objectives and contents can be concretised.

The participants go home the first day with the idea that culture learning is a matter of raising awareness and a matter of attitude, not only of acquiring culture-specific knowledge. They are able to formulate objectives and contents of intercultural language-and-culture teaching courses and have carried out a number of experiential tasks also suited for the foreign language classroom.

2 A curriculum for intercultural language teaching

2.1 Intercultural competence and language production

Activity 9: Fluency-oriented tasks
The second day starts with some materials taken from Seelye's *Teaching Culture: Strategies for Intercultural Communication* (1988), where the objectives for intercultural language-and-culture teaching have been translated into a number of concrete tasks. The tasks include: (1) Through an example illustrate how an element of folklore may mirror the attitudes or cultural themes of a nation's thoughts and actions. (2) List key questions you would ask to elicit how people of the target culture satisfy the need for food and shelter, for love and affection, for pride in oneself. (3) Continue the story: What became of Snow White and her prince after they left for the USA?

The participants choose a number of tasks and exchange ideas on their adequacy for the secondary classroom and with regard to the attainment targets for intercultural language teaching discussed the previous day. The tasks suggested by Seelye facilitate substantial language production while practising at the same time the reflective skills essential to the acquisition of intercultural competence.

2.2 Linguistic awareness of cultures: an exercise typology

In this section an exercise typology will be presented which concentrates on what Attinasi and Friedrich (1988) call 'linguaculture' or Helmot and Müller (1993) 'Linguistic Awareness of Culture', both stressing the inseparability of language and culture. The exercise types help to explore the cultural dimensions of the language that is taught and sensitise people to verbal and non-verbal markers of cultural differences. Attention is devoted to elements of vocabulary, grammar, non-verbal and para-verbal communicative clues and to differences in communicative styles which may cause reciprocal comprehension difficulties in direct encounters between people of different cultures.

2.2.1 Conjunctions, adverbs, particles and negations (Grammar)

The choice of conjunctions is culturally determined and can help reinforce or undermine stereotypical images. An interculturally orientated grammar lesson could focus on conjunctions (and negations), not from a linguistic point of view, i.e. pointing out what linguistic equivalent exists in language Y for a particular conjunction in language X, but from a sociocultural one, reflecting on the values expressed when choosing a particular conjunction. An example will make this clear. One can link 'He's from Madrid' and 'he's very nice' in a number of different ways. One could say: '*Although* he's from Madrid he's very nice.' The speaker is then clearly negatively prejudiced against people living in Madrid. One could also say: 'He's from Madrid *and* he's very nice', which is a neutral description of that person. A third possibility would be: '*Because* he's from Madrid, he's very nice', the speaker here being positively biased.

Activity 10: Conjunctions
The participants are asked to combine a number of sentences and explain why they chose a particular conjunction or particle and what meanings other particles would convey and would, from a Flemish cultural point of view, not be adequate. The sentences include (1) Helen is married. She would like a baby. (2) He doesn't make bad money. He's driving a VW Polo. (3) We had planned to leave at 9.00. We left at 9.30.

2.2.2 Concepts and their culture-specific meaning (Vocabulary)

In this section the participants experience how culture-specific the meaning of words is and learn a number of techniques to pass this awareness on to their learners. From a perceptional point of view it is interesting to see that people very often associate only those ideas with the object under consideration that are conventionally/stereotypically mentioned. When asked for instance what 'Sunday' means, many people will answer: 'going to church, being with the family'. When then asked if they actually go to church or stay with the family they have to admit they do not. Therefore, associogrammes for instance, a well-known technique in vocabulary learning, can not only be used to show that members from two different cultures bear different images of an object in mind and more or less systematically associate it with some culturally pre-set objects, feelings, beliefs and processes. They can also indicate how unconsciously one may live one's own culture.

Activity 11: Is it work when . . .?
The participants are presented with a number of exercises, published in Hog, Müller and Wessling (1984), which can be used to point out that words are assigned culture-specific meanings. 'Was ist Arbeit?' (see Appendix 10) is an exercise type in which a number of statements are formulated in a controversial way so as to force learners to put explicitly into words the criteria they use to define a particular concept, in this case 'work'. The statements inviting learners to make their views on work explicit include 'After the baptismal ceremony the priest drinks a cup of coffee with the family'; 'a teacher of German goes to see a play at the theatre'; 'after having dug a hole in the ground a man fills it up again'. The participants then define concepts such as 'tolerance', 'tidiness', 'freedom', 'laziness', 'greed' in a similar way, drawing up statements for their learners to judge.

Activity 12: Prototypes
The participants are invited to classify a number of representations of a particular prototype, in this case 'house' in descending order of 'prototypicality'. The representations include 'hotel', 'flat', 'opera house', 'cabin', 'garden house', etc. (See Appendix 11.)

When trying to classify what we perceive into a coherent world view we produce prototypical images of a concept in our minds (Müller 1983). Prototypes vary between cultures. What person X in culture 1 perceives as possessing all the characterising features of, for instance, the concept 'house', 'tree' or 'family' will not be the same as what person Y in culture 2 defines to be a prototypical 'house', 'tree' or 'family' respectively. Other realisations of the concept possessing only some of the required characteristics will be perceived as still belonging to the same category but will be assigned to a lower level of prototypicality. An example may clarify this. When considering the abstract concept 'bird', Americans may prototypically think of a sparrow whereas members from some Asian culture may think of another concretisation of that same abstract category. The concretisation then becomes the point of reference of the members of that culture. Americans will for example regard a duck as less birdlike than a sparrow. In multicultural classes this classification type of exercise can trigger off lively attempts at clarifying what societal circumstances make for one house to be more prototypical than another. Other topics could be: weather, evening meal, gift, invitation, day, vocabulary lesson, holiday, etc.

2.2.3 Non-verbal communicative behaviour

Effective communicative behaviour is one of the most relevant topics to cover in intercultural training. This is probably best done by also including experiential exercises that illustrate variations in non-verbal and para-verbal communicative behaviour, followed by discussion and interpretation. Non-verbal clues include sign and body language and proxemics; para-verbal clues include the 'sounds' of the language used, such as intonation, loudness and its variation, modulation of pitch, pausing. Within one culture, non-verbal clues are used to modify the meaning of what is said. They may reinforce it, weaken it or render it ironic. These non-verbal modifiers of speech differ from culture to culture. People learn them as they grow up. They betray their membership of a particular culture not merely through their accent but also through the way they express or do not express their emotions, the way they stand, the way they look or do not look into the eyes of their communication partner. Para-verbal clues, too, influence the message being communicated and may alter its meaning.

Activity 13: Non-verbal clues
The '9 Guidelines for More Successful Intercultural Communication' formulated by Leathers (1986) serve as a good introduction to this aspect of intercultural communicative behaviour. The participants are presented with a number of pictures illustrating some signs used by the Dutch (originating from Andrea and De Boer 1993) but unfamiliar to Flemings. (See Appendix 12 for an example.) They have to link the written explanations and the pictures. The participants are also asked to complete sentences like the following: 'When a Frenchman kisses his attractive female friend on the cheek, this can be perceived as ..., whereas it was possibly meant as ...'; 'When a German looks straight into somebody's eyes while negotiating, this can be perceived as ..., whereas it was possibly meant as ...'. In a total physical response activity individual participants are asked to use the body language conveying the meaning of the sentence(s) they receive on a slip of paper, while the others try to verbalise that meaning. The sentences include: 'This is delicious', 'I'm angry', 'I don't know' or 'come in, please'.

2.2.4 Communicative styles

Rules of para-verbal, non-verbal and verbal expression of meaning and intention build, as a set of rules, communicative styles. These styles are characterised by referring more explicitly versus more implicitly to facts; expressing more directly versus more indirectly one's wishes; using more verbal versus more non-verbal expressions; showing more overtly versus more indirectly self-disclosure (Knapp and Knapp-Potthoff 1990). Being unaware of these differences may leave one with unjustified irritation and rejection.

Activity 14: You may give me a kiss ...
The participants are presented with a grid to analyse critical incidents, as suggested by Knapp and Knapp-Potthoff (1990), which they can use to analyse critical incidents arising because of differences in communicative style. Trying to make sense of the situation presented in Appendix 13, the participants discuss topics such as: How does a Japanese woman feel at stage 5? What emotions do both experience at stage 25? What is important in a relationship in both cultures? What could the 30 different stages be? Other topics which could be discussed with regard to differences in communicative style as described by Knapp and Knapp-Potthoff are 'the way someone asks for a small loan and the way the addressee reacts to that question', 'the way people are let into the community', 'ways of opening a conversation'. Travel guides are particularly revealing in these respects as they make the rules of verbal and non-verbal behaviour in another culture explicit.

2.3 Prejudices and stereotypes

Many people believe that stereotypical views can be countered, if only one deals with them explicitly. However, as people *need* stereotypes in order to classify people and objects into a coherent world view, they will probably resist explicit attempts at making them set stereotypes aside altogether. Only humorous irony and pleasant exaggeration can tone down and moderate stereotypical ideas.

Activity 15: Himmel und Hölle
On the overhead projector, line after line of this poem (see Appendix 14) is revealed, as a kind of eye-opener. The participants are invited to replace the nationalities by others, including their own, while at the same time also changing their attributions.

Activity 16: Germans are boring
Adjectives popping up when thinking of a particular nationality are collected. They are written in one column on the blackboard. Completing a second eye-opening column together with the participants offers the possibility to tone the attributions down and view these ideas from a different perspective. One can always interpret something positively and negatively. What is said to be irritating behaviour from the point of view of one culture will be regarded as very positive from the point of view of another. Thus, adjectives associated with Germans such as hardworking, rich and punctual find their counterparts in well-organised, economical and programmed.

3 Evaluating existing teaching materials

A last important activity involves the participants in carrying out a 'home ethnography' of an aspect of their teaching, viz. the materials they use in the classroom. At first sight, existing materials seem quite acceptable for teaching-and-learning language-and-culture. Systematic investigation, however, reveals how biased and prejudiced textbooks – and more recent media such as the internet or multimedia (Brammerts 1995; Ingesman 1995) – often are. Their contents may be outdated and may fail to present a coherent picture of the foreign culture (Byram 1993). Generalising statements leave wrong impressions, as Kubanek (1987) shows in an analysis of the presentation of the Third World in English textbooks used in Germany. Intercultural situations may not occur. Exercises may pick out cultural elements which then stay in the mind. The tasks set may be very superficial. As stated before, a good ethnographer asks the right kind of questions. In what follows a number of criteria are listed, which help teachers decide on the adequacy of their textbooks for teaching intercultural competence. The criteria are organised in four groups, a number of questions concretising each criterion.

Representativeness and realism

The first group of questions aims at examining whether the textbook offers a complete, up-to-date, realistic and representative picture of the foreign intercultural society. Leaving out certain aspects or points of view makes statements false and one-sided. This biased picture is reinforced by means of a stereotypical and generalising characterisation of cultures merely on the basis of what they produce on the material level (factories, economy, export), leaving out references to what cultures have to offer, for instance, in the field of philosophy, and devoting no attention whatsoever to the great diversity within each culture.

The following questions could help teachers decide on the acceptability of their textbook with respect to representativeness and realism:

- What image is presented: a royal image or a realistic one? Only a royal visit could run so smoothly. No distorting sound is heard. Everything passes off easily and perfectly.
- Does the textbook only present a tourist point of view? Tourism-oriented textbooks only discuss situations which are marginal to the ordinary everyday situations members of the foreign culture find themselves in. Tourism-oriented textbooks do not usually concern themselves with values and opinions central to a foreign society.

- Are negative and problematic aspects of the foreign culture touched upon?
- Does the textbook offer an authentic reflection of the multicultural character of the foreign society? Do cultural incidents occur? Are all nationalities living in the foreign country represented?
- Do situations occur in which someone with a good mastery of the foreign language is not understood because of differences in culture-specific reference frames? Is the relationship between language and culture dealt with?
- Are teachers and learners encouraged to consult additional material on the topics dealt with or do the textbook authors present the information in their books as the true and only picture of the foreign culture?
- Do the textbooks include materials/texts written by members of the different nationalities living in the foreign country or do they merely present the white male point of view?
- Are mentality, values, ideas dealt with?
- Is a historical perspective presented and used to explain certain present-day features of mentality or national character?
- Is the information on the foreign culture integrated in the course or is it added at the end of every chapter or even presented in a separate chapter at the end of the book?

Characters in the book

Characters reveal a lot about textbook authors' opinions on and conceptions of the foreign culture. Very often one nationality is over-represented in the textbook whereas others are scarcely present. One nationality may be represented as being superior to the others.

The following questions could be asked:

- Are the characters in the book representative of the foreign society with regard to their age, social class, interests, mentality, family situation, etc.?
- Do the characters meet foreigners or members from other nationalities living in their country and are misunderstandings which might arise from these encounters dealt with?
- Do textbook authors comment on their characters' behaviour? Are the characters' ways of behaving linked with the society they live in?
- Do photographs show ordinary people?
- In what mood are the characters: always happy? Happy one moment, sad the next? Irritated, angry, aggressive, racist, tolerant, etc.?

Language

The language chosen may betray implicit value judgements and opinions. The usage of words with a negative connotation may create a negative image of a certain nationality. Some examples taken from Van der Vegt (1987) will illustrate this: '*dirty* Turk', '*Although* he's a black doctor he's very competent', 'a *well-dressed* Moroccan'. When talking about members from the dominant group in the foreign cultures this kind of (derogatory) 'coloured' usage is absent.

Learners

Finally, we want to devote some attention to what the textbook expects of the learners. Does it merely pass on knowledge or does it aim at enhancing awareness of the riches of intercultural encounters?

The following questions can be asked:

- Do learners get the chance to reflect on their own culture?
- Are alternative perspectives on some aspect of the foreign culture presented and are learners invited to choose between them and account for their choice?
- What opinion do textbook authors hold on the comprehension ability of their audience? Can learners only handle data and petty facts or should they be able to compare and judge materials? Should learners be able to think in an abstract way and understand differences in value systems and mentality?
- Do activities invite learners to take in a foreign perspective?
- Do activities prepare learners to behave adequately when in contact with members from other cultures?
- Are questions like 'What do you think about ...' preceded by 'What do you know about ...'? One first has to have essential knowledge on a foreign culture before one can give one's opinion on something.
- Have the cultural elements taken from the text and used in follow-up activities been carefully selected? The elements popping up in exercises are often the only ones learners will remember. They may reinforce certain over-simplified judgements and distort the more diversified message of a text.
- Are discussions used to help learners gain a true understanding of a foreign culture? When discussing, however, one should be careful not to offer too many elements in advance. This might limit learners' creativity and interest and keep them from gaining new insights.
- Are insights that have been gained previously re-used in the course of the textbook? Is there progression?

Conclusion

This chapter started by setting out a number of principles that underlie the in-service teacher training course presented. We hope to have illustrated how these principles have been realised in a concrete course outline and how the application of these principles culminated in the realisation of a 'home ethnography' of a textbook. This particular project requires participants to integrate theory and practice as well as apply culture-general and culture-specific principles.

It is certainly too optimistic to presume that the participants' attitudes, knowledge and skills can be completely changed by one training programme. What is important, however, is that carrying out this demanding task gives the teachers a sense of having acquired a number of insights and tools that will allow them to take an active part in the search for contemporary language teaching's contribution to international understanding and peacemaking at home and abroad. If more teachers become confident in dealing with intercultural issues, which call for a more pronounced treatment of the affective and behavioural aspects of learning, and are better informed about the major possibilities opened up by intercultural language-and-culture teaching, contacts at home and abroad will benefit from it, as will society as a whole.

Achievements of this kind obviously require long-term planning and resources. National teacher training institutions, therefore, must support in-service teacher training seminars dealing with the acquisition of intercultural competence, at home and abroad, providing the opportunity for teachers of different languages and cultures to exchange learning and teaching experiences in the field.

Note: The programme presented here was developed partly on the basis of materials presented during a workshop organised at Bayreuth University in July 1993 and partly on the basis of my own reading. I am grateful to Saskia Bachman (Goethe-Institut Barcelona), Gerd Wessling (Goethe-Institut Barcelona) and Bernd Müller (University Chemnitz-Zwickau) for providing me with some ideas for the course outlined in this paper. The teaching materials they presented at the Bayreuth seminar have now been published in a new edition of *Sichtwechsel*.

Appendices

The course materials are at present unpublished. The teacher's guide is only available in its original Dutch version, the course materials themselves in their original Dutch, French, German or English version. Both can be obtained from Lies Sercu, KULeuven, Blijde-Inkomststraat 21, 3000 Leuven, Belgium.

Appendix 1: Cartoon

(from: *Knack*, Nr. 29, 20.07.1994: 11)

Appendix 2: Views of a country

(from H. Behal-Thomsen, A. Lundquist-Mog and P. Mog. 1993. *Typisch Deutsch? Arbeitsbuch zu Aspekten deutscher Mentalität*. Langenscheidt: 96)

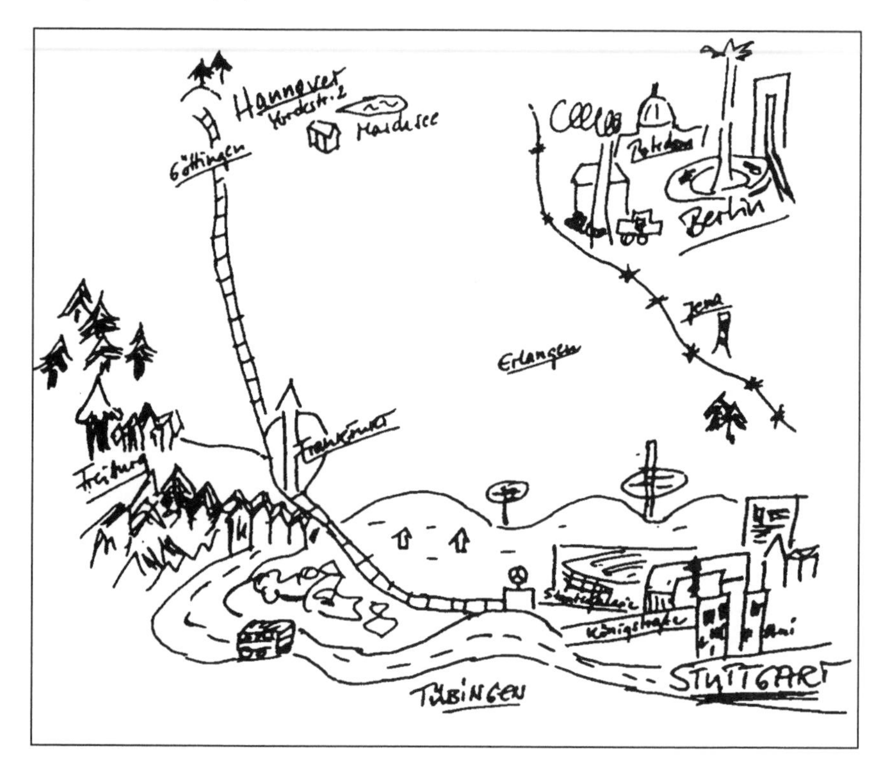

Appendix 3: Policeman

(from M. Hog, B. Müller and G. Wessling. 1984. *Sichtwechsel. Elf Kapitel zur Sprachsensibilisierung. Ein Deutschkurs für Fortgeschrittene*. Ernst Klett Verlag: 114)

Appendix 4: Mücke, Henne und Löwe

(G. Anders. 1982. 'Der Löwe' aus *Blick vom Turm*. München: Beck)

Als die Mücke zum erstenmal den Löwen brüllen hörte,
da sprach sie zur Henne: 'Der summt aber komisch'
'Summen ist gut', fand die Henne
'Sondern?' fragte die Mücke.
'Er gackert', antwortete die Henne.
'Aber das tut er allerdings komisch.'

[*As the mosquito heard the lion roar for the first time*
She spoke to the hen and said: 'Now he buzzes in a peculiar way.'
'Buzzing is good', the hen said.
'But?' the mosquito asked.
'He cackles', the hen answered,
'In a very peculiar way.']

Appendix 5: Grid of questions: café (=X)

Based on B. Müller. 1983. Begriffe und Bilder. Bedeutungscollagen zur Landeskunde. In: *Zielsprache Deutsch* 2, 5–14 (My translation)

1 **Inside–outside**
- Is X a private rather than a public place?
- Is X a closed rather than an open space?
- Does one go to X alone or in company?

2 **Top–bottom**
- What social class do the people who go to X belong to?
- Does the bartender own the place or does s/he rent it?
- Do you find younger rather than older people in X?

3 **Distribution in time and space**
- When does one go to X?
- How often?
- How long does one stay in X?
- Whereabouts in the city, in the country do you find X?

4 **A historical point of view**
- Has X always been there?
- Is X in fashion now?
- What did X look like in the past?
- How did X develop?

5 **An emotional point of view**
 - Do people associate positive or negative ideas/feelings with X?
 - Can X make people react positively or negatively?

6 **An intracultural point of view**
 - How do X and Y (e.g. restaurant) differ?

7 **Function**
 - Why do people go to X?
 - What secondary reasons do people have to go to X?

8 **A symbolic point of view**
 - How is X looked upon?
 - What social class is X associated with?

Appendix 6: Concept investigation

Based on B. Müller. 1985. Bedeutungsanalytische Praxisforschung in der Lehrerausbildung. In J. Gerighausen and P. C. Seel. *Sprachpolitik als Bildungspolitik. Werkstattgespräch der Goethe-Instituts*. München: Goethe-Institut. The grid presented by Müller is intended for use in teacher training courses. I translated it and adapted it for use in the secondary language classroom.

1 **Before you start**
 - In your group decide on an everyday concept to investigate (e.g. bicycle, dog, shoe, bread, plastic bag, walk, bargain, freedom, etc.).
 - Formulate a number of hypotheses with regard to what X means to the members of the culture you are investigating.

2 **Carry out the investigation**
 - Go out, alone or in twos, and observe X, live it, meet it, establish a relationship with it.
 - Meet with your group, exchange experiences.
 - Now write down what at present seem individual rather than generalisable interpretations of X.
 - Decide on what aspect of X you are now going to concentrate on (e.g. café: loneliness).
 - Investigate the aspect you chose (make pictures, recordings, drawings, notes; collect documents, statements, etc.).

3 **Prepare your presentation**
 - Look for generalisable aspects.
 - Compare your results with the hypotheses you formulated at the start.
 - What concept in your own culture is comparable to X?
 - Represent your findings, in writing, drawing or combining the two.

Appendix 7: Ways of presenting concept investigation findings

Americans in Bayreuth[1]

When we entered the class, our ideas over what we were going to do were somewhat unclear. Was it going to be more of a traditional language course or was it going to be more culture orientated? When we started to write out the questions we were going to ask it soon became clear. Everyone was naturally more interested in the experiences of the Americans than in grammar. It also became clear that our ideas about the project were influenced by our own stereotypes. Our opinions and pictures of the Americans certainly affected what we asked as well as what we did not ask.

The stereotypes we had about the Americans were basically the typical ones that everybody has. We thought that they would not be very well informed about current affairs, on the whole less educated than Europeans and of course that they had no culture and no history. There were also the other typical stereotypes of baseball caps, bubble gum and junk food (McDonald's, popcorn etc.). It was also thought that Americans would perhaps be hyper-nationalistic. The pride and love for their country, often seen in Americans, could become exaggerated and have this result. We felt that the United States was similar to Germany in that they tried to make people adapt to their own culture (on vacation, etc.) rather than try to experience a new culture. Also mentioned were Americans being more violent, having more weapons and more crime and also of course more drugs.

Most of the people interviewed were young (under 30) and came from various parts of the United States. We received many interesting answers about why they had come to Germany and the various experiences in their daily lives. We decided to center this paper around the themes of *Ausländerfeindlichkeit* and racism for two reasons. First of all because it was what the interviewees were most interested in. The questions asked about these topics received much more complete and emotional answers than almost any others asked. They were clearly on the minds of those we talked to. Secondly because it was what we were most interested in. When the interviews were discussed in class, it was about these subjects that we spoke the most. So we decided to focus our paper on these topics.

All of the interviewees agreed that racism was a problem in both the US as well as in Germany and many other countries of the world. One person said that the racial problems in the US could be compared to a "sleeping dog", nobody is aware of it and therefore it might be a greater danger to society. Many agreed that even though the situation in the US has improved since the 60s, there are still a large number of problems to be solved. People still do not realize that everyone is a foreigner in the United States and that everyone deserves equal rights. It doesn't matter if you have been here 5 years or 15. One of the results of this is that in the States multi-racial relationships are still not as accepted as in France, England, etc. It was mentioned for example that it was

[1] Written by: Cristoph Gütinger, Karin Meisinger, Jens Müller, Sebastian Siebzehnrübl, Michael Wisser.

easier to have a black-white relationship in Germany than in the United States. But it was also mentioned that conversely a marriage to a Turk would be easier in the States. It was mentioned that the average American is perhaps a bit too obsessed with achieving the "American Dream". They concentrate on what is seen as an American lifestyle and therefore try to assimilate other cultures instead of tolerating them. This sometimes blinds them on a deeper level to other cultures and peoples. This of course also makes the integration of various nationalities even more difficult. Another person said that Americans cannot even remember the racial problems of the previous week and this hinders their solving the problem. In contrast, Germany is quite focused on solving its problem because of the intense documentation of the racial conflicts. The Germans are made very aware of the situation and of Germany's past.

Although the Germans seem to be handling the problems better than the Americans, the interviewees were of the opinion that there was a greater number of racist acts in Germany than in the US. It was mentioned that in Germany, as everywhere, racism was passed from generation to generation subconsciously. Prejudices and stereotypes are never really beaten, they just lie dormant until the next generation, or even the one after that, finds them and revives them. Ideals from the past are still alive. Yet compared to the situation during the Third Reich, things are still different. Today it can be seen that a majority is standing up to a minority. Our interviewees were also of the opinion that not a majority, but a minority was responsible for the current violence. Although Germans were not seen as racists, it was not believed that they were as open to different people, especially other races and even sub-cultures. Germans are loyal to their traditions and adapt less easily to new cultures. One interesting point was that the interviewees had the impression that it was not only Germans against foreigners, but also Germans against Germans. Even the expression *Ossis gegen Wessis* was used. We did not expect to find this level of insight into the German culture among our interviewees. The reason for this hostility between Germans, from the American point of view, could be found in the worsening economic condition in Germany. Especially the eastern part of Germany, as they are still searching for their identity and thus needing an outlet. Many of those interviewed said that only so can the brutality be understood.

At the end of this course one thing that we realized is that our perception of Americans had changed. We no longer considered them to be ill-informed, but on the contrary, able to make intelligent judgements about the events that were occurring around them. We were glad to have found out that *Ausländerfeindlichkeit* was not a major problem for the people we interviewed. With one notable exception, they did not seem to have experienced any violence or excessive hostility towards them. It was informative for us to find out how people from a foreign country judge the situation in Germany that worries us as much as anyone. It was also a relief to us that they could see the problem in a better light than it was presented in many foreign publications.

(from U. Jung. 1994. *Der Eszettelkasten/2*. Bayreuth University)

Appendix 8: A questionnaire

CULTURAL AWARENESS/THE CULTURAL DIMENSION

31a The following statements are taken from the national curriculum working group's list of the 'educational purposes of modern foreign language teaching'. Please put them in *your* order of importance, first to least: 1 to 8.

- ☐ to develop an awareness of the nature of language and language learning
- ☐ to encourage positive attitudes to foreign language learning and to speakers of foreign languages and a sympathetic approach to other cultures and civilisations
- ☐ to promote learning of skills of more general application (e.g. analysis, memorising, drawing interferences)
- ☐ to develop the ability to use the language effectively for purposes of practical communication
- ☐ to develop the learners' understanding of themselves and their own culture
- ☐ to form a sound basis of the skills, language and attitudes required for further study, work and leisure

- ☐ to offer insights into the culture and civilisation of the countries where the language is spoken
- ☐ to provide enjoyment and intellectual stimulation

31b What do *you* understand by 'cultural awareness'?
32 To what extent do you use textbooks?
33 If you use mainly one course, what is it?
34 With respect to the courses *you* use the most, does it live up to the demands you think should be made in the cultural dimension?
35 Do you have – in addition to what the coursebook offers – sufficient possibilities of producing teaching materials which live up to the demands you think should be made in the cultural dimension?
36 If in 35 you think there are inadequacies, where do you think they lie?

THE AIMS OF THE CULTURAL DIMENSION

37 Which of the following aims of the cultural dimension do you think are the most important? Please tick only the 4 most important.

- ☐ Giving learners knowledge and understanding of the relevant culture
- ☐ Breaking down prejudices and developing learners' tolerance
- ☐ Giving learners understanding of their own cultural identity
- ☐ Developing learners' ability to see similarities and differences between countries.
- ☐ Helping learners to get personal contacts in the foreign country
- ☐ Helping learners to acquire an interested and critical attitude to cultural/social issues
- ☐ Making language teaching more motivating
- ☐ Other (specify) . . .

TOPICS/THEMES IN LANGUAGE TEACHING

38 Which topics or themes should learners – as a minimum – be introduced to? (Tick a *maximum* of 10 for each language.)

Specify language	Lang. 1: . . .	Lang. 2: . . .
political system	☐	☐
history	☐	☐
daily life and routines	☐	☐
shopping and food and drink	☐	☐
youth culture (fashion, music, etc.)	☐	☐

Specify language	Lang. 1: . . .	Lang. 2: . . .
literature	☐	☐
school and education	☐	☐
geography and regions	☐	☐
family life	☐	☐
film, theatre, art	☐	☐
social and living conditions	☐	☐
festivities and customs	☐	☐
ethnic relations, racism	☐	☐
tourism and travel	☐	☐
gender roles and relationships	☐	☐
religious life and traditions	☐	☐
working life and employment	☐	☐
environmental issues	☐	☐
stereotypes	☐	☐
the country's significance for Britain	☐	☐
other (specify)	☐	☐

Appendix 9: Four savoirs (M. Byram and G. Zarate)

Attitudes and values/Savoir-être

An affective capacity to relinquish ethnocentric attitudes towards and perceptions of otherness, and a cognitive ability to establish and maintain a relationship between native culture and foreign cultures.

Ability to learn/Savoir apprendre

An ability to produce and operate an interpretative system with which to gain insight into hitherto unknown cultural meanings, beliefs and practices, either in a familiar or a new language and culture.

Skills/knowing how/Savoir faire

A capacity to integrate savoirs and savoir-être in specific situations of bicultural contact, i.e. between (the) culture(s) of the learner and of the target language.

Knowledge/knowing what/Savoirs

A system of cultural references which structures the implicit and explicit knowledge acquired in the course of linguistic and cultural learning, and which takes into account the specific needs of the learner in his/her interaction with speakers of the foreign language.

Appendix 10: Was ist Arbeit?

(from M. Hog, B. Müller and G. Wessling. 1984. *Sichtwechsel. Elf Kapitel zur Sprachsensibilisierung. Ein Deutschkurs für Fortgeschrittene*. Ernst Klett Verlag: 22)

Bitte entscheiden Sie jeder für sich, ob es sich bei den folgenden Tätigkeiten um ARBEIT handelt. Wählen Sie dann 5 Fälle aus und geben Sie die Kriterien für Ihre Entscheidung an.

	Tätigkeit	Arbeit ja = x; nein = o	Kriterium
1	Ein Priester trinkt nach einer Taufe mit der Familie Kaffee.		
2	Ein Arbeiter trägt ein Werkzeug von einer Seite der Halle zur anderen, damit der Meister nicht sieht, daß er keine Arbeit hat.		
3	Kinder bauen am Strand eine Burg.		
4	Ein Unteroffizier zielt auf einen Pappkamaraden.		
5	Ein Chauffeur wartet auf den Direktor.		
6	Ein Angestellter wartet auf der Toilette auf das Ende der Arbeitszeit.		
7	Ein Deutschlehrer geht ins Theater.		
8	Eine Animierdame läßt sich zum Whisky einladen.		
9	Frau Karla S. hat Kurzarbeit und näht sich einen Rock.		
10	Bauern Kippen Obst ins Meer.		
11	Schüler diskutieren in der Pause über den Unterrichtsstil des Lehrers.		
12	Ein Mann gräbt ein Loch in der Erde und schüttet es wieder zu.		
13	Ein Hand bellt den Briefträger an.		
14	Eine Ehefrau macht sich jeden Abend um 19 Uhr für ihren Mann schön.		
15	Eine Ameise repariert mit anderen ihren Bau, den ein Spaziergänger zerstört hat.		

Appendix 11: Prototypes

Presented at the Bayreuth workshop July 1993. Unpublished.

Zum Begriff HAUS

Aufgabe: Ordnen sie die folgenden Wörter danach, wie sehr ähnlich bzw. wie wenig ähnlich ihre Bedeutung zum Begriff HAUS ist:

Ferienhaus Hotel Jugendzentrum Hütte Villa Bungalow Museum Einfamilienhaus Oper Reihenhaus Hochhaus Rathaus Wohnung Gartenhaus

1.
2.
3.
4.
5.
6.
7.
8.
9.
10.
11.
12.
13.
14.

Appendix 12: Sign and body language

(from P. Andrea and H. P. De Boer. 1993. *Het Gebarenboekje*. Baarn: De Fontein: 118, 120, 135, 171)

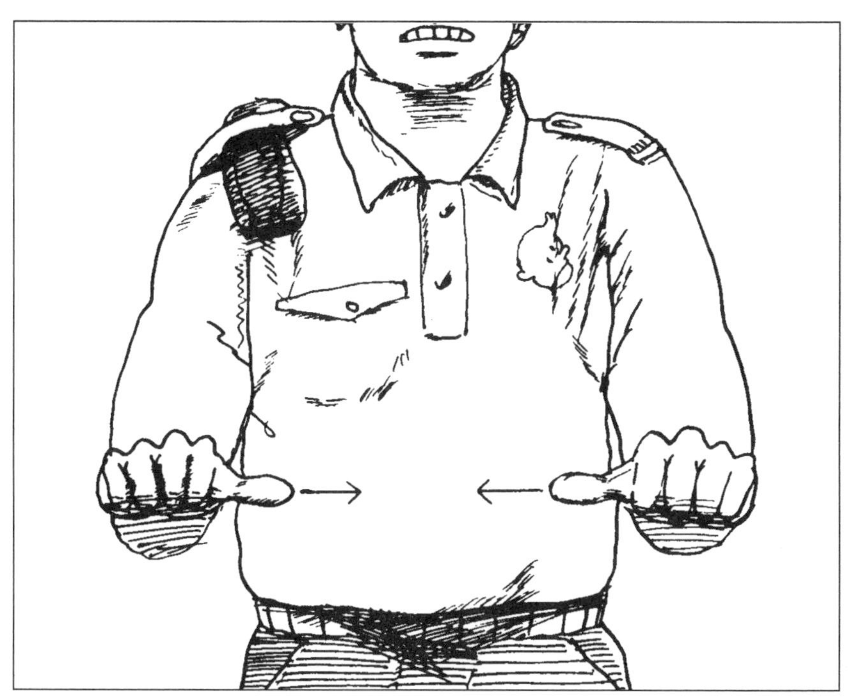

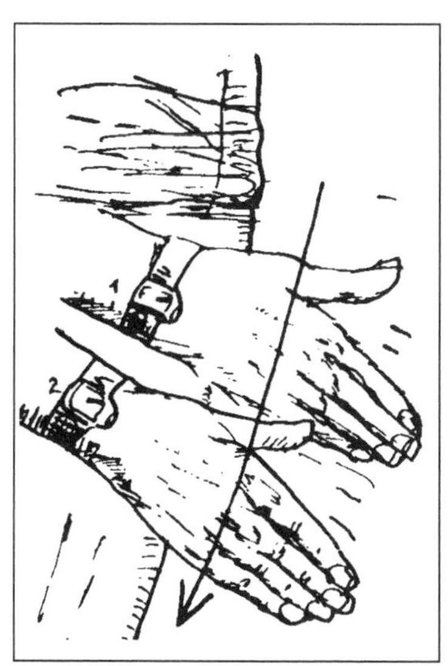

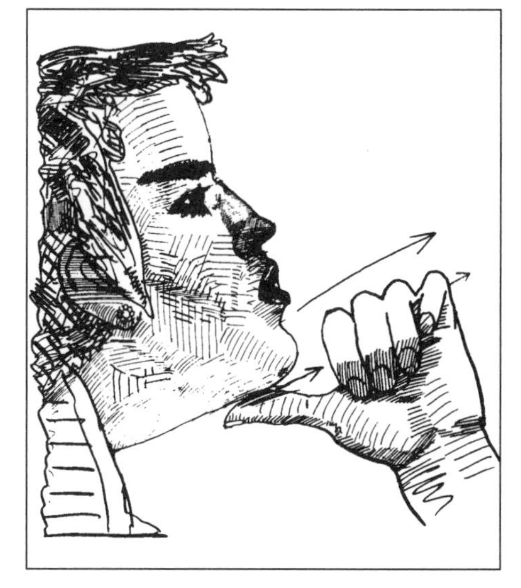

Appendix 13: Stages in a relationship

(from M. Hog, B. Müller and G. Wessling. 1984. *Sichtwechsel. Elf Kapitel zur Sprachsensibilisierung. Ein Deutschkurs für Fortgeschrittene*. Ernst Klett Verlag: 105. (My translation))

	USA		Japan
1.		Establishing contact	
2.			
3.			
4.			
5.	To kiss		
.			
.			
.			
25.			To kiss
.			
.			
30.		Sexual intercourse	

Appendix 14: Himmel und Hölle

Presented at the Bayreuth workshop July 1993.

Im Himmel sind
die Engländer Polizisten
die Franzosen Köche
die Deutschen Mechaniker
die Italianer Liebhaber
und die Schweizer organisieren das Ganze.

In der Hölle sind
die Polizisten Deutsche
die Köche Engländer
die Mechaniker Franzosen
die Liebhaber Schweizer
und die Italiener organisieren ...

[*In heaven*
the British are policemen
the French cooks
the Germans mechanics
the Italian lovers
and the Swiss organise everything.

In hell
the policemen are Germans
the cooks British
the mechanics French
the lovers Swiss
and the Italians organise ...]

References

Aarup Jensen, A., K. Jæger and A. Lorentsen (Eds.) 1995. *Intercultural Competence: A New Challenge for Language Teachers and Trainers in Europe: Volume II*. Aalborg University Press.

Abbs, P. 1994. *The Educational Imperative*. London: Falmer Press.

Adelman, M. B. and D. R. Levine. 1982. *Beyond Language: Intercultural Communication for English as a Second Language*. Englewood Cliffs, N.J.: Prentice Hall.

Adent-Hoecklin, L. 1993. Managing Cultural Differences for Competitive Advantage, Special Report No P656, The Economist Intelligence Unit.

Agar, M. 1994. *Language Shock*. New York: William Morrow.

AIESEC International. 1994. Survey of Management and Business Education Students, B–1050 Brussels, Belgium.

Alix, C. and G. Bertrand (Eds.) 1994. *Pour une pédagogie des échanges. (Le français dans le monde: numéro special)*. Paris: EDICEF.

Alvesson, M. 1993. *Cultural Perspectives on Organizations*. Cambridge: Cambridge University Press.

Ammon, U. 1991. *Die internationale Stellung der deutschen Sprache*. Berlin, New York: Walter de Gruyter.

Anders, G. 1982. 'Der Löwe' aus *Blick vom Turm*. München: Beck.

Anderson, B. 1983. *Imagined Communities: reflections on the origin and spread of nationalism*. London: Verso.

Andrea, P. and H. P. De Boer. 1993. *Het Gebarenboekje*. Baarn: De Fontein.

Apitzsch, G. and N. Dittmar. 1987. Contact between German and Turkish Adolescents: A Case Study. In K. Knapp, W. Enninger and A. Knapp-Potthoff (Eds.) *Analyzing Intercultural Communication*. Berlin: Mouton de Gruyter.

Archer, C. 1986. Culture bump and beyond. In J. M. Valdes (Ed.) *Culture Bound: Bridging the Cultural Gap in Language Teaching*. Cambridge: Cambridge University Press.

Argyle, M. 1982. Intercultural communication. In S. Bochner (Ed.) *Cultures in Contact: Studies in Cross-Cultural Interaction*. Oxford: Pergamon.

Asad, T. 1980. Anthropology and the Analysis of Ideology. *Man*, 14:60–77.

Asad, T. and J. Dixon. 1984. Translating Europe's Others. In F. Barker (Ed.) *Europe and its Others*. Colchester: University of Essex.

ASEAN-New Zealand English for Business and Technology Project. 1992. SEAMEO Regional Language Centre, Singapore 1025.

Association of Graduate Recruiters. 1994. Summer Update Survey, Cambridge.

Attinasi, L. and P. Friedrich. 1988. Dialogic Breakthrough: Catalysis and Synthesis in Life-changing Dialogue. Unpublished manuscript.

Bachman, L. 1990. *Fundamental Considerations in Language Testing*. Oxford: Oxford University Press.

Bachmann, S., S. Gerhold, B.-D. Müller and G. Wessling. 1995. *Sichtwechsel neu. Mittelstufe Deutsch als Fremdsprache*. Ernst Klett Verlag.

Bailey, F. 1971. *Gifts and Poisons*. Oxford: Blackwell.

Bandler, R. 1990. *Using Your Brain – for a Change*. Utah: Real People Press.

Barley, N. 1989. *The Innocent Anthropologist*. London: Penguin.

Barth, F. 1989. The Analysis of Culture in a Complex Society. *Ethnos*, 54: 120–42.

Barthes, R. 1964. *Essais Critiques*. Paris: Seuil.

Bartsch, R. 1988. *Norms of Language*. London: Longman.

Bateson, G. 1972. *Steps to an Ecology of Mind. Collected Essays in Anthropology, Psychiatry, Evolution and Epistemology*. Chandler Publishing Company.

Bauman, R. and J. Sherzer (Eds.) 1989. *Explorations in the Ethnography of Speaking*. Cambridge: Cambridge University Press (2nd edition).

Baumgratz, G. 1987. Esquisse d'une conception pédagogique de l'enseignement des langues étrangères visant la compétence de communication transnationale, les conséquences pour le role et la compétence du professeur et les perspectives de la formation continue. In G. Baumgratz and R. Stephan (Eds.) *Fremdsprachenlernen als Beitrag zur internationalen Verständigung*. München: Iudicium, 64–75.

Beattie, J. 1962. Tis the season to be jolly – why? *New Society*, 27(12) 62.

Behal-Thomsen, H., A. Lundquist-Mog and P. Mog. 1993. *Typisch Deutsch? Arbeitsbuch zu Aspekten deutscher Mentalität*. Langenscheidt.

Billig, M. 1987. *Arguing and Thinking: A Rhetorical Approach to Social Psychology*. Cambridge: Cambridge University Press.

Birkenbihl, V. F. 1992. *Die Birkenbihl-Methode, Fremdsprachen zu lernen*. Munich: mvg-Verlag.

Blyth, C. 1995. Redefining the boundaries of language use: the foreign language classroom as a multilingual speech community. In C. Kramsch (Ed.) *Redefining the Boundaries of Language Study*. Boston: Heinle and Heinle.

Bochner, S. 1982a. The social psychology of cross-cultural relations. In S. Bochner (Ed.) *Cultures in Contact: Studies in Cross-Cultural Interaction*. Oxford: Pergamon.

Bochner, S. 1982b. Outcomes of cross-cultural interaction. In S. Bochner (Ed.) *Cultures in Contact: Studies in Cross-Cultural Interaction*. Oxford: Pergamon.

Bond, M. H. 1991. *Beyond the Chinese Face*. Hong Kong: Oxford University Press.

Bond, M. H. (Ed.) 1986. *The Psychology of the Chinese People*. Hong Kong: Oxford University Press.

Bozon, M. 1984. *Vie quotidienne et rapports sociaux dans une petite ville de province: la mise en scène des différences*. Lyon: Presses Universitaires de Lyon.

Brammerts, H. 1995. Tandem Learning and the Internet. Using New Technology to Acquire Intercultural Competence. In A. Aarup Jensen *et al.* (Eds.) *Intercultural Competence. A New Challenge for Teachers and Teacher Trainers in Europe. Volume II*. Aalborg: Aalborg University Press.

Bredella, L. and M. Legutke. 1985. *Schüleraktivierende Methoden im Fremdsprachenunterricht Englisch*. Bochum: Kamp.

Brislin, R. 1981. *Cross-Cultural Encounters: Face-to-Face Interaction*. Oxford: Pergamon.

Brislin, R., K. Cushner, C. Cherrie and M. Yong. 1986. *Intercultural Interactions – A Practical Guide*. London: Sage.

Broadfoot, P. and M. Osborn, with M. Gilly and A. Bucher. 1993. *Perceptions of Teaching: Primary School Teachers in England and France*. London: Cassell.

Brook, P. 1968. *The Empty Space*. Harmondsworth: Penguin Books.

Brook, P. 1988. *The Shifting Point*. London: Methuen.

Brown, A. 1995. *Organisational Culture*. London: Pitman Publishers.

Brown, P. and S. Levinson. 1987. *Politeness*. Cambridge: Cambridge University Press.

Brownell, J. A. 1992. *Quality and Equality in Education*. 1992 ILE Conference Proceedings, Institute of Education, Hong Kong.

Brumfit, C. 1984. *Communicative Methodology in Language Teaching*. Cambridge: Cambridge University Press.

Buchanan, D. and A. Huczynski. 1985. *Organizational Behaviour*. London: Prentice Hall International.

Burton, J. and W. Rusek. 1994. The Learner as Curriculum Resource in English for Professional Employment courses. *Prospect*, 9(3).

Buttjes, D. and M. Byram (Eds.) 1991. *Mediating Languages and Cultures: Towards an Intercultural Theory of Foreign Language Education*. Clevedon: Multilingual Matters.

Byram, M. 1989a. *Cultural Studies in Foreign Language Education*. Clevedon, UK: Multilingual Matters.

Byram, M. 1989b. Intercultural education and foreign language teaching. *World Studies Journal*, 7(2) 4–7.

Byram, M. 1991. Background studies in English foreign language teaching: lost opportunities in the comprehensive school debate. In D. Buttjes and M. Byram (Eds.) *Mediating Languages and Cultures: Towards an Intercultural Theory of Foreign Language Education*. Clevedon: Multilingual Matters.

Byram, M. (Ed.) 1993. *Germany: its representation in textbooks for teaching German in Great Britain*. Frankfurt am Main: Diesterweg.

Byram, M. 1997. Cultural Studies and Foreign Language Teaching. In S. Bassnett (Ed.) *Studying British Cultures: an introduction*. London: Routledge.

Byram, M. (Ed.) 1997. *Face to Face. Learning Language and Culture through Visits and Exchanges*. London: CILT.

Byram, M. and V. Esarte-Sarries. 1991. *Investigating Cultural Studies in Foreign Language Teaching*. Clevedon: Multilingual Matters.
Byram, M., V. Esarte-Sarries and S. Taylor. 1991. *Cultural Studies and Language Learning: a Research Report*. Clevedon: Multilingual Matters.
Byram, M., C. Morgan *et al.* 1994. *Teaching-and-Learning Language-and-Culture*. Clevedon: Multilingual Matters.
Byram, M. and G. Zarate. 1994. *Definitions, Objectives and Assessment of Socio-cultural Competence*. Strasbourg: Council of Europe.
Byrne, D. 1969. Attitudes and Attraction. In L. Berkowitz (Ed.) *Advances in Experimental Social Psychology*, Vol. IV, 35–69. New York: Academic Press.
Cain, A. 1990a. French Secondary School Students' Perceptions of Foreign Cultures. *Language Learning Journal*, September: 48–52.
Cain, A. 1990b. Les pays de langue anglaise vus par les lycéens français. *Cahiers de l'EREL*, No spécial, APLV, FIPLV Nantes, p. 20.
Cain, A. (Ed.) 1996. *Culture, civilisation: propositions pour un enseignement en classe d'anglais*. Paris: Gap, Ophrys.
Cain, A. and C. Briane. 1994. *Comment collégiens et lycéens voient les pays dont ils apprennent la langue. Représentations et stéréotypes*. Paris: Institut National de Recherche Pédagogique.
Canale, M. 1983. From communicative competence to language pedagogy. In J. Richards and J. Schmidt (Eds.) *Language and Communication*. London: Longman.
Canale, M. and M. Swain. 1980. Theoretical Bases of Communicative Approaches to Second Language Teaching and Testing. *Applied Linguistics*. 1(1) 1–47.
Carolle, R. 1987. *Evidences invisibles: américains et français au quotidien*. Paris: Seuil.
Cazden, C. B. 1992. Performing expository texts in the foreign language classroom. In C. Kramsch and S. McConnell-Ginet (Eds.) *Text and Context: Cross-Disciplinary Perspectives on Language Study*. Lexington, MA: D C Heath, 67–78.
Chen, J. 1990. *Confucius as a Teacher*. Beijing: Foreign Languages Press.
Chomsky, N. 1991. Towards a Humanistic Conception of Education and Work. In D. Corson (Ed.) *Education for Work: Background to Policy and Curriculum*. Clevedon: Multilingual Matters.
Christ, H. 1993. Schüleraustausch zwischen Verstehen und Missverstehen. In L. Bredelle und H. Christ (Hrsg.) *Zugänge zum Fremden*. Giessener Diskurse 10, Verlag der Felber'schen Universitätsbuchhandlung.
Clarke, L. and W. Grünzweig. 1988. Integrating the apparently disparate: Landeskunde and international education. In M. Wright (Ed.) *Dynamic Approaches to Culture Studies*. Frankfurt am Main: Peter Lang.
Clarke, M. 1976. Second language acquisition as a clash of consciousness. *Language Learning*, 26(2) 377–90.
Clement, R. 1980. Ethnicity, contact and communicative competence in a second language. In H. Giles, W. P. Robinson and P. M. Smith (Eds.) *Language: Social Psychological Perspectives*. Oxford: Pergamon.

Cohen, A. (Ed.) 1982. *Belonging*. Manchester: Manchester University Press.
Coleman, J. A. 1994. What motivates British students of German? An interim report on a study of learners' progress, background and attitudes. *Fremdsprachen und Hochschule*, 42:39–50.
Coleman, J. A. 1995a. The current state of knowledge concerning student residence abroad. In G. Parker and A. Rouxeville (Eds.) *The Year Abroad: Preparation, Monitoring, Evaluation*. AFLS/CILT.
Coleman, J. A. 1995b. Progress, Proficiency and Attitudes among University Language Learners. Centre for Language and Communication Studies (Trinity College Dublin), Occasional Paper No 40.
Coleman, J. A. 1995c. Developing a Questionnaire to Investigate the Advanced Language Learner. *Language Learning Journal*, 12:20–25.
Coleman, J. A. 1996a. *Studying Languages: A Survey. The Proficiency, Background, Attitudes and Motivations of Students of Foreign Languages in the United Kingdom and Europe*. London: Centre for Information on Language Teaching and Research.
Coleman, J. A. 1996b. Attitudes of British language students towards target language communities, with some European comparisons. In G. Aub-Buscher (Ed.) *The Linguistic Challenge of the New Europe*. Plymouth: CERCLES.
Collee, J. 1996. *The Observer*, Observer Life, 7 January 1996, London.
Collie, J. and S. Slater. 1992. *Literature in the Language Classroom. A resource book of ideas and activities*. Cambridge: Cambridge University Press.
Collier, M. J. and M. Thomas 1988. Cultural Identity, an interpretative perspective. In Y. Y. Kim and W. B. Gudykunst (Eds.) *Theories in Intercultural Communication*. Newbury Park, CA: Sage.
Cope, B. and M. Kalantzis. 1995. Why Literacy Pedagogy has to Change. *Education Australia*, Issue 30 UT, Australia.
Coppieters, R. 1987. Competence differences between native and near-native speakers. *Language*, 63(3) 544–73.
Corson, D. (Ed.) 1991. *Education for Work: Background to Policy and Curriculum*. Clevedon: Multilingual Matters.
Cortazzi, M. and L. Jin. 1966. Changes in Learning English Vocabulary in China. In H. Coleman and L. Cameron (Eds.) *Change and Language*. Clevedon: Multilingual Matters.
Cortazzi, M. and L. Jin. 1997. Cultures of Learning: Language Classrooms in China. In H. Coleman (Ed.) *Society in the Language Classroom*. Cambridge: Cambridge University Press.
Council of Europe. 1973. *Systems Development in Adult Language Learning*. Pergamon Press.
Creel, H. G. 1970. *What is Taoism?* Chicago: University of Chicago Press.
Crystal, D. 1978. *Linguistics*. London: Penguin Books.
Davies, A. 1991. *The Native Speaker in Applied Linguistics*. Edinburgh: Edinburgh University Press.
Davies, A. 1994. Native speaker not dead! Alive and well in Standard Languages. Paper presented at the Annual Applied Linguistics Association of Australia (ALAA) Conference, Melbourne, July 1994.

Davis, J. 1977. *People of the Mediterranean*. London: Routledge.

Davis, J. 1992. *Exchange*. Oxford: Oxford University Press.

Delamont, S. 1995. *Appetites and Identities: an Introduction to the Anthropology of Western Europe*. London: Routledge.

Denzin, N. K. 1989. *The Research Act*. New Jersey. Prentice Hall.

DES (Department of Education and Science, and the Welsh Office). 1990. *Modern Foreign Languages for ages 11 to 16: proposals of the Secretary of State for Education and Science and the Secretary of State for Wales*. London: HMSO.

Doyé, P. 1992. Fremdsprachenunterricht als Beitrag zu tertiärer Sozialisation. In Buttjes *et al.* (Eds.) *Neue Brennpunkte des Englishunterrichts*, Frankfurt am Main: Peter Lang.

Drucker, P. F. 1989. *The New Realities*. London: Heinemann.

Duff, T. (Ed.) 1988. *Explorations in Teacher Training. Problems and Issues*. London: Longman.

Duncker, L. 1995. Spiel und Phantasie. Eine kreative Form der Weltaneignung: *Spielzeit – Spielräume in der Schulwirklichkeit. Friedrich Jahresheft* XIII, Seelze: Erhard Friedrich Verlag.

Eagleton, T. 1985. *Literary Theory. An introduction*. Oxford: Basil Blackwell.

Edelhoff, C. 1987. Lehrerfortbildung und interkulturelles Lehren und Lernen im Fremdsprachenunterricht. In G. Baumgratz and R. Stephan (Eds.) *Fremdsprachenlernen als Beitrag zur internationalen Verständigung. Inhaltliche und organisatorische Perspektiven der Lehrerfortbildung in Europa*. München: Iudicium.

Edelhoff, C. 1992. In-Service Teacher Training and Teaching Through Activities. A Progress Report from Germany. In A. Van Essen and E. I. Burkart (Eds.) *Homage to W R Lee. Essays in English as a Foreign and Second Language*. Berlin/New York: Foris.

Educational Testing Service. 1994. Learning by Degrees, Centre for the Assessment of Educational Progress at ETS, USA.

Eisner, E. 1991. The Misunderstood Role of the Arts in Human Development. Paper for the International Symposium on Human Development and Education. Madrid, October 1991.

Ellis, R. 1994. *The Study of Second Language Acquisition*. Oxford: Oxford University Press.

Ely, C. M. 1986. Language Learning Motivation: a Descriptive and Causal Analysis. *Modern Language Journal*, 70(1) 28–35.

Enzensberger, H. 1985. Ein bescheidener Vorschlag zum Schutze der Jugend vor den Errungenschaften der Poesie. In H. Hoven (Ed.) *Literatur und Lernen. Zur berufsmäßigen Aneignung von Literatur*. Darmstadt/Neuwied: Luchterhand.

Evans, C. 1988. *Language People*. Oxford: Oxford University Press.

Fairclough, N. 1989. *Language and Power*. London: Longman.

Fiske, H. 1989. *Understanding Popular Culture*. Boston: Unwin Hyman.

Fleming, M. 1997. *The Art of Drama Teaching*. London: David Fulton Publishers.

Frake, C. 1964. How to Ask for a Drink in Subanun. *American Anthropologist*, 66(6) 127–32.

Friedrichs, U. 1995. Das Fremde erfahren. Interkultureller Kontakt als Rollenspiel. *Spielzeit – Spielräume in der Schulwirklichkeit. Friedrich Jahresheft* XIII, Seelze: Erhard Friedrich Verlag.

Fung, Yu-lan. 1961. *A Short History of Chinese Philosophy*. New York: Macmillan.

Furnham, A. 1994. Communicating in Foreign Lands: The Cause, Consequences and Cures of Culture Shock. In M. Byram (Ed.) *Culture and Language Learning in Higher Education*. Clevedon: Multilingual Matters.

Furnham, A. and S. Bochner. 1982. Social difficulty in a foreign culture: an empirical analysis of culture shock. In S. Bochner (Ed.) *Cultures in Contact: Studies in Cross-Cultural Interaction*. Oxford: Pergamon.

Furnham, A. and S. Bochner. 1986. *Culture Shock: Psychological Reactions to Unfamiliar Environments*. London: Routledge.

Gardner, R. and W. Lambert. 1972. *Attitudes and Motivation in Second Language Learning*. Rowley, Mass.: Newbury House.

Garfinkel, H. 1972. Remarks on ethnomethodology. In J. J. Gumperz and D. Hymes *Directions in Sociolinguistics. The Ethnography of Communication*. Oxford: Basil Blackwell, 301–23.

Geertz, C. 1975. *The Interpretation of Cultures*. New York: Basic Books.

Gertsen, M. C. 1995. Intercultural Training as In-Service Training. A Discussion of Possible Approaches. In Aarup Jensen *et al.* (Eds.) *Intercultural Competence: A New Challenge for Language Teachers and Trainers in Europe: Volume II*. Aalborg: Aalborg University Press.

Giles, H. and Coupland, N. 1991. *Language: Contents and Consequences*. Milton Keynes: Open University Press.

Gilmore, D. (Ed.) 1987. *Honour and Shame and the Unity of the Mediterranean*. Washington DC: American Anthropological Association.

Goffman, E. 1967. On Face Work. In E. Goffman (Ed.) *Interactional Ritual*. New York: Anchor Books.

Goldstein, L. 1987. Standard English: The only target for non-native speakers of English? *TESOL Quarterly*, 21(3) 417–36.

Gombrich, E. 1960. *Art and Illusion*. Oxford: Phaidon.

Grosjean, F. 1982. *Life with Two Languages. An Introduction to Bilingualism*. Cambridge, Mass.: Harvard University Press.

Grossberg, L., C. Nelson and P. Treichler. 1992. *Cultural Studies*. London: Routledge.

Grotjahn, R., C. Klein-Braley and U. Raatz. 1997. C-Tests: an overview. In J. A. Coleman (Ed.) *University Language testing and the C-Test*. Portsmouth: University of Portsmouth,

Grünzweig, W. 1988. Adopting a different culture: An appreciation of intercultural dialogue in a Cultural Studies curriculum. In M. Wright (Ed.) *Dynamic Approaches to Culture Studies*. Frankfurt am Main: Peter Lang.

Gudykunst, W. B. and M. Hammer. 1983. Basic Training Design: Approaches to Intercultural Training. In D. Landis and R. Brislin (Eds.) *Handbook of Intercultural Training, Vol I*. New York: Pergamon.

Gumperz, J. and D. Hymes (Eds.) 1972. *Directions in Sociolinguistics: the Ethnography of Communication*. New York: Oxford University Press.
Hall, E. T. 1961. *The Silent Language*. New York: Fawcett.
Hall, E. T. 1966. *The Hidden Dimension*. New York: Doubleday.
Hall, E. T. 1976. *Beyond Culture*. New York: Anchor Press/Doubleday.
Hall, E. T. 1983. *The Dance of Life. The Other Dimension of Time*. New York: Anchor Press/Doubleday.
Hall, E. T. and Hall, M. R. 1981. *Understanding Cultural Differences: Germans, French and Americans*. Yarmouth, Maine: Intercultural Press.
Hall, S., D. Hobson, A. Lowe and P. Willis (Eds.) 1980. *Culture, Media, Language*. London: Hutchinson.
Halliwell, S. 1990. Aristotelean Mimesis Re-evaluated. *Journal of the History of Philosophy*, 28: 487–510.
Hammersley, M. and P. Atkinson. 1983. *Ethnography: Principles in Practice*. London: Tavistock.
Hannerz, U. 1992. *Cultural Complexity. Studies in the Social Organization of Meaning*. New York: Columbia University Press.
Hatch, E. 1992. *Discourse and Language Education*. Cambridge: Cambridge University Press.
Hawkins, B. 1993. Back to Back: Drama Techniques and Second Language Acquisition. In M. Schewe and P. Shaw (Eds.) *Towards Drama as a Method in the Foreign Language Classroom*. Frankfurt am Main: Peter Lang.
Heider, F. 1944. Social perception and phenomenal causality. *Psychological Review*, 51, 358–74.
Heider, F. 1957. *The Psychology of Interpersonal Relationships*. New York: Wiley.
Heilpern, J. 1977. *Conference of the Birds. The Story of Peter Brook in Africa*. Harmondsworth: Penguin Books.
Helmot, K. and B. Müller. 1993. Zur Vermittlung interkultureller Kompetenz. In B. Müller. *Interkulturelle Wirtschaftskommunikation*. München: Iudicium.
Herzfeld, M. 1992. *The Social Production of Indifference*. New York: Berg.
Hinton, L. 1994. *Flutes of Fire. Essays on California Indian Languages*. Berkeley, CA: Heyday Books.
Hofstede, G. 1991. *Cultures and Organizations – Software of the Mind*. London: AMED.
Hofstede, G. 1994. *Cultures and Organizations*. London: HarperCollins Publishers.
Hog, M., B. Müller and G. Wessling. 1984. *Sichtwechsel. Elf Kapitel zur Sprachsensibilisierung. Ein Deutschkurs für Fortgeschrittene*. Frankfurt: Ernst Klett Verlag.
Hölderlin, F. 1970. *Hyperion, Zweites Buch*. Berlin: Aufbau Verlag, v2.
Holec, H. 1981. *Autonomy and Foreign Language Learning*. Oxford: Pergamon.
Holliday, A. 1994. *Appropriate Methodology and Social Context*. Cambridge: Cambridge University Press.

Howard, M. C. 1993. *Contemporary Cultural Anthropology.* London: Harper-Collins College Publishers.

Hua, Y. 1988. *Qizhuuang de Jitan (Mournful and Heroic Sacrificial Altar).* Beijing: International Culture Publishing Company.

Hunt, B. and D. Targett. 1996. *The Japanese Advantage?* Oxford: Butterworth Heinemann.

Ingesman, L. 1995. Multimedia in Language Learning. In A. Aarup Jensen *et al.* (Eds) *Intercultural Competence: A New Challenge for Language Teachers and Trainers in Europe: Volume II.* Aalborg: Aalborg University Press.

Iser, W. 1994. Die Appellstruktur der Texte. In R. Warning (Ed.) *Rezeptionsästhetik.* Munich: 228–52.

Jackson, T. 1993. *Organizational Behaviour in International Management.* Oxford: Butterworth Heinemann.

Jæger, K. 1995. Teaching Culture – State of the Art. In L. Sercu (ed.) *Intercultural Competence. A New Challenge for Language Teachers and Trainers in Europe: Volume I.* Aalborg: Aalborg University Press.

Jan, K. 1981. *Ik hou van dit land, zijn leiders, zijn bevolking. Politiek is de vlag in top van de lading die niet gedekt is.* Gent: Masereelfonds.

Jaspars, J. and M. Hewstone. 1982. Cross-cultural interaction, social attribution and intergroup relations. In S. Bochner (Ed.) *Cultures in Contact: Studies in Cross-Cultural Interaction.* Oxford: Pergamon.

Jin, L. 1992. *Academic Cultural Expectations and Second Language Use: Chinese Postgraduate Students in the UK – A Cultural Synergy Model.* PhD thesis, University of Leicester, UK.

Jin, L. and M. Cortazzi. 1993. Cultural Orientation and Academic Language Use. In D. Graddol, L. Thompson and M. Byram (Eds.) *Language and Culture.* Clevedon: Multilingual Matters.

Jin, L. and M. Cortazzi, 1995. A Cultural Synergy Model for Academic Language Use. In P. Bruthiaux, T. Boswood and B. Du-Babcock (Eds.) *Explorations in English for Professional Communication.* Hong Kong: City University.

Judd, E. 1987. The English Language Amendment: A case study on language and politics. *TESOL Quarterly.* 21(1) 113–36.

Jung, H. 1994. *Der Eszettelkasten/2.* Bayreuth: University of Bayreuth.

Kachru, B. 1985. Standards, codification and sociolinguistic realism: the English language in the outer circle. In R. Quirk and H. G. Widdowson (Eds.) *English in the World: Teaching and Learning the Language and Literatures.* Cambridge: Cambridge University Press.

Kelly, G. A. 1955. *The Psychology of Personal Constructs.* New York: W. W. Norton.

Kim, Y. 1989. Intercultural Adaptation. In M. K. Asante and W. B. Gudykunst (Eds.) *Handbook of International and International Communication.* Newbury Park: Sage.

King, A. Y. C. and M. H. Bond. 1985. The Confucian Paradigm of Man: a sociological view. In W. S. Tseng and D. Y. H. Wu (Eds.) *Chinese Culture and Mental Health.* Orlando: Academic Press.

Klein-Braley, C. 1997. C-Tests in the context of reduced redundancy testing: an appraisal. *Language Testing*, 14(1) 47–84.

Klineberg, O. 1982. Contact between ethnic groups: a historical perspective of some aspects of theory and research. In S. Bochner (Ed.) *Cultures in Contact: Studies in Cross-Cultural Interaction*. Oxford: Pergamon.

Knapp, K. and A. Knapp-Potthoff. 1990. Interkulturelle Kommunikation. *Zeitschrift für Fremdsprachenforschung*, 1: 62–93.

Knights, L. C. 1989. Literature and the Education of Feeling. In P. Abbs (Ed.) *The Symbolic Order. A Contemporary Reader on the Arts Debate*. London: Falmer Press.

Kræmer, A. J. 1973. *Development of a Cultural Self-Awareness Approach to Instruction in Intercultural Communication*. Alexandria V.A.: Human Resources Research Organisation.

Kramsch, C. 1991. Culture in Language Learning: A View from the United States. In K. de Bot, R. Ginsberg and C. Kramsch (Eds.) *Foreign Language Research in Cross-Cultural Perspective*. Philadelphia: John Benjamin.

Kramsch, C. 1993. *Context and Culture in Language Teaching*. Oxford: Oxford University Press.

Kramsch, C. 1995. Rhetorical models of understanding. In T. Miller (Ed.) *Functional Approaches to Written Texts: Classroom Applications. TESOL-France*, 2:2, 61–78.

Kramsch, C. 1996a. Stylistic choice and cultural awareness. In L. Bredella and W. Delanoy (Eds.) *Challenges for Pedagogy: Literary Texts in the Foreign Language Classroom*. Tübingen: Gunter Narr.

Kramsch, C. 1996b. The cultural component of language teaching. *Language, Culture and Curriculum*, 2: 83–92.

Kramsch, C. and P. Sullivan. 1996. Appropriate pedagogy. *ELT Journal*, 50(3) 199–212.

Kramsch, C., A. Cain and E. Murphy. 1996. Why should language teachers teach culture? *Language, Culture and Curriculum*, 9(1) 1–9.

Kress, G. 1988. Language as social practice. In G. Kress (Ed.) *Communication and Culture. An Introduction*. Kensington, Australia: New South Wales University Press.

Kristeva, J. 1988. *Étrangers à nous-memes*. Paris: Gallimard.

Krusche, D. 1993. Text und Erfahrung. *Jahrbuch Deutsch als Fremdsprache*, 11:390–401.

Kubanek, A. 1987. *Dritte Welt im Englischlehrbuch der Bundesrepublik. Aspekte der Darstellung und Vermittlung*. Regensburg: Verlag Friedrich Pustet.

Lasnel, C. 1994. Entre histoire coloniale et migration. ... changes méditerranéens et éducation interculturelle. *Le français dans le monde. Numéro spéciale: Pour une pédagogie des échanges*. Février–mars: 39–44.

Lave, J. 1991. Situated learning in communities of practice. In L. B. Resnick, J. M. Levine and S. D. Teasley. *Socially Shared Cognition*. Washington DC: American Psychological Association.

Lazar, G. 1993. *Literature and Language Teaching. A guide for teachers and trainers*. Cambridge: Cambridge University Press.

Le Page, R. and A. Tabouret-Keller. 1985. *Acts of Identity. Creole-Based Approaches to Language and Ethnicity.* Cambridge: Cambridge University Press.

Leathers, D. G. 1986. *Successful Non-verbal Communication. Principles and Applications*. London: Collier Macmillan.

Li, Ze-hou. 1986. *Zhongguo Gudai Sixiang Shilun (Essays on Classical Chinese Thinking)*. Beijing: People's Press.

Lin, Yu-tang. 1955. *The Wisdom of China*. Bombay: Jaico Publishing House.

Lo, T. and C. Lee. 1993. A Sociocultural Framework for a Critical Analysis of English as a Foreign Language in Hong Kong. In *Language and Content*, 1993 ILE Conference Proceedings, Institute of Education, Hong Kong.

London University Survey of Science Undergraduates. 1994. Department of Genetics and the Queen's English Society, University of London.

Louie, K. 1984. Salvaging Confucian Education (1949–1983). *Comparative Education*, 20(1) 27–38.

Luo, Chi. 1985. *Zhongguo Zhexue Jianshi (History of Chinese Philosophies)*. Beijing: China Zhanwang Press.

Maclean, H. 1990. *Britain and a Single Market Europe: Prospects for a Common School Curriculum*. London: Kogan Page.

Malinowski, B. 1923. The Problem of Meaning in Primitive Languages. In C. K. Ogden and I. A. Richards (Eds.) *The Meaning of Meaning*. New York: Harcourt, Brace & World Inc.

Manes, J. 1983. Compliments: a mirror of cultural values. In N. Wolfson and E. Judd (eds.) *Sociolinguistics and Language Acquisition.* London: Newbury House.

Martin, J. N. 1993. Intercultural Communication Competence, a review. In R. L. Wiseman and J. Koester. *Intercultural Communication Competence.* Newbury Park, CA: Sage.

Mauss, M. 1954. *The Gift: form and functions of exchange in archaic societies.* London: Cohen and West.

McRobbie, A. 1994. *Postmodernism and Popular Culture*. London: Routledge.

Meara, P. 1994. What Should Language Graduates Be Able to Do? *Language Learning Journal*, 9:36–40.

Mei, Y. P. 1967. The basis of social, ethical, and spiritual values in Chinese philosophy. In C. A. Moore (Ed.) *The Chinese Mind, essentials of Chinese philosophy and culture*. Honolulu: University of Hawaii Press.

Meyer, M. 1991. Developing transcultural competence: Case studies of advanced language learners. In D. Buttjes and M. Byram (Eds.) *Mediating Languages and Cultures: Towards an Intercultural Theory of Foreign Language Education*. Clevedon: Multilingual Matters.

Milroy, L. 1980. *Language and Social Networks*. Oxford: Basil Blackwell.

Mole, J. 1990. *Culture Clash in the European Single Market: Mind Your Manners*. London: The Industrial Society.

Moore, C. A. 1967. *The Chinese Mind. Essentials of Chinese Philosophy and Culture*. Honolulu: University of Hawaii Press.

Moran, T. and P. Harris. 1991. *Managing Cultural Differences*. Houston: Gulf Publishing Co.

Morgan, C. 1993. Attitude change and foreign language culture learning. *Language Teaching*, 26(2) 63–75.
Mortimer, J. 1994. *Murderers and Other Friends*. London: Penguin.
Mughan, T. 1998. The Integration of Foreign Culture Awareness into Business Language Teaching Materials and Methods. *Language Learning Journal*, 17.
Müller, B. 1983. Begriffe und Bilder. Bedeutungscollagen zur Landeskunde. *Zielsprache Deutsch* 2:5–14.
Müller, B. 1985. Bedeutungsanalytische Praxisforschung in der Lehrerausbildung. In J. Gerighausen and P. C. Seel. *Sprachpolitik als Bildungspolitik. Werkstattgespräch der Goethe-Instituts*. München: Goethe-Institut.
Müller, B. 1986. Interkulturelle Verstehensstrategien – Vergleich und Empathie. In G. Neuner (Ed.) *Kulturkontraste im DaF-Unterricht*. München: Iudicium.
Murphy, E. 1988. The cultural dimension in foreign language teaching: four models. *Language, Culture and Curriculum*, 1(2) 147–63.
New London Group. 1995. Occasional Paper No 1, CWCC, University of Technology, Sydney, Australia.
Nunan, D. 1992. *Research Methods in Language Learning*. Cambridge: Cambridge University Press.
Oliver, R. T. 1971. *Communication and Culture in Ancient India and China*. New York: Syracuse University Press.
Oxford, R. and J. Shearin. 1994. Language Learning Motivation: Expanding the Theoretical Framework. *Modern Language Journal*, 79(1) 1–28.
Paikeday, T. 1985. *The Native Speaker is Dead!* Toronto: Paikeday Publishing Inc.
Pavis, P. 1990. *Le Théâtre au Croisement des Cultures*. Paris: Corti.
Peabody, D. 1984. *National Characteristics*. Cambridge: Cambridge University Press.
Pearce, O. 1982. Tourists and their hosts: some social and psychological effects of inter-cultural contact. In S. Bochner (Ed.) *Cultures in Contact: Studies in Cross-Cultural Interaction*. Oxford: Pergamon.
Peirce, B. N. 1995. Social identity, investment, and language learning. *TESOL Quarterly*, 29(1) 9–32.
Pennycook, A. 1994. *The Cultural Politics of English as an International Language*. London: Longman.
Phillipson, R. 1992. *Linguistic Imperialism*. Oxford: Oxford University Press.
Pickett, L. 1993. *The Effects of Cultural Distancing on Attitudes and Motivation in Foreign Language Learning*. MA thesis, University of Portsmouth.
Poirier, F. 1990. L'enseignement/l'apprentissage de la civilisation en cours de langue. Aspects épistémologiques, contenus, modalités et objectifs. Paper given at the Institut National de Recherche Pédagogique.
Posner, R. 1991. Kultur als Zeichensystem. Zur semiotischen Explikation kulturwissenschaftlicher Grundbegriffe. In A. Assmann and D. Harth (Eds.) *Kultur als Lebenswelt und Monument*. Frankfurt/M: Fischer Verlag.
Preston, D. 1981. The ethnography of TESOL. *TESOL Quarterly*, 15(2) 105–16

Puren, C. 1988. *Histoire des méthodologies de l'enseignement des langues*. Paris: Clé International.
Quirk, R. and H. G. Widdowson (Eds.) 1985. *English in the World: Teaching and Learning the Language and Literatures*. Cambridge: Cambridge University Press.
Rich, A. 1986. *Your Native Land, Your Life*. New York: W. W. Norton.
Rieder, E. 1993. Elektronische Post en Machtsrelaties in Organisaties. Thesis submitted to University of Amsterdam, departments: Sociaal Wetenschappelijk Informatica and Arbeids-en Organisatiepsychologie.
Risager, K. 1988. Fremmedsprog og nationalkultur. In *Kultur og samfund 1*. Roskilde University: 1–17.
Risager, K. 1993. Buy some petit souvenir au Dänemark. Viden og bevidsthed om sprogmødet. In K. Risager *et al.* (Eds.) *Sproglig mangfoldighed*. Roskilde: ADLA, Roskilde University.
Risager, K. 1995. Language teachers' identity and the process of European integration. In A. Aarup Jensen *et al.* (Eds.) *Intercultural Competence. A New Challenge for Teachers and Teacher Trainers in Europe. Volume II*. Aalborg: Aalborg University Press.
Roberts, C. 1993. Cultural studies and student exchange: Living the ethnographic life. *Language, Culture and Curriculum*, 6(1) 11–17.
Roberts, C. 1995. Language and Cultural Learning. An Ethnographic Approach. In A. Aarup Jensen *et al.* (Eds.) *Intercultural Competence. A New Challenge for Teachers and Teacher Trainers in Europe. Volume II*. Aalborg: Aalborg University Press.
Roberts, C. and P. Sayer. 1987. Keeping the gate: How judgements are made in interethnic views. In K. Knapp, W. Enninger and A. Knapp-Potthoff (Eds.) *Analyzing Intercultural Communications*. Berlin: Mouton de Gruyter.
Roberts, L. P. 1992. Attitudes of Entering University Freshmen toward Foreign Language Study: A descriptive analysis. *Modern Language Journal*, 76: 273–83.
Robinson, G. 1988. *Crosscultural Understanding*. London: Prentice Hall.
Sallmann, (Michael) Salli. 1983. *Nix Besonderes*. Berlin: Dirk Nishen Verlag.
Sampson, E. 1971. *Social Psychology and Contemporary Society*. New York: Wiley.
Saville-Troike, M. 1989, 2nd edition. *The Ethnography of Communication*. Oxford: Blackwell.
Scarino, A., D. Vale, P. McKay and J. Clark. 1988. *Language Learning in Australia*. Curriculum Development Centre, Woden ACT 2606.
Schewe, M. and P. Shaw. 1993. *Towards Drama as a Method in the Foreign Language Classroom*. Frankfurt: Peter Lang.
Schewe, M. and H. Wilms. 1995. *Texte lesen und inszenieren*. Munich: Klett Verlag.
Schulz-Ojala, J. 1992. Alfred Andersch: Fluchtpunkt Sansibar. *Konturen*, 4:5–12.
Schumann, J. 1978. Social and psychological factors in second language acquisition. In J. Richards (Ed.) *Understanding Second and Foreign Language Learning: Issues and Approaches*. Rowley, Mass.: Newbury House.

Schumann, J. 1978. The acculturation model for second language acquisition. In R. Gingras (Ed.) *Second Language Acquisition and Foreign Language Teaching*. Arlington, VA: Center for Applied Linguistics.

Schumann, J. 1986. Research on the acculturation model for second language acquisition. *Journal of Multilingual and Multicultural Development*, 7: 379–92.

Scollon, R. and S. Scollon. 1983. Face in interethnic communication. In J. Richards and R. Schmidt (Eds.) *Language and Communication*. London: Longman.

Scollon, R. and S. Scollon. 1995. *Intercultural Communication*. Oxford: Blackwell.

Seely Brown, J. and P. Duguid. 1991. *Organizational Science*, Vol 2, No 1.

Seelye, H. N. 1988. *Teaching Culture: Strategies for Intercultural Communication*. Lincolnwood, Illinois: National Textbook Company.

Shipman, M. D. with D. Bolam and D. Jenkins. 1974. *Inside a Curriculum Project: A Case Study in the Process of Curriculum Change*. London: Methuen.

Siegal, M. 1994. Second Language Learning, Looking East: Learning Japanese and the Interaction of Race, Gender, and Social Context. Unpublished PhD dissertation, Berkeley, CA: UC Berkeley.

Singleton, D. and E. Singleton. 1992. *University-level learners of Spanish in Ireland*. Trinity College Dublin, Centre for Language and Communication Studies Occasional Paper No. 35.

Skutnabb-Kangas, T. and R. Phillipson (Eds.) 1994. *Linguistic Human Rights*. Berlin: M. de Gruyter.

Slater, P. (Ed.) 1977. *The Measurement of Intrapersonal Space by Grid Technique*. Vol 2 *Dimensions of Interpersonal Space*. London: Wiley.

Smith, D. H. 1985. *Confucius and Confucianism*. London: Paladin Books.

States, B. 1994. *The Pleasures of the Play*. Cornell: Cornell University Press.

Steele, R. and A. Suozzo. 1994. *Teaching French Culture. Theory and Practice*. Lincolnwood, Ill.: National Textbook Company.

Street, B. 1993. Culture is a verb. In D. Graddol, L. Thompson and M. Byram (Eds.) *Language and Culture*. Clevedon: Multilingual Matters.

Styan, R. 1981. *Modern Drama in Theory and Practice 1 Realism and Naturalism*. Cambridge: Cambridge University Press.

Sullivan, P. 1997. Historical, Pedagogical, and Cultural Influences on English Language Education in Vietnam: Implications for American Educators. PhD dissertation, Berkeley, CA: UC Berkeley.

Tajfel, H. 1981. *Human Groups and Social Categories*. Cambridge: Cambridge University Press.

Thomas, J. 1983. Cross-cultural pragmatic failure. *Applied Linguistics*, 4(2) 91–112.

Thornton, R. 1988. Culture: a Contemporary Definition. In E. Boonzaeir and J. Sharp (Eds.) *Keywords*. Capetown: David Philip.

Ting-Toomey, S. 1993. Communicative resourcefulness, an identity negotiation perspective. In R. L. Wiseman and J. Koester (Eds.) *Intercultural Communication Competence*. Newbury Park, CA: Sage.

Tomalin, B. and S. Stempleski. 1993. *Cultural Awareness*. Oxford University Press.

Triandis, H. C. 1995. *Individualism and Collectivism*. Boulder, Colorado: Westview Press.

Trompenaars, F. 1993. *Riding the Waves of Culture*. London: Economists Books.

Tu, W. M., M. Hejtmanek and A. Wachman (Eds.) 1991. *The Confucian World Observed, a contemporary discussion of Confucian Humanism in East Asia*. Honolulu: Institute of Culture and Communication, the East–West Centre.

Undervisningsministeriet. 1994. *Formål og centrale kundskabs- og færdighedsområder. Folkeskolens fag*. Copenhagen: Undervisningsministeriet.

University of Central England. 1994. Employer Satisfaction Summary, Quality in Higher Education Project. Birmingham: UCE.

Valdes, G. 1995. The teaching of minority languages as academic subjects: pedagogical and theoretical challenges. *The Modern Language Journal*, 79(3) 299–328.

Valdman, A. 1992. Authenticity, variation, and communication in the foreign language classroom. In C. Kramsch and S. McConnell-Ginet (Eds.) *Text and Context: Cross-disciplinary Perspectives on Language Study*. Lexington, MA: D. C. Heath.

Van der Vegt, N. 1987. *Op vooroordelen bekeken. Het toetsen van leermiddelen voor intercultureel onderwijs*. Enschede: SLO.

Victor, D. A. 1992. *International Business Communications*. New York: HarperCollins.

Watts, A. 1979. *Tao: The Watercourse Way*. London: Penguin Books.

Weaver, G. 1986. Understanding and coping with cross-cultural adjustment stress. In R. M. Page (Ed.) *Cross-Cultural Orientations: New Conceptualizations and Applications*. London: University Press of America.

Welsch, W. 1995. Transculturality – the puzzling form of cultures today. Paper for the conference 'Culture and Identity: City, Nation, World', Berlin 10–14 August, 1995:21.

Widdowson, H. G. 1987. *A Rationale for Language Teacher Education. Council for Cultural Co-operation. Working Document CC-GP12(87)14*. Strasbourg: Council of Europe.

Widdowson, H. G. 1988. Aspects of the relationship between culture and language. *Triangle 7: Culture and Language Learning*. Paris: Didier.

Widdowson, H. G. 1994. The ownership of English. *TESOL Quarterly*, 28(2) 377–88.

Willis, F. M., G. Doble, U. Sankarayya and A. Smithers. 1977. *Residence Abroad and the Student of Modern Languages: a preliminary survey*. University of Bradford, Modern Languages Centre.

Winter, G. 1986. German-American student exchange: adaptation problems and opportunities for personal growth. In R. M. Page (Ed.) *Cross-Cultural Orientations: New Conceptualizations and Applications*. London: University Press of America.

Wolfson, N. 1988. The Bulge: A theory of speech behavior and social distance.

In J. Fine (Ed.) *Second Language Discourse: A Textbook of Current Research*. Norwood, N.J.: Ablex.

Wolfson, N. 1989. The social dynamics of native non-native variation in complimenting behaviour. In M. Eisenstein (Ed.) *The Dynamic Interlanguage*. New York: Plenum.

Wringe, C. 1991. Education, Schooling and the World of Work. In D. Corson (Ed.) *Education for Work: Background to Policy and Curriculum*. Clevedon: Multilingual Matters.

Young, A. S. 1994. Motivational State and Process within the Sociolinguistic Context: an Anglo-French comparative study of school pupils learning foreign languages. Unpublished PhD thesis, The University of Aston in Birmingham.

Young, L. W. L. 1994. *Crosstalk and Culture in Sino-American Communication*. Cambridge: Cambridge University Press.

Zarate, G. 1986. *Enseigner une culture étrangère*. Paris: Hachette.

Zarate, G. 1987. Etranger dans la ville: Appropriation de l'espace urbain en classe de langue. *Langues Modernes*, 81, 3/4, 15–21.

Zarate, G. 1988. La déscription d'une culture étrangère dans la classe de langue: deux modèles didactiques. *Triangle 7: Culture and Language Learning*. Paris: Didier.

Zarate, G. 1993. *Représentations de l'étranger et didactique des langues*. Paris: Didier.

Index

 0775